ARGUMENTS AND CASE

LINGUISTIK AKTUELL/LINGUISTICS TODAY

Linguistik Aktuell/Linguistics Today (LA) provides a platform for original monograph studies into synchronic and diachronic linguistics. Studies in LA confront empirical and theoretical problems as these are currently discussed in syntax, semantics, morphology, phonology, and systematic pragmatics with the aim to establish robust empirical generalizations within a universalistic perspective.

Series Editor

Werner Abraham
Germanistisch Instituut
Rijksuniversiteit Groningen
Oude Kijk in 't Jatstraat 26
9712 EK Groningen
The Netherlands
E-mail: Abraham@let.rug.nl

Advisory Editorial Board

Guglielmo Cinque (University of Venice)
Günther Grewendorf (J.W. Goethe-University, Frankfurt)
Liliane Haegeman (University of Lille, France)
Hubert Haider (University of Salzburg)
Christer Platzack (University of Lund)
Ian Roberts (University of Stuttgart)
Ken Safir (Rutgers University, New Brunswick NJ)
Höskuldur Thráinsson (University of Iceland, Reykjavik)
Lisa deMena Travis (McGill University)
Sten Vikner (University of Stuttgart)
C. Jan-Wouter Zwart (University of Groningen)

Volume 34

Eric Reuland (ed.)

Arguments and Case: Explaining Burzio's Generalization

ARGUMENTS AND CASE

EXPLAINING BURZIO'S GENERALIZATION

Edited by

ERIC REULAND
Utrecht institute of Linguistics OTS

JOHN BENJAMINS PUBLISHING COMPANY
AMSTERDAM / PHILADELPHIA

∞ ™   The paper used in this publication meets the minimum requirements of
American National Standard for Information Sciences — Permanence of Paper
for Printed Library Materials, ANSI Z39.48-1984.

Library of Congress Cataloging-in-Publication Data

Arguments and case : explaining Burzio's generalization / edited by Eric Reuland.
   p.   cm. -- (Linguistik aktuell / Linguistics today, ISSN 0166-0829; v. 34)
Includes bibliographical references and index.
   1. Grammar, Comparative and general--Case. 2. Grammar, Comparative and general--Syntax.
3. Burzio, Luigi, 1943- I. Reuland, Eric J. II. Linguistik aktuell ; Bd. 34.
P240.6.A74   2000
415--dc21   99-462297
ISBN 90 272 2755 1 (Eur) / 1 55619 918 X (US) (Hb; alk. paper)   CIP

© 2000 – John Benjamins B.V.
No part of this book may be reproduced in any form, by print, photoprint, microfilm, or any other
means, without written permission from the publisher.

John Benjamins Publishing Co. · P.O.Box 75577 · 1070 AN Amsterdam · The Netherlands
John Benjamins North America · P.O.Box 27519 · Philadelphia PA 19118-0519 · USA

This book is dedicated to the memory of Teun Hoekstra

Table of Contents

List of Contributors	ix
Preface	xi
Explaining Burzio's Generalization: Exploring the Issues *Eric Reuland*	1
Case and Licensing *Alec Marantz*	11
The License to License: Licensing of Structural Case Plus Economy Yields Burzio's Generalization *Hubert Haider*	31
The Nature of Verbs and Burzio's Generalization *Teun Hoekstra*	57
Oblique Subjects and Burzio's Generalization *Anoop Mahajan*	79
Thetablind Case: Burzio's Generalization and its Image in the Mirror *Itziar Laka*	103
The Aspect-Case Typology Correlation: Perfectivity and Burzio's Generalization *Werner Abraham*	131
Anatomy of a Generalization *Luigi Burzio*	195
Name Index	241
Subject Index	245

List of Contributors

Werner Abraham
Department of German
University of Groningen
P.O. Box 716
NL-9700 AS Groningen
The Netherlands
abraham@let.rug.nl

Luigi Burzio
Department of Cognitive Science
Johns Hopkins University
Baltimore, MD 21218
USA
burzio@jhu.edu

Hubert Haider
Institute of Linguistics
University of Salzburg
Muehlbacherhofweg 6
A-5020 Salzburg
Austria
Hubert.Haider@sbg.ac.at

Teun Hoekstra[†]
Leiden University/HIL

Itziar Laka
University of the Basque Country
Departemento Filologia Española
Campus de Alava
c\Paseo de la Universidad 5
E-01006 Vitoria-Gasteiz
Spain
feplamui@vc.ehu.es

Anoop Mahajan
UCLA
Department of Linguistics
BOX 951543
Los Angeles, California 90095–1543
USA
mahajan@humnet.ucla.edu

Alec Marantz
MIT
Dept. of Linguistics and Philosophy
Cambridge, MA 02139
USA
marantz@MIT.edu

Eric Reuland
Utrecht institute of Linguistics OTS
Trans 10
NL-3512 JK Utrecht
The Netherlands
eric.reuland@let.uu.nl

Preface

This volume is based on a workshop on Burzio's generalization which was held at the Utrecht institute of Linguistics OTS on June 3 and 4 1994, and organized by Ad Neeleman, Fred Weerman and myself. At the time of the workshop we were struck by the high degree of convergence of a couple of presentations. This resulted in the plan to bring out a volume that would take the ideas in those presentations as its point of departure. As most people who have ever been involved in such enterprises will know, there is a considerable risk involved in such an undertaking. Contributors have pressing schedules, reviewers have to reconcile their desire to do a proper job with the fact that other academic activities are by far more visible. It is therefore with pleasure that I am able to present this volume, not without expressing my gratitude to the anonymous reviewers for their very helpful comments. Pleasure, also since I am convinced that, together, these works make an important contribution to our understanding of a set of intriguing, and theoretically important questions. The insights they offer pose strong empirical constraints on the further development of current syntactic theories such as the *Minimalist program* or even point in alternative directions.

The volume brings together an elaboration of the orginal statement of the workshop theme, and contributions by Hubert Haider, Teun Hoekstra, Anoop Mahajan, Itziar Laka and Luigi Burzio which all originated as presentations at the workshop. It further includes an article by Alec Marantz, who also participated in the workshop, and which originally appeared in the proceedings of the Eighth Eastern States Conference on Linguistics (ESCOL 1991), edited by Germán Westphal, Benjamin Ao and Hee-Rahk Chae. This article is included because it profoundly influenced the discussion in the workshop and the contributions as they were subsequently written. I am grateful to the department of linguistics of The Ohio State University and its chairman Peter Culicover for granting permission to reprint this article. In a later stage during the preparation of this volume I learnt about the work by Werner Abraham on the nature of ergativity. This work provides an interestingly different perspective on the issues involved and thus nicely complements the discussion in the other contributions.

My pleasure at this occasion is overshadowed by the untimely death of Teun Hoekstra who contributed a chapter on the nature of verbs and Burzio's generalization. He is sadly missed by all who knew him. This volume is dedicated to his memory. Teun died before he could send me the finalized version of his contribution to this book. I am very grateful to Nina Hyams for her generous help in this matter under circumstances that were so difficult for her.

Utrecht, October 19, 1999
Eric Reuland

Explaining Burzio's Generalization
Exploring the Issues

Eric Reuland
Utrecht University

1. Background

In its original form, Burzio's Generalization (BG) states that a verb that does not assign an external θ-role to its subject does not assign structural accusative Case to an object and conversely. This is represented in (1).

(1) $-ACC_{struct} \leftrightarrow -T_{ext}$

It thus connects cross-linguistic similarities between e.g. passives, regardless of their morpho-syntactic trigger, and unaccusatives (see Burzio 1986, Chomsky 1981 for discussion). However, it does so by linking very different properties of a predicate, i.e. whether or not it assigns a particular thematic role and whether or not it assigns structural case. Therefore, since Chomsky (1981), considerable attention has been given to the following question and its various suggested answers:

(2)   What is BG's theoretical basis, and how can it be explained?

This question can be made more specific as follows:

(3)   Does BG in any way reflect an intrinsic dependency between the ways the verb relates to its subject and object arguments, or is BG just an epiphenomenon due to the interaction between independent principles of grammar?

One line of research focussed on the conditions on NP-movement as in (4). I.e., movement of the NP to the subject position was taken to be triggered by the impossibility for the NP to receive structural Case in its source position.

(4) a. *John arrived t*
    b. *John was killed t*

However, what triggers dethematization of the target? Though such dethematization is a condition for movement to be possible, the question is how it is enforced. Passive morphology and reflexive clitics have been proposed as elements that may absorb an external role, facilitating movement when required.

This line raised a number of other well-known questions. For instance, why is the NP in passives and unaccusatives licensed by movement to the nominative position, rather than by inherent Case assignment or by insertion of a preposition (as is possible in NPs and APs)? Or, by contrast, how can similar constructions be licensed with an expletive element in subject position and the thematic argument in situ? Clearly, in such cases, the subject position is non-thematic as well, although there is no syntactic movement.

As an alternative to Case, the EPP (the requirement that VP have a subject) has been suggested as the driving force behind the movements in (4). If correct, this leads to the view that in general "move NP" has nothing to do with Case theory. Much of the evidence for (abstract) Case theory would then appear in a different light, which should lead to a fundamental discussion of the relation between Case theory and θ-theory.

One may then ask to what extent this shift from Case to the EPP as the force behind NP-movement helps solve questions (2) and (3). How can the the absence of accusative Case for the object be related to the absence of a thematic role for the structural subject?

A recent line of research essentially sets out to capture the effect of the EPP in terms of conditions on nominative Case assignment: "if nominative is available it must be used" (for relevant discussion see Weerman 1989; Marantz 1991; Laka 1993; Bobaljik 1993 and others). So structures as in (5) are excluded since nominative has not been used.

(5) a. $*e_{-Case}$ arrived [John$_{inh}$]
    b. $*e_{-Case}$ was killed [John$_{ACC}$]

Underlying this approach is the claim that the two structural Cases, both being assigned/checked by elements of the verbal agrement system, are thereby interconnected. C_t is the Case checked by T, C_v the Case checked by V. Languages may vary in the way this Case system operates. Of the Case pair one member is more active than the other: that one is assigned first. In Nominative/Accusative languages the active Case is C_t, while in ergative languages this is C_v. Economy prescribes 1 Case per argument. Hence, in a Nominative/

Accusative language, if there is only one argument, C_t is the Case to be assigned. This gives the effects of BG in one direction: $-T \rightarrow -A$. If there are two arguments, after C_t has been assigned, the remaining argument receives C_v.

What about the effects of BG in the other direction: $-A_{struct} \leftrightarrow -T_{ext}$? In principle, a 2-place predicate requires two arguments to saturate its roles. $-A$ implies that the structure is one Case short. So, it will come out as illformed unless one of the arguments need not be realized. Therefore, if there is some process available that may absorb one of the θ-roles, that process must apply.

So, now Burzio's generalization comes out as the result of the parameter that expresses that the first Case that is suppressed in a Nominative/Accusative language is the accusative Case, in conjunction with the general availability of independent processes that may cause a θ-role to be absorbed.

This still leaves open whether there might be a 'causal' relation between 'checking accusative', and 'assigning an external θ-role'. That is, if some morpheme absorbs accusative Case (as one might say about certain reflexive elements), is that by itself enough to suppress the external θ-role, or would one rather say that the θ-roles of the predicate get merged, and that as a result one argument suffices?

Note that the EPP or "nominative first" approaches do not imply that accusative is absent per se in passives and unaccusatives. If somehow NP-movement to the structural subject position is blocked, the EPP may be satisfied by an expletive in the structural subject position, and the "nominative first" condition may well be compatible with checking C_v by the (only) argument as a last resort (the position in which C_t is checked being inaccessible).

The first type of evidence that this is indeed possible comes from languages with morphological Case. In Russian, for instance, verbs can be used impersonally with an accusative direct object. In Ukrainian participial passives the direct object can occur in the accusative. Similarly, BG is violated in existential constructions in German, while in Middle Dutch one can observe accusative subjects in passives and unaccusatives.

Another type of evidence might come from the behaviour of predicates. To some extent these have the same distribution as objects: in Dutch both arguments and predicates precede the verb, in English both follow the verb, while in Old English and Middle Dutch arguments and predicates could appear (independently) on either side of V. This suggest that predicates, like arguments, are licensed by Case. Crucially, predicates do show up with passives and unaccusatives, indicating that these can assign Case.

On the other hand, facts recently discussed by Pollock 1994 point in the other direction, suggesting that for reasons unrelated to "move NP" at least passives are not able to assign Case. Pollock argues that bare infinitives in English must be licensed by Case as opposed to *to*-infinitives. The assumption that Case is absorbed in passives now derives the following pattern:

(6) a. *John made Mary (*to) leave*
    b. *Mary was made *(to) leave*

Coming back to the specifics of the "nominative first" approach, the idea that the two structural Cases are somehow connected is possibly supported by the behaviour of indefinite NPs. De Hoop (1992) suggests that in Dutch the interpretation of indefinites is dependent on the type of Case they have. If an indefinite bears the canonical objective Case, it receives a strong interpretation. If it is assigned special (inherent) Case, it receives a weak (non-specific) interpretation. Interestingly, under neutral intonation a weak subject is preferably combined with a weak object:

(7) a. *?dat er   een man het boek leest*
        that there a man the book reads
    b. *dat er   een man een boek leest*
        that there a man a   book reads

One might say that C_t may not be 'weaker' than C_v, and that structural Case is stronger than inherent Case. This means that if C_v is strong, C_t cannot be weak, but if C_v is weak, C_t is allowed to be weak as well. If dependencies of this sort indeed exist, the two structural Cases must reflect a single system. It is not a priori clear how this can be expressed if the two Cases are checked in separate projections.

To summarize, the following important questions arise in connection with Burzio's generalization:

1. Can there be a direct relation between the absorption of a θ-role and the absorption of accusative Case?
2. Is it possible to derive BG from the "obligatory subject" hypothesis? How can this approach be developed and what consequences does it have for Case theory and the relation between Case and θ-theory?
3. Is it possible to derive BG from the "nominative first" hypothesis? How does this appoach solve the problems raised above?
4. Is there a relation between nominative Case and accusative Case as suggested by the dependency between these Cases in terms of the 'activity' parameter, and by the facts in (6). If so, how can we acount for such a relation?

A further question is:

5. What is the nature of the checking mechanisms for Case? When, if at all, does it involve the mediation of an Agr-projection? Does structural case differ from inherent, oblique, and lexical Cases in this respect?

These, and other questions are addressed in the contributions to this volume.

2. The Issues

All contributions give a negative answer to the first question, thus, either implicitly or explicitly agreeing with Luigi Burzio's statement (in Chapter 8) that Burzio's generalization is an epiphenomenon; however, in their specifics of deriving BG they differ.

Chapter 2 is a contribution by Marantz. This seminal article was published earlier in the proceedings of ESCOL 1991, and is included here because it directly addresses the topic of this volume, and in fact served as a starting point for most of the other contributions. In this contribution Marantz argues that the facts covered by Burzio's generalization split into two sets both explained by independent principles. One of these principles is the extended projection principle (Chomsky 1986), the other necessary ingredients emerge from a reassessment of the relation between structural and morphological Case. Marantz shows that the proper treatment of morphological case requires a complete break between abstract and morphological case, leading to the elimination of abstract Case theory from the theory of syntax. Case and agreement morphemes are inserted only "after" S-structure, at a level of Morphological Structure, which is strictly interpretive and at the PF branch of the grammar. Crucial for deriving Burzio's generalization is the claim that the V-I complex may assign a case to one argument position in opposition to what it has assigned to another argument position. ACC(usative) and ERG(ative) are the dependent cases (on NOM(inative) and ABS(olutive) respectively), in the sense that ACC and ERG case on an NP is dependent not only on properties of the NP itself, but also of another NP position governed by V-I. As Marantz shows the direction of the dependency is different, though. Dependent case assigned up to the subject is ERG, dependent case assigned down to the object is ACC. Thus, in a nominative/accusative language the head of a chain governed by (finite) V-I will typically be realized as NOM; due to the different direction of the dependency of ERG in ergative languages no derived subject will be realized with ERG. This derives what Marantz considers the relevant part of Burzio's generalization for NOM/ACC languages and its counterpart for ergative languages.

Haider, in Chapter 3 takes as the basis of his explanation the notion of economy of checking. In his approach UG has two default checking environments for structural Case. One involves checking by a functional head, yielding nominative, the other involves checking by a lexical head, and yields accusative. The difference between nominative/accusative and ergative/nominative languages comes from the choice of the argument for the default. In nominative/accusative languages the highest ranked structural argument (the external argument) is linked to the default checking; in a nominative/ergative system the converse obtains. BG reflects that whereever the checking configuration is ambiguous, allowing both functional and lexical checking, functional checking is preferred. Consider, for example, a nominative/accusative system. The nominative argument is not only Case marked, but it also exhibits agreement with the finite verb. Therefore, two types of features are checked, namely both Case and φ-features. Thus, suppose a structure contains a 1-argument verb. If the argument first receives accusative Case, as a next step, still the φ-features of the verb will have to be checked. This implies a 2-step checking process. Haider now formulates the following axiom:

The BG-axiom: Minimize checking

From this axiom the nominative first property follows in that configuration. Only checking the nominative will allow checking to take place by one operation only. Note, that if the inflectional system of a language provides an impersonal paradigm, accusative checking is not in competition with checking by I/Agr. Hence, a well-known class of exceptions to BG (varying from existential sentences in German to accusative passives in Polish, Russian and Ukranian) is accounted for.

Hoekstra in Chapter 4 starts out with a discussion of the 'nominative first' property as underlying Burzio's generalization. Hoekstra argues that this property reflects a distinction between T-related Cases and V-related Cases. T is a primitive, and having T is a property of all sentences. Moreover, T always licenses nominative Case. Lexical verbs, however, are not primitive, but always the result from incorporating a lexical primitive, such as A or N, into functional material. Not all verbs license a V-related Case (accusative). Verbs that do, i.e. transitive lexical verbs, are formed by the additional incorporation of an (oblique) preposition which is associated with the external argument. Thus, without an external argument to provide this preposition, no accusative Case can be assigned. This effectively derives Burzio's generalization. If in some language the oblique preposition of the external argument cannot be incorporated this argument will be marked ergative, and it is the internal argument that must receive nominative. Thus, an ergative system goes with the impossibility to assign accusative to the internal argument. This view is essentially in agreement with Haiders position. In fact, Haider's BG-axiom may well be directly linked to Hoekstra's T-invariance.

In Chapter 5 Mahajan starts out to show that Burzio's generalization does not hold in Hindi and many other Indic Indoeuropean languages. Hindi has construction types with predicates that are unable to assign structural accusative Case (due to their participial nature). Yet, as Mahajan shows in great detail, they license an argument that must be considered a structural thematic subject. Hence, Burzio's generalization is not a true generalization. Whatever it is must be due to the interaction of universal grammar and language particular properties of structures. The analysis is based on Marantz's (this volume) notion of a dependent Case. Subjects of transitive verbs can receive a morphological Case if the verbs themselves are not structural Case assigners (this case can be compared to the genitive Case in nominals). This option is universally available. Mahajan discusses both transitive participial constructions and passives. In both cases, Mahajan argues, the participle does not assign structural Case. Hence, the subject is marked for dependent Case, in the former case by an ergative preposition, in the latter case by *by*. The ergative preposition may incorporate into the higher Aux, yielding *have*. This *have* will provide accusative Case to the object (see also Hoekstra 1994 and this volume)), the subject, then, moves on to a nominative position. In similar constructions in Hindi incorporation is blocked for structural reasons. Hence, the resulting verb is *be*, and it is the object, rather than the subject that has to move. In the case of passive, it is both English and Hindi that block incorporation into Aux of the dependent Case marker on the subject. Here the difference is that, independently, English does not allow PP-subjects, the reason why the by-phrase is demoted to adjunct position.

In Chapter 6 Laka derives the pattern reflected in Burzio's generalization from a particular elaboration of Case theory. Laka argues that the Case assigners in the clause are Tense and Aspect. Languages may differ as to which of these is active. A Tense active system assigns nominative when a one-place predicate is involved, and the effect of Burzio's generalization follows. An Aspect active system assigns absolutive in a one-argument case, hence the absence of BG-effects. Again, Burzio's generalization derives from a conspiracy between independent principles. Although, by itself, this account leaves open why in one language type Tense is active, and in another Aspect, it seems that this issue can be understood from the perspectives of Haider's result about the priority of agreement-checking and Hoekstra's and Mahajan's proposals about the relation between Case and P-incorporation. In this sense, then, Laka's contribution provides confirmation from yet a different angle of the pattern that keeps emerging.

In Chapter 7, Abraham focuses on the notion of ergativity and the way it should be understood. His contribution puts the topic in a different perspective since it brings into the discussion a wealth of considerations from the typological literature. Starting out from an analysis of 'split ergativity', his discussion addresses two main issues, one conceptual, the other empirical. Conceptually, it is an important issue whether the term 'ergativity' as it being used in the literature really reflects one notion. Alternatively, as some have claimed, the notion of ergativity, or unaccusativity, as it is employed in most of the current syntactic literature is unrelated to the notion of ergativity employed in the typological literature. Abraham sketches these positions and the grounds on which they rest in considerable detail. Basing himself on an extensive discussion of, occasionally rather intricate, empirical considerations, Abraham argues that the two notions are in fact related, but that this relation can only be given substance, if ergativity is understood as an aspectual phenomenon. More specifically, it is certain types of realizations of perfectivity which give rise to the phenomena subsumed under ergativity. There is a residue, concerning VP-internality of subject arguments, which Abraham argues is independent, and reduceable to conditions on non-specificity of subjects.

In Chapter 8, finally, Burzio provides an anatomy of his generalization, approaching it from a novel angle. In line with the other contributors, Burzio argues that BG is an epiphenomenon. What is observed results from the interaction between movement and conditions on Case. Where a predicate lacks an external argument, movement is triggerred by the extended projection principle, requiring the external position to be occupied. However, there is no reason for the argument moving into this position to be Case-less. In fact, in Burzio's view it cannot be, since Cases basically reflect grammatical relations. What is affected, then, is not the possibility for some predicate to assign a Case, but the possibility for some argument to realize it. Burzio argues that Cases are subject to a number of constraints of an optimality-theoretic nature. These are ranked and not inviolable. The two main constraints are: (i) Case uniqueness (associate each Case with a single θ-role and vice-versa) and (ii) GR consistency of Case (associate each specific Case with one specific grammatical relation). Since the extended projection principle imposes a subject at all cost if there is no θ-role for an external argument, (i) and (ii) impose conflicting requirements. A chain will be formed with two Cases. Assuming that constraint (i) is more highly ranked than (ii) the conflict will be resolved by suppressing one Case. In nominative/accusative languages the object Case is suppressed, in ergative languages the subject Case. The longstanding difference between structural and inherent Case, finally, is understood in terms of a principle of θ-role consistency of Case (associate each specific Case with one specific θ-role). This principle can be understood as one more constraint on Case realization ranked below constraints (i) and (ii). Cases that are called inherent are those Cases where θ-consistency is directly observable. Finally, Burzio discusses at length quirky Case assignment in Icelandic. In fact, Icelandic represents one more option to resolve the potential Case conflict resulting from movement, namely by superimposing one Case on the other (an idea that can be traced back to Belletti (1988)). It creates a violation of Case uniqueness, but because both cases are present on the chain it permits double satisfaction of GR consistency. The reason that this device is not available throughout follows from the idea that it is costly. That is, universal grammar accomodates a constraint to avoid quirky subjects, that may be ranked highest in languages such as English, but low enough in Icelandic.

Burzio's conlusion is that the notion of optimization is directly relevant to Case realization, explaining among others the effect of Burzio's generalization where it obtains. If so, perhaps more far reaching conclusions about the domain of optimality theory can be warranted.

3. Conclusion

At this point one can see that all the questions we started out with have been extensively addressed. There is full consensus that there can be no direct relation between the absorption of a θ-role and the absorption of accusative Case. The "obligatory subject" hypothesis has played an important role in the discussion, and has in fact been corroborated. Where BG holds the "nominative first" hypothesis has played an important role as well, though not as a primitive, but as a property that can be derived. The availability of accusative Case has been shown to directly reflect the structural relations into which subjects and their morphological markers can enter. Finally, the relation between Case and agreement has been fundamentally challenged, each being licensing relations in their own right. Finally, new light has been shed on the relation between structural and inherent Case.

References

Bobaljik, J. 1993. "Ergativity and ergative unergatives". In *Papers on Case and Agreement* II [Working Papers in Linguistics 18], J. Bobaljik and C. Philips (eds). Cambridge, MA: MIT Press.
Burzio, L. 1986. *Italian Syntax*. Dordrecht: Reidel.
Chomsky, N. 1981. *Lectures on Government and Binding*. Dordrecht: Foris.
Chomsky, N. 1986. *Barriers*. Cambridge, MA: MIT Press.
Hoekstra, T. 1994. Possession and Transitivity. Ms. Leiden: HIL, Leiden University.
Hoop, H. de. 1992. Case Configuration and Noun Phrase Interpretation. PhD Dissertation, Groningen University.
Laka, I. 1993. "Unergatives that assign case". In *Papers on Case and Agreement* I [Working Papers in Linguistics 18], J. Bobaljik and C. Philips (eds). Cambridge, MA: MIT Press.
Marantz, A. This volume. "Case and licensing." [Published earlier in G. Westphal, B. Ao, and H.-R. Chae (eds), *ESCOL* 8].
Pollock, J.-Y. 1994. Checking Theory and Bare Verbs. Ms. Univ. de Picardie, Amiens.
Weerman, F. 1989. *The V-2 Conspiracy*. Dordrecht: Foris.

Case and Licensing

Alec Marantz
Massachusetts Institute of Technology

It is fairly well understood that noun phrases (or DPs) occupy argument positions in sentences (or bear grammatical relations or functions) by virtue of the semantic roles they bear with respect to predicates. Current Principles and Parameters theories, following Chomsky (1981), add an additional condition on licensing NP (DP) arguments: they must also be assigned (abstract) Case. Recent investigations of languages with rich morphological case and agreement systems strongly indicate that the relationship between abstract Case and morphological case and agreement is indirect, at best. In this paper, I argue that the proper treatment of morphological case necessitates a complete break between abstract Case and morphological case. I show that the facts covered by "Burzio's generalization" (Burzio 1986) split into two sets explained by independently motivated principles. One set is covered by the "Extended Projection Principle" (see, e.g., Chomsky 1986: 4), in particular the requirement that sentences have subjects. The remainder is handled by the correct universal characterization of "accusative" and "ergative" morphological case, a characterization that also successfully explains a peculiar fact about the distribution of ergative case. Giving content to the theory of morphological case allows for the elimination of abstract Case theory from the theory of syntax. The mapping between semantic roles and argument positions, augmented by the subject requirement of the Extended Projection Principle, is sufficient to license NPs in argument positions.

1. Ergative case and Burzio's generalization

The examples in (1)–(3) illustrate an interesting feature of what's called ergative case in many languages — here I draw on Georgian (Harris 1981; Aronson 1982). In present, future, and other "Series I" tenses,[1] Georgian shows nominative case on the subject and dative case on the object (in Georgian, dative and accusative morphological case have fallen together into what's called the dative case) — see (1a, c). However, in the aorist or simple past ("Series II"), we find ergative case on the subject and nominative case on the object. This is true for regular (Class 3) intransitive verbs — unergative in Relational Grammar terms — as in (1b) and for transitive (Class 1) verbs as in (1d). The contrast in the case-marking patterns between the Series I INFL in (1a, c) and the aorist from Series II in (1b, d) should be clear: only the aorist yields ergative case on the subject NP (and nominative case on the object of a transitive verb).

(1) a. *vano   [pikr-ob]-s   marikaze.*
       Vano-NOM [think$_3$]-INFL$_I$ Marika-on
       'Vano is thinking about Marika.'
    b. *vano-m   [i-pikr]-a   marikaze.*
       Vano-ERG [think$_3$]-INFL$_{II}$ Marika-on
       'Vano thought about Marika.'
    c. *nino   gia-s   surateb-s   [a-čven-eb]-s.*
       Nino-NOM Gia-DAT pictures-DAT [show$_1$]-INFL$_I$
       'Nino is showing pictures to Gia.'
    d. *nino-m   gia-s   surateb-i   [a-čven]-a*
       Nino-ERG Gia-DAT pictures-NOM [show$_1$]-INFL$_{II}$
       'Nino showed the pictures to Gia.'

The examples in (2) illustrate what happens when we put unaccusative (Class 2) verbs in the aorist; these verbs, like passives, have syntactically derived subjects. For the present and future (Series I) tenses, intransitive unaccusative verbs have nominative subjects, as shown in (2a). In the aorist, the subject remains nominative — it does not become ergative, as shown in (2b). The sentences in (3) show that unaccusative psychological verbs (Class 4) in Georgian that have dative subjects and nominative objects also do not change the case marking on subject and object in the aorist. Class 4 psych verbs resemble Class 2 unaccusatives in that, like the nominative subject of the Class 2 verbs, the dative subject of the psych verb is syntactically derived from some VP internal position.

(2) a. *es saxl-i   ivane-s   a=[u-šendeb]-a.*
       this house-NOM Ivan-DAT PreV=[built$_2$]-INFL$_{I3SG}$
       'This house will be built for Ivan.'
    b. *es saxl-i   ivane-s   a=[u-šend]-a.*
       this house-NOM Ivan-DAT PreV=[built$_2$]-INFL$_{II3SG}$
       'This house was built for Ivan.'

(3) a. šen pelamuš-i g-[i-qvar]-s.
you-DAT pelamusi-NOM AGR-[like₄]-INFL₁
'You like pelamusi.'
b. šen pelamuš-i g-[e-qvar]-e.
you-DAT pelamusi-NOM AGR-[like₄]-INFL₁₁
'You liked pelamusi.'

The same patterning of ergative case, summarized in (6), is observed for ergative case on the subjects in sentences with perfect tense/aspect in Hindi (examples from Mahajan 1991) and for ergative case with all tenses in Basque (examples from the discussion in Marantz 1984b). Note that ergative case is prohibited on the subject of unaccusative verbs in the perfect in Hindi — (4a). Ergative is optional for the subject of unergative verbs, as shown in (4b, c), and obligatory on the subjects of transitives, (4d). In Basque, ergative case occurs across tenses. As in Georgian and Hindi, ergative does not occur on the subject of an unaccusative — (5a). It is obligatory, however, on the subject of unergatives and transitives — (5b, c).

(4) a. siita (*ne) aayii. (unaccusative)
Sita-FEM (*ERG) (arrived/came-FEM
b. kutte bhoNke.
dogs-MASC.PL barked-MASC.PL
c. kuttoN ne bhoNkaa.
dogs-PL ERG barked-MASC.SG
d. raam ne roTii khaayii thii.
Ram-MASC ERG bread-FEM eat-FEM be-PAST.FEM

(5) a. Ni etorri naiz. (unaccusative)
I-ABS come 1SG-be
b. Nik lan egin dut.
I-ERG work do have-1SG
c. Nik libura ekarri dut.
I-ERG book-ABS bought have-1SG

(6) Ergative case generalization: Even when ergative case may go on the subject of an intransitive clause, ergative case will not appear on a derived subject.

The sentences in (7) raise another interesting aspect of Georgian ergative case in the aorist. Although the case marking changes from NOM-DAT to ERG-NOM in (1a, c)–(1b, d), the agreement morphology sticks to the NOM-DAT pattern. In particular, the suffixal agreement that normally agrees with a nominative subject will agree with the ergative subject in the aorist.

(7) a. *da=v-[mal]-e.*
    PreV=AGR-[hide₁]-INFL_II
    'I hid something'
  b. *da=Ø-[mal]-e.*
    PreV=AGR-[hide₁]-INFL_II
    'you hid something'
  c. *da= [mal]-a.*
    PreV=[hide₁]-INFL_II
    'he hid something'
  d. *da= [mal]-es.*
    PreV=[hide₁]-INFL_II
    'they hid something'

In the aorist sentences (7), the suffixal agreement, glossed as INFL, changes with the person and number of the subject, which would be in the ergative case if expressed as an overt NP. This is the same suffixal agreement that would agree with a nominative subject in other tenses. Thus Georgian shows a split ergative pattern in the aorist. Some Indo-Iranian languages closely related to Hindi show a similar split ergative pattern in the tenses that trigger ergative case (see, e.g., Mahajan 1991).

These data raise the problem of what accounts for the generalization in (6), which seems well-supported cross-linguistically. Generalization (6), restated in (8b), is tantalizingly similar to Burzio's generalization, written as a generalization about accusative case as in (8a).

(8) a. Burzio's generalization: no accusative case on an object in a sentence with a non-thematic subject position
  b. Ergative generalization: no ergative case on a non-thematic subject (i.e., on an argument moved into a non-thematic subject position)

Although it would be tempting to try to collapse the generalizations in (8), Burzio's generalization is not put correctly in (8). Rather, it is more accurately formulated as in (9):

(9) Burzio's generalization (as a one way implication): If a verb's subject position is non-thematic, the verb will not assign accusative structural Case.

That is, Burzio's generalization is about abstract Case, Case that licenses NPs in object positions. The Ergative generalization isn't about abstract Case but about the morphological realization of case on subjects. The subject position in

Georgian is always licensed by tense/aspect inflection; that is, abstract Case is always (able to be) assigned to the subject position whether the verb is in the present, future, or aorist tense. The agreement patterns illustrated by (7) reinforce the fact that the subject is licensed by INFL; INFL agrees with the subject whether in nominative or in ergative case. However, the morphological shape of the case on the subject is different depending on the tense/aspect and the realization of ergative morphological case is subject to the Ergative generalization. Thus the Ergative generalization doesn't seem to have anything to do with abstract Case, while Burzio's generalization does.

Suppose then it is correct to relate the Ergative generalization to Burzio's generalization and it is also correct that the Ergative generalization is not about abstract Case but about the morphological realization of case. Then Burzio's generalization too may not treat abstract Case but rather the realization of accusative morphological case.

2. Burzio's generalization isn't about Case

Burzio's generalization seems to be about Case because objects are not licensed in a clause if the clause has a non-thematic subject, as in (10). Recall that "the man" in (10a) and "the porcupine" in (10b) should be licensed in the argument positions in which they appear by virtue of the semantic roles they bear in the sentences; these phrases are "projected" into the post-verbal argument positions. Case theory, governed by Burzio's generalization, specifically accounts for these situations in which NPs do not seem to be licensed to appear in the positions into which they are projected.

(10) a. *It arrived the man.
b. *It was sold the porcupine.

Despite its ability to account for structures like (10), there are many examples in the literature of violations of Burzio's generalization — situations in which objects are in fact licensed when there is a non-thematic subject. I've chosen the examples in (11)–(13) since they also violate the morphological accusative case version of Burzio's generalization — it seems that morphological accusative is being realized in a sentence with a non-thematic subject. We want whatever principle that replaces the generalizations in (8) to account for these constructions as well.

Consider the Japanese example in (11a) from Kubo (1989). Kubo argues that this sort of passive, in which the derived subject is the possessor of an object, patterns with the so-called "direct" passives in Japanese and not with the "indirect" or adversity passives as in (11b). In particular, passives like those in (11a) behave on a variety of tests like other passives with traces in direct or indirect object positions and not like indirect passives like (11b) in which there is no gapped position. Kubo argues that direct passives like (11a) involve movement into a non-thematic subject position while indirect passives like (11b) contain a thematic subject position, into which arguments may be projected at DS. Despite the fact that the subject position in (11a) is non-thematic, the object seems to be licensed by structural accusative Case and appears with morphological accusative case as well.

(11) a. *Hanako$_i$-ga (dorobo-ni) [t$_i$ yubiwa-o] to-rare-ta.*
Hanako-NOM (thief-by) ring-ACC steal-PASS-PAST
'Hanako had a thief steal her ring on her.'
b. *Hanako-ga ame-ni hu-rare-ta.*
Hanako-NOM rain-DAT fall-PASS-PAST
'Hanako had rain fall on her.'

Bresnan and Moshi (1990) show that in what they call symmetrical object languages like Kichaga, passivization of one of the objects of a double object verb leaves the other object with all syntactic object properties. The Kichaga sentence (12a) is an active double object construction; the verb shows object agreement with both objects. (12b, c) contain possible passives of the verb in (12a). Either object may become the subject of the passive verb. Although movement in (12b, c) is into a non-thematic subject position, the object that does not become subject still seems to be assigned abstract accusative structural Case, realized via object agreement on the verb, in violation of Burzio's generalization. If we correlate accusative morphological case with object agreement morphology, (12b, c) violate the morphological version of Burzio's generalization as well as the abstract Case version.

(12) a. *N-ä-ï-lyì-í-à `m-kà k-élyà.*
(He$_i$) AgrS$_i$-AgrO$_j$-AgrO$_k$-eat-BEN wife$_j$ food$_k$
'He is eating food for his wife.'
b. *`M-kà n-ä-ï-lyì-í-ò   k-èlyâ.*
food$_k$ AgrS$_k$-AgrO$_j$-eat-BEN-PASS wife$_j$
'Food is being eaten for the wife.'
c. *K-èlyá k-ï-lyì-í-ò   `m-kà.*
wife$_j$ AgrS$_j$-AgrO$_k$-eat-BEN-PASS food$_k$
'The wife is being beneficially/adversely affected by someone eating food.'

English raising examples like those in (13b, c) are well-known challenges to Burzio's generalization in any formulation. In (13) the objects of "strike" look as if they are being assigned structural Case by "strike" even though the subject position of "strike" is non-thematic. Note also that the morphological case on "me" and "her" is apparently accusative in (13), although it might be dative.

(13) a. *It struck me that I should have used "Elmer" in this sentence.*
b. *There struck me as being too many examples in his paper.*
c. *Elmer$_i$ struck her as [t$_i$ being too stubborn for the job].*

If, as the examples in (11)–(13) suggest, Burzio's generalization doesn't govern abstract Case, why then are the sentences in (10) bad; why don't we just assign Case to the objects in such structures and be done with it? On standard assumptions, the structures in (10) would have underlying structures as in (14), with empty subject positions.

(14) a. *e arrived the man.*
b. *e was sold the porcupine.*

Suppose we assume the "Extended Projection Principle" or some sort of "subject condition" — some condition that sentences (IPs) require (structural) subjects (cf. the final 1 law of Relational Grammar and the subject condition of LFG). By any such condition, the structures in (14) will have to get subjects to be well-formed. Assuming that movement comes for free while insertion of a dummy subject in environments like (14) is a last-resort option for satisfying the Extended Projection Principle (EPP),[2] we predict the ungrammaticality of (10) without recourse to Case theory at all; the EPP and standard assumptions about the "economy" of derivations (move for free rather than insert a dummy at cost) will suffice. That is, the issue surrounding examples like (10) is not whether or not Case may be assigned in such environments but rather whether sentences are licensed if there is no subject. Since objects may freely solve the subject requirement through movement, it misleadingly appears as if objects are not licensed (assigned Case) if there is no subject.

If this line of thinking is correct, then NPs (DPs) may be licensed to appear in the positions that they do by the EPP; that is, argument structure to syntax mappings plus the need for sentential subjects would account for the distribution of NPs (DPs). So licensing might follow from projection without Case theory. If abstract Case is sufficiently distinct from morphological case, the Case theory might be entirely superfluous.

3. "Case" (=licensing) isn't "case" (morphology)

Linguists have already established that the connection between abstract Case as the means to license NPs and morphological case as what you see on NPs can't be too close. The literature on Icelandic provides the clearest examples of the separation of Case and case (here I rely on Maling 1990; Sigurðsson 1991; and Zaenen, Maling and Thráinsson 1985).

Icelandic quirky case marking shows instances of NPs that get morphological case by virtue of being objects of certain verbs but are not necessarily licensed as objects by getting this case. (15a) contains an example of a double object verb both of whose objects get quirky case. The DATive object is optional. You can passivize the verb with just its genitive object, as in (15b), but in this case the object must become the subject of the passive verb — it may not stay in object position. I'll refer you to the literature on Icelandic for convincing evidence that the GEN must become a subject and is in fact a subject in (15b). Although the GEN NP gets genitive case as an object in (15b), this case does not license the NP in object position; quirky GEN case isn't abstract Case. Note that (15c) is consistent with the notion that it's the EPP, not the need for abstract Case, that is forcing the GEN NP to become a subject in (15b). If we add back the DAT argument in the passive in (15c), it satisfies the EPP by becoming the subject and now the GEN NP is licensed as an object. If we try to explain the obligatory movement of the GEN NP to subject position in (15b) by saying that the GEN NP lacks abstract Case as an object in the passive, we raise the question of why this NP can suddenly get abstract Case as an object in the passive in (15c) when there's a DAT argument around.

(15) a. María   óskaði (Ólafi)   alls   góðs.
        Mary-NOM wished Olaf-DAT everything-GEN good-GEN
     b. Þess   vas óskað.
        this-GEN was wished
     c. Henni   var óskað þess.
        her-DAT was wished this-GEN

The examples in (15) illustrated how an NP could get (morphological) case without being licensed. In (16) we see the opposite situation — a NP is licensed as an object without getting case. Icelandic has a number of verbs that show a DATive subject and a NOMinative object. One could claim that the NOM object is getting abstract Case from inflection, and in fact the verb may agree with a NOM object. But if tensed inflection with agreement is the source of NOM case on the objects of DAT subject verbs, we would expect the object to lose its NOM case in an infinitive, because infinitive inflection does not assign NOM. Instead, as illustrated in (16), such DAT subject/NOM object verbs still take a NOM object in infinitival constructions although there is no element around to assign NOM case.

(16) *Ég tel   henni   hafa   alltaf   þótt   Ólafur   leiðinlegur.*
     I   believe her-DAT to-have always thought Olaf-NOM boring-NOM

To review, Icelandic shows clear examples of NPs being assigned (quirky) morphological case in a position without being assigned abstract Case in that position and clear examples of NPs being assigned Case in a position without being assigned morphological case there. In short, the Icelandic facts argue for a clean separation of licensing and morphological case realization. The data we have examined lead us to suggest a grammar in which NPs are licensed via projection (and the EPP). Morphological case interprets the syntactic structures licensed by projection but does not itself figure into licensing.

Within such a grammar, we want ergative and accusative cases to be morphological cases whose very definition prevents them from being realized in certain syntactic configurations, those covered by the generalizations in (8).

4. The structure of the grammar

I will assume a standard model of grammar as in (17), in which lexical properties are projected into DS and in which the Extended Projection Principle demands the presence of subjects at SS. This is a model without Case theory.

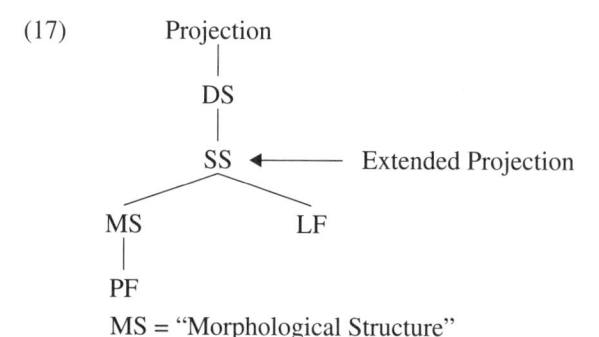

(17)
```
            Projection
                |
               DS
                |
               SS  ←———— Extended Projection
              /  \
            MS    LF
            |
            PF
```
MS = "Morphological Structure"

The present paper is not the appropriate space in which to sketch an entire theory of morphology to go along with this picture of grammar (see e.g., Halle 1991 for some discussion). For present purposes, I will assume that case and agreement morphemes are inserted only after SS at a level we could call "MS" or morphological structure. The presence of such case and agreement morphemes is a language particular option. Thus English has case only on pronominals while languages like Russian require a case suffix on every noun.

It's crucial that in this model, case and agreement are part of the PF branch of the grammar, an interpretative component. Government relations at SS determine the features of case and agreement morphology but the PF will find a way to interpret any well-formed SS. Syntactic ungrammaticality will not result from the realization of case and agreement. In particular, there is always a default case realization. If no principle or language particular property determines the case features for a case morpheme on a noun in a particular language, there will be default case features for the language that this morpheme will pick up.

I've been arguing for a principle like that in (18).

(18) Nominal arguments are licensed by (extended) projection, not by Case or by morphological properties.

The distribution of PRO immediately raises problems for this principle. The near complementary distribution between PRO and lexical NPs is summarized in (19). I put the "never" in quotations in (19) because, of course, there are often ways to realize lexical NPs as the subjects of infinitivals — e.g., in English making them the object of the preposition "for" or placing the infinitival clause as the complement to an ECM (raising to object) verb.

(19) a. PRO is only licensed in the subject position of infinitivals.
b. Lexical NPs are "never" licensed in the subject position of infinitivals.

Another way to state this problem is that (extended) projection alone does not license PRO or pro. If projection were sufficient to license PRO, we should find PRO in the object position in (20a), since it could be projected and thus licensed there.

(20) a. *Elmer bought PRO.
b. Elmer preferred [PRO$_i$ to be given t$_i$ the bigger porcupine].

One might say the PRO is only projected as the subject of infinitivals, thus PRO is licensed via projection. However, (20b) shows that PRO can't be projected only in the subject position of infinitivals; PRO in (20b) is projected as an object and moves to subject position to satisfy the EPP. Thus PRO must be allowed to be projected into a position where it may or may not be licensed.

Extended projection also doesn't explain why lexical nominals are not licensed in subject position of infinitivals, as in (21).

(21) *Hortense tried [Elmer$_i$ to be given t$_i$ a porcupine].

Although (extended) projection doesn't determine the distribution of PRO, neither does Case theory in other approaches. The explanation for the distribution of PRO and lexical nominals is distributed among a few principles, as listed in (22).

(22) a. PRO theorem: PRO cannot be (lexically) governed
b. PRO does not need Case
c. Lexical NPs need Case

As Sigurðsson (1971) shows, PRO does in fact get morphological case in languages like Icelandic. Standard theories still require a stipulation that PRO doesn't need abstract Case as in (22b) and that lexical NPs do, as in (22c), in addition to the stipulation that PRO is a pronominal anaphor or whatever determines that PRO cannot be lexically governed, as stated in (22a).

We must admit that it is not (extended) projection that determines the distribution of PRO and the complementary distribution of PRO and lexical nominals. It is something about the S-structure position of PRO and lexical nominals that licenses PRO in environments where lexical nominals are impossible. Therefore, we need something that would be the RESidue of Case theory. Marantz (1984a: 85) gives one version of such a principle:

(23) The Surface Appearance Principle: A constituent X will appear in the surface structure tree by virtue of bearing a relation with respect to some item Y iff Y is a lexical item (i.e., not a phrase).

In Marantz (1984a), (23) insured that phonologically realized constituents had to be governed by lexical items or tense. PRO was precisely that NP that did not appear in surface structure, by virtue of not being lexically governed. Sigurðsson (1991: 343) argues for a similar principle:

(24) Proper Head Government Condition: pro and lexical NPs in A-positions must be properly head governed.

And, of course, for Sigurðsson, PRO must not be properly head governed. For present purposes, we acknowledge that something remains of Case Theory besides projection theory, as stated in (25):

(25) RES(Case Theory): an NP argument is PRO iff not governed at S-structure by a lexical item or [+tense] INFL

Again, (25) acknowledges a role for S-structure or PF beyond the EPP in the licensing of arguments.

Small pro would seem to be licensed by the morphological properties of agreement, in contradiction to principle (18) (see the papers in Jaeggli and Safir 1989). However, it is not the property of a particular agreement affix itself that is supposed to license pro on theories that tie the licensing of pro to agreement. Rather, it is the agreement system of a language as a whole that determines whether pro is licensed by agreement (see, again, Jaeggli and Safir 1989). Still, since the licensing of pro is tied to an S-structure position (the position connected to Agr at S-structure) and not to (extended) projection by itself, the licensing of pro is also an exception to the generalization in (18).

To review, in a grammar without Case theory, (extended) projection plus independently required principles governing the distribution of PRO and pro license the appearance of NPs (DPs) in argument positions. Morphological case and agreement appear at MS, as part of the phonological component. The morpho-phonology of case and agreement interprets S-structure relations between constituents but does not determine the distribution of NPs in argument positions.

5. case realization at Morphological Structure

Recall that in the theory diagrammed in (17), case morphemes are added to stems at MS according to the morphological requirements of particular languages. When a word contains a CASE affix, this affix will acquire its particular CASE features according to the syntactic relations of its host stem at SS (assume that MS preserves all the syntactic relations of SS). Consider a noun that appears with a CASE affix at MS, as in (26a), because it's a morphological fact about the language in question that nouns require such affixes. To simplify matters, let's suppose that markers like NOM, ACC, ERG, etc. as in (26b) are the morphological features that the CASE affix is looking for. What determines which of these features the CASE affix will acquire?

(26) a. N+CASE
 b. CASE features: NOM, ACC, ERG, DAT, GEN, etc.

The CASE features on the affix will depend on which elements at MS govern the maximal projection of the N to which the CASE affix is attached (or which elements govern the DP that is headed by the D that governs the NP that is headed by the N in question). For the purposes of all syntactic principles, including the realization of CASE, the relevant objects at MS are not NPs per se but chains — A-chains (argument chains) that include the traces of NP-movement. Thus the CASE features on the CASE affix may depend on what governs any link in the chain of the NP headed by the N+CASE.

(27) CASE features are assigned/realized based on what governs the chain of the NP headed by N+CASE

Given the principle in (27), consider an example of NP-movement as in (28). The chain of the subject NP is governed both by the V+I that governs the subject itself and the trace of the V that governs the trace of the subject. Either the V+I or the V, then, might determine CASE features on the CASE suffix.

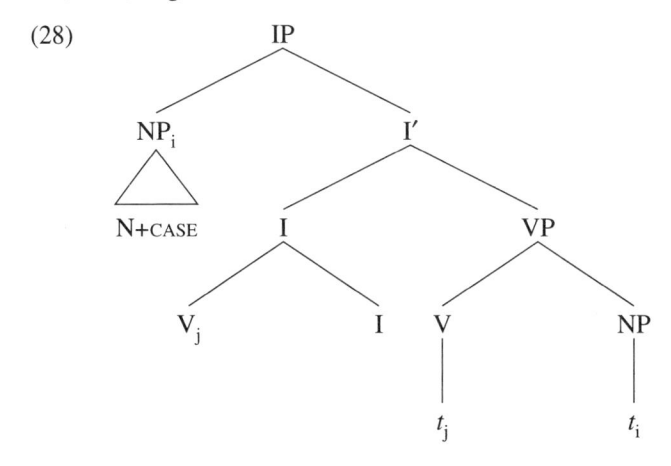

(28)

```
                    IP
                   /  \
                 NP_i   I'
                 /\    /  \
              N+CASE  I    VP
                     / \  /  \
                   V_j  I V   NP
                        |  |  |
                        t_j   t_i
```

In particular, if the verb in (28) realizes a quirky case, this case would be realized on the subject N because the verb governs a link in the subject's chain. It is principle (27) (taken with the disjunctive CASE realization hierarchy (29) to be discussed below) that accounts for the well-known preservation of quirky case in Icelandic passive and raising constructions. The chain of an NP involved in passive and raising will always be governed by the V of which it is a semantic argument; thus, this V may determine the CASE features on the NP no matter where the NP ends up at SS, MS, or PF.

The subject N in (28) looks like a candidate for at least three different CASES. It might get quirky DAT CASE if the verb that governs the object position requires DAT. It might get ACC CASE since the object trace, part of the chain of the subject, is in object position. And it might get NOM CASE since part of its chain, the subject position, is governed by Inflection. As a matter of fact, we know that in such configurations, the subject will appear as DAT, not NOM or ACC, if the verb that governs its trace requires a quirky DAT CASE. And we know that the subject will never appear with (non-quirky) ACC. What insures these results?

Case realization obeys a disjunctive hierarchy that is typical of morphological spell-out, as discussed, e.g., in Halle (1989, 1991). The more specific, more particular CASE requirements win out over the more general, less particular CASE requirements. The hierarchy is roughly that in (29). Again, this is a disjunctive hierarchy: going down the list, as soon as a CASE affix finds some CASE feature that it is eligible for, it takes that CASE and leaves the list.

(29) case realization disjunctive hierarchy:
– lexically governed case
– "dependent" case (accusative and ergative)
– unmarked case (environment-sensitive)
– default case

Lexically determined case takes precedence over everything else, explaining the preservation of quirky case when an NP moves from a position governed by a quirky case verb to a position of NOM or ECM ACC case realization. "Dependent" case is what we will call accusative and ergative; dependent case will be explained immediately below. Unmarked case may be sensitive to the syntactic environment; for example, in a language GEN may be the unmarked case for NPs inside NPs (or DPs) while NOM may be the unmarked case inside IPs. Finally, there is a general default case in the language when no other case realization principle is applicable.

The universal availability of a default case realization mirrors the universal existence of default phonological "spell-out rules" for the phonological realization of morphemes. Disjunctive hierarchies with defaults are characteristic of the morphology (of the morpho-phonological component). A sentence will never be ungrammatical because no case features are assigned to a CASE affix; there will always be a default case realization. Thus case, like morpho-phonology in general, merely interprets syntactic structures and does not filter them.

6. Dependent case

What now about ACC and ERG case, which I have called the "dependent" cases? ACC and ERG are assigned by V+I to one argument position in opposition to another argument position; hence ACC and ERG case on an NP is dependent on the properties not only of the NP itself but also of another NP position governed by V+I. We assume here that, when V moves and adjoins to I, the resulting V+I governs object positions that are governed by the trace of V either (i) directly (because the VP headed by the trace of V is no longer a barrier to such government), or (ii) because the antecedent of the trace is part of the V+I unit, or (iii) through the trace of V; for present purposes, we do not need to decide which combination of these possibilities is correct. ACC is the name for the dependent case that is assigned downward to an NP position governed by V+I when the subject position governed by V+I has certain properties. ERG is the name for the dependent case assigned upward to the subject position when V+I governs downward an NP position with certain properties. These certain properties are listed in (30a, b).

(30) Dependent case is assigned by V+I to a position governed by V+I when a distinct position governed by V+I is:
   a. not "marked" (not part of a chain governed by a lexical case determiner)
   b. distinct from the chain being assigned dependent case
   Dependent case assigned up to subject: ergative
   Dependent case assigned down to object: accusative

Condition (30a) is something of a stipulation as written. It prevents ACC case on an object if the subject is assigned a quirky case by a verb. There are ways of making (30a) follow from other principles, but they involve an investigation of quirky case that would take us beyond the concerns of this paper. (30b) simply clarifies what it means for the dependent case to depend on a *distinct* NP from the NP that gets dependent case. One link in a chain can't count as distinct from another link for the assignment of dependent case. Since case is assigned to chains, all the links are part of the same entity.

Condition (30b) explains why we couldn't get either ACC or ERG on the derived subject NP in (28). Both positions governed by V+I in (28) are in the same chain; thus there are not two distinct positions to set in opposition for the assignment of dependent case. On this theory, it is the definition of dependent case itself that explains the data covered by Burzio's generalization and the Ergative generalization in (8). A slight conceptual jump is required to see why Georgian, Hindi, and Basque can get ERG case on the subject of an intransitive verb when the subject is not raised from an object position — i.e., when the verb is unergative (subjects of unergatives can bear ergative case, unfortunately for the terminology). In the case of normal intransitives, the object position will be empty and thus available to count as the distinct "unmarked" position in opposition to which ERG case may by realized. Should an unfilled position be considered visible for the realization of dependent case? Apparently Georgian and Basque obligatorily count such an unfilled position as visible while Hindi, which shows optional ERG on the subjects of intransitives in the perfect, only optionally "sees" such an unfilled position. So-called "ergative" languages such as Inuktitut that never allow ERG on the subject of an intransitive verb, either unergative or unaccusative, apparently never consider an unfilled position as a distinct position for the realization of dependent case.

The definition in (30) explains the situations in which the generalization in (8) seemed appropriate. It looks like ACC case can't be assigned when there's a non-thematic subject because in most situations in which there's a non-thematic subject, an NP governed by V+I raises to this non-thematic subject position and thus the subject and object positions are filled by members of the same chain. Similarly, ERG case will not generally be assigned when an NP moves into a non-thematic subject position because again the subject and object positions will belong to the same chain. Although the examples in (11)–(13) violate (8a), they are consistent with the definition of dependent case. Although these sentences have non-thematic subject positions, the derived subject and the NPs getting ACC case are in distinct chains, allowing for dependent case assignment.

The present approach to dependent case should be distinguished from superficially similar approaches that use case hierarchies for the distribution of cases within a clause (see, e.g., Yip et al. 1987) or that rely on notions of dependent case requiring that one case be assigned in a clause only after some other case is assigned or realized. On the present theory, although the CASE feature in an NP may depend on syntactic properties of other NPs in a clause, CASE in an NP does not depend on the CASE features in other NPs. Thus the assignment of dependent case does not depend on the previous assignment of NOM or some other "independent" case but rather on the existence of an independent argument position with certain syntactic properties. ECM clauses such as, "I consider [him to have discovered her too late]," in which both the subject and object receive ACC dependent case (the subject from a higher V+I), show that ACC in a clause does not obviously depend on the prior assignment of NOM in the clause. The hierarchy in (29) serves to determine the CASE features for an individual CASE affix; it does not serve to distribute cases through a clause. Thus this hierarchy reverses what might be expected for a hierarchy of cases for a clause; for a particular NP, dependent case (ACC) takes precedence over independent case (NOM).

7. Split ergativity between case and agreement

On the theory under discussion, Agr is a morpheme added to I at MS for those languages that demand morphological agreement to create a well-formed inflected verb as a word; agreement, like case, is a morphological property of certain syntactic categories of words in certain languages. While the CASE morpheme picks up case features keyed to the syntactic environment of the NP with which CASE is associated, Agr picks up person and number features from NPs governed by the V+I that Agr attaches to. Although the features on CASE and Agr reflect similar syntactic relations, the actual determination of these features depends on potentially idiosyncratic properties of governors such as particular tenses in I or quirky case requirements of Vs. It is not necessary that the governing properties of a particular tense in I that determine, for example, that dependent case will be assigned upward (=ERG case) correlate with a particular property of the Agr on that I that determines that Agr will pick up the features of the ERG NP or of some other NP. Thus the theory leaves open the possibility of split ergative systems, like that described above in Georgian, for which the ERG-NOM patterning of case with certain tenses does not correlate with a NOM-ACC pattern in the agreement system.

Assuming that an Agr morpheme on V+I picks up the features of an NP (DP) that is governed by V+I, the question, of course, is which NPs governed by V+I determine the person and number features of Agr. Here, the story is very similar to that given for the determination of CASE features above. In particular, there is dependent agreement, unmarked agreement, and of course, default agreement that stand in the same disjunctive hierarchy as dependent, unmarked and default case as in (29) (I leave open here the issue of what "lexically-governed" Agr might be). Dependent Agr picks up features of one NP governed by V+I in opposition to a distinct, unmarked NP also governed by V+I, where the definitions of distinct and unmarked are as in (30b, a). Dependent Agr with the subject in opposition to an object position we might call "ergative" Agr while dependent Agr with an object in opposition to a subject we could call "accusative" Agr. Unmarked agreement would be with any NP governed by V+I. Finally, default agreement would provide a set of person and number features for Agr when V+I does not govern any NP (or perhaps, any "unmarked" NP in the sense of (30a)).

We saw above that CASE in Georgian depends on the Series of the tense/aspect in I(NFL). Series I INFL assigned dependent case downward, yielding a NOM-ACC(=DAT) pattern, while Series II INFL assigned dependent case upward, yielding an ERG-NOM pattern. Regardless of the case-determining properties of INFL, the Agr on V+I in Georgian has its own properties and works the same way across the board. In particular, the Agr in V+[I+Agr] triggers dependent up agreement, coupled with unmarked and default agreement, as shown in the disjunctive hierarchy in (31) — again, since this is a disjunctive hierarchy, Agr will leave the hierarchy as soon as it picks up features from an eligible NP.

(31) Georgian suffixal Agr on I:
- dependent up (picks up the features of an unmarked NP in subject position in opposition to a distinct NP position governed by V+I)
- unmarked Agr (picks up the features of an unmarked NP governed by V+I, but only the person features of a (3rd person) NP inside the VP)
- default Agr (if no NP is governed by V+I, the Agr is 3rd person singular)

The one notable peculiarity of the Georgian Agr in (31) is that it will not agree in number with a (3rd person) NP that is VP internal, i.e., when Agr governs this NP downward (for example, when there's a DAT — "marked" — NP in subject position).

On the theory under discussion, canonical "subject agreement" is a combination of dependent agreement upward and unmarked agreement, as in (31). Subjects of transitive clauses would trigger dependent agreement, while subjects of intransitives and objects of verbs with "marked" subjects (e.g., quirky case-marked subjects) would trigger unmarked agreement.

Since the subject that gets ERG in Georgian Series II sentences and the subject that gets NOM in Series I sentences are equally unmarked in the relevant sense, the Agr described in (31) will pick up the person and number features of both sorts of subjects. Since DAT subjects are marked in the relevant sense, this Agr will not pick up the features of a dative subject but will pick up the features of a NOM object instead.

Again, the agreement properties of Georgian Agr hold across the Series I Inflections that assign dependent case downward and the Series II Inflections that assign dependent case upward. There is no reason to expect a correlation between the "directional" features of INFL for case marking and the "directional" features of Agr for agreement. Split ergativity of the Georgian sort simply exploits this lack of correlation.

We have seen that the work of Burzio's generalization could be split between the definition of dependent case and the requirement for sentential subjects encoded in the EPP. Making the realization of morphological case and agreement explicitly depend on government relations at SS allowed for the complete elimination of Case theory as involved in the licensing of NP arguments or the spell-out of case or agreement. Licensing now generally follows from the semantics to syntax interface and the subject requirement of the EPP. The theory that results from abandoning Case theory and fleshing out the realization of morphological case has the added advantage of providing an explanation for the Ergative generalization in (8) and the connection between the Ergative and Burzio's generalizations.

Acknowledgments

This is a lightly revised version of the talk I read at the ESCOL conference; since the paper was written as a talk, I invite the reader to read it out loud to herself. I thank audiences at ESCOL and at Cornell for helpful comments and Germán Westphal for his patience.

Notes

1. The Series of the tense is indicated by a roman numeral on INFL (= tense); I follow Harris's (1981) presentation of tense "Series" and verb "Classes."
2. Or that expletive subject constructions have their own peculiar semantics and thus must be projected directly in DS as expletive subject sentences.

References

Aronson, H. I. 1982. *Georgian: A reading grammar*. Columbus, OH: Slavica.
Bresnan, J. and Moshi, L. 1990. "Object asymmetries in comparative Bantu syntax". *LI* 21: 147–185.
Burzio, L. 1986. *Italian Syntax*. Dordrecht: Reidel.
Chomsky, N. 1981. *Lectures on Government and Binding*. Dordrecht: Foris.
Chomsky, N. 1986. *Barriers*. Cambridge, MA: MIT Press.
Halle, M. 1989. "An approach to morphology". *NELS* 20:150–184.
Halle, M. 1991. "The Russian declension: An illustration of distributed morphology and a rebuttal of some criticisms levelled at the theory". To appear in *The Organization of Phonology: Features and domains*. Stanford University: CSLI.
Harris, A. 1981. *Georgian Syntax: A study in relational grammar*. Cambridge: CUP.
Jaeggli, O. and Safir, K. (eds). 1989. *The Null Subject Parameter*. Dordrecht: Kluwer Academic Publishers.
Kubo, M. 1989. Japanese Passives. MS, MIT.
Mahajan, A. 1990. The A/A-Bar Distinction and Movement Theory. PhD dissertation, MIT. (Available from MITWPL)
Maling, J. 1990. "The hierarchical assignment of grammatical case". Paper presented at the Symposium on Icelandic Linguistics, Reykjavik, June 13th, 1990.
Marantz, A. 1984a. *On the Nature of Grammatical Relations*. Cambridge, MA: MIT Press.
Marantz, A. 1984b. "Predicting ergative agreement with transitive auxiliaries". *ESCOL '84*, Columbus, Ohio, pp. 58–68.

Sigurðsson, H. 1991. "Icelandic case-marked PRO and the licensing of lexical arguments". *NLLT* 9: 327–363.
Yip, M., Maling, J. and Jackendoff, R. 1987. "Case in tiers". *Language* 63: 217–250.
Zaenen, A., Maling, J. and Thráinsson, H. 1985. "Case and grammatical functions: The Icelandic passive". *NLLT* 3: 441–483.

The License to License
Licensing of Structural Case Plus Economy Yields Burzio's Generalization

Hubert Haider
Department of Linguistics, Univ. Salzburg

Introduction

This paper defends the claim that Burzio's generalization[1] (henceforth *BG*), which correlates θ-assignment to the subject with case assignment to the object, should be reformulated as a pure constraint on case licensing. This constraint is argued to be reducible to an economy condition on case licensing. A particular instance of the more general licensing constraint is the dependency of accusative licensing on nominative licensing in a finite clause: In a NOM-ACC-system, ACC-licensing by V^0 is dependent on a structural case being licensed by a superordinate element. In a finite clause this is nominative, licensed by finiteness features. This was pointed out in Haider (1984: 72, 88; 1985: 13, 30) and more recently by Marantz (1991). Reference to θ-assignment is dispensable.

The German data sample in (1) illustrates the core effect described by BG: Accusative (as in (1a)) cannot be licensed unless the licensing of nominative has applied (as in (1c)). This leaves nominative as the only option for the internal argument in (1b). Dative, a lexical, not a structural case, remains unaffected, as (1d) exemplifies.

(1) a. *Wurde ihm **den Fehler** vergeben? (German)
 was him-DAT the mistake-ACC forgiven?
 b. Wurde ihm **der Fehler** vergeben?
 was him-DAT the mistake-NOM forgiven?
 'was he forgiven the mistake?'
 c. Hat man ihm **den Fehler** vergeben?
 has one-NOM him-DAT the mistake-ACC forgiven?
 'Has one forgiven him the mistake?'

d. *Wurde **ihm**-DAT vergeben?*
   'was   him-DAT forgiven?'

The relevant condition that will be worked out in more detail below can be characterized in a simplified form as follows: If two case licensing options are applicable alternatively — which is easy to demonstrate for nominative and accusative in German — the case system provides a principled choice. The principle in question will be shown to be a priority principle, whose particular implementation is based on economy: It is more economic to exploit the licensing of nominative (as in (1b)) than the licensing of accusative (as in (1a)).

The idea is this: In (1a), *two* licensing relations must be checked *independently*, namely the licensing of the accusative for the DP, and the licensing of the φ-features of the finite verb. In (1b), the licensing of the nominative and the licensing of the φ-features constitute a *single* interdependent licensing operation: The nominative-licensing provides the feature values for the agreement features of the finite verb. In the absence of a DP licensed for nominative (as in (1d) and the ungrammatical (1a)), these features nevertheless are present and must receive a default specification. Thus, a principle that gives nominative-licensing priority over accusative-licensing has the effect of minimizing the number of independent licensing operations.

A dependency-relation analogous to the accusative-nominative dependency is found in pure NOM-ERG-systems, namely the dependency of ergative case on nominative/absolutive case: The licensing of ergative case presupposes the licensing of nominative/absolutive case. BG is a descriptive characterization of these dependencies which needs to be derived from general principles. The subject matter of BG will be characterized as a priority condition on case licensing whose particular implementation reflects an economy effect in case licensing systems. The priority condition is equivalent to the specification of a default licensing relation for structural case.

The paper is organized as follows: In the first section, evidence will be provided for the reformulation of BG as a pure case dependency relation. The next section introduces the priority principle and the discussion of its consequences for a nominative-accusative language. In Section 3, the economy constraint is generalized in order to capture the BG-effects of ergative systems and to account for differences and apparent exceptions.

1. BG should exclusively refer to case licensing, not to θ-assignment

In Burzio's (1986) account and in earlier versions, the BG relates θ-assignment to the subject with the potential of the verb to assign structural case. In Haider (1984: 72, 82) it has been pointed out that BG needs to be reformulated as a pure case dependency, both for conceptual and empirical reasons. The conceptual difficulty was obvious from the beginning: BG correlates two independent sets of conditions in a triggering configuration, namely θ-marking and case licensing. Even if BG were descriptively adequate, one would have to ask oneself how to derive this cross-modular constraint: BG as a primitive principle of grammar would contradict a basic assumption of the modular organization: A sub-rule of one module (i.e. θ-marking of subject) cannot directly interfere with a sub-rule of another system (i.e. case assignment by V^0). The empirical difficulties, most of them raised in Haider (1984), are discussed in due order below.

Before doing so, I have to briefly specify how the basic theoretic notions used in the paper should be read. Misunderstandings would be unavoidable since I will use concepts of the P&P-System (Chomsky & Lasnik 1995) in a somewhat modified form. Moreover I take the freedom to not adopt or presuppose the premises of the Minimalist Program with respect to Case licensing. In particular, I assume a licensing system for case that applies to S-structure, not to LF, and does not restrict case licensing to Spec–Head configurations (see the discussion of the examples 2 below).[2]

BG can, and in fact must, be reformulated as a generalization about the licensing of structural cases. *Structural cases* are the cases of arguments that are not prespecified for inherent case in the lexical entry. Let us start with English as a language without inherent case for verbal arguments. There are three alternative licensing relations for the very same argument, depending on the syntactic environment, namely nominative (1a), accusative (1b), and PRO (1c), for which Chomsky & Lasnik (1995) suggested *zero case* as licensing relation. (1d) is an example with multiple licensing of accusative. For each accusative there is a unique licensing element, on the assumption that the licensing of accusative is effected by a V^0-element.

(1)   a. *She* smiles
       b. [Make [*her* smile]]
       c. [*PRO* to smile] ...
       d. [Make [*her* [forgive$_i$ [*him* [[$_{V^0}$ e]$_i$ *everything*]]]]][3]

Nominative and zero case in (1a) and (1c), are licensed *functionally*, accusative is licensed *categorially*. Functional licensing is licensing by functional features (like tense and/or agreement). Categorial licensing is licensing by a head of a specific category in a local environment. In (1d), all occurences of accusative are categorially licensed by a V^0-head, one of which is an empty V^0. Functional licensing is not necessarily constrained to a Spec–Head configuration. Relevant empirical evidence for the need of a relational implementation of functional licensing comes from German: It is well-established that a topicalized VP can contain a nominative:

(2) a. *[Gute Beispiele eingefallen] sind ihm noch nie*
good examples in-fallen are him never ever
'Good examples never ever came to his mind'
b. **[Gute Beispiele ein-e$_i$] fielen$_i$ ihm noch nie*
good examples in fell him never ever
c. *Ihm fielen$_i$ noch nie gute Beispiele ein-e$_i$*
him fell never ever good examples in

The ungrammaticality of the example (2b) shows that the topicalized phrase must be a VP and not a higher functional projection, since it cannot contain the trace of the finite verb. If the nominative in (2a) would be analyzed as a DP in a functional Spec-position, the fronted constituent would be a functional projection that contains a functional head targeted by the finite verb, given that nominative is licensed by functional feature that is related to the finite verb. So, (2a) would have a trace of the finite verb in the topicalized constituents. This can be ruled out, however, in clear cases, as in (2b): If the trace of the finite verb is contained in the topicalized phrase, a particle verb would be a good indicator: V2-movement strands the particle, as in (2c). The stranded particle marks the trace. The ungrammaticality of particle stranding in a fronted constituent as in (2b), therefore, is evidence against reanalyzing VP-topicalization as topicalization of a functional projection. So, the nominative must be licensed in a VP-internal position.

Licensing of the nominative in (2a) by means of feature checking in a Spec–Head configuration on a covert representation is not plausible either: The nominative DP or at least its features would have to be extracted out of a constituent in a Spec-position and moved to a position *lower* than the constituent that contains the extraction site. First, the constituent in (2a) occupies the SpecC-position. This position — as a functional Spec-position — is in uncontroversial cases opaque for extraction. Second, the topicalized constituent occupies the Spec-position of the highest functional projection in the clause. So, extraction would amount to extraction plus lowering. This is an unattractive consequence, too.

BG, in a first approximation, describes the effect of a constraint on licensing structural case: Functional licensing has priority over categorial licensing, that is, accusative cannot be licensed unless the available functional licensing option has been exploited. This informal characterization will be refined and formalized in Section 2.

If BG is reformulated as a dependency relation between two modes of structural case licensing — categorial versus functional — the empirical obstacles the original version of BG has to cope with do not arise: The passive of *double object constructions*, the V-projections of transitive *psych*-verbs, and accusative assignment in transitive *middle constructions* are in conflict with the original version of BG, because accusative is assigned despite the lack of a primary subject θ-role.

(3)   a.   She$_i$ was offered e_i *one*
       b.   *One$_i$ was offered *her* e_i

In (3), the subject-position is θ-free and nevertheless a structural case is licensed for the second object in (3a). It is neither necessary not revealing to invoke a specific, morphologically unidentifiable oblique case for the second object in (3a). In languages with overt morphological case paradigms (for instance German or Icelandic), the second object in contexts corresponding to (3a) is marked accusative while the first object is marked with an inherent case, namely dative.

If BG is reformulated as a case-dependency restriction, (3) does not pose a problem: The internal structural case (i.e. licensed categorially by V^0) can be licensed in (3a) since the external structural case (i.e. case by a functional head) has been assigned. The unacceptability of (3b) is not the reflex of an oblique case but rather the result of a case conflict in the chain: The trace of the fronted DP in (3b) is licensed for accusative, but the head of the NP-movement chain is licensed for nominative. This may sound strange, but it follows from the assumptions so far. The licensing of accusative by V^0 in (3b) with the VP-structure (4) cannot be blocked:

(4)   *One$_i$ was [$_{VP}$ offered$_j$ [her [V^0_j e_i]]]

The licensing context for the second object in (4) is the same as in any double object construction. In particular, it is unaffected by whatever effect passive has for the higher object: If the fronted object in (4) is assigned nominative, *her* is licensed for accusative and nothing can prevent V^0 from licensing accusative on the lowest DP-position. Consequently, the fronted object in (4) cannot be assumed to be assigned nominative. If so, *her* is not licensed for accusative, because of the BG-restriction. So, in either perspective, (3c) is predicted to be ungrammatical without having to invoke oblique case.

The VP-structure of transitive psych-verbs as proposed by Belletti & Rizzi

(1988) is an immediate problem for BG, and at first glance also for what has been said so far. The first problem is a real one, the second only an apparent one. Binding facts as in (5a) constitute the principal reason for Belletti & Rizzi to generate the subject argument of a psych-verb like *annoy* in a position lower than the object. Given that the binding asymmetry in (5) is indicative of different base positions of the respective subject-DP in the specI-position, a verb like *annoy* projects its two arguments in a double object structure. The surface structure is like the structure of a passivized double object verb. If this is correct, the derived subject of (5a) originates in a VP-internal position, while the subject of (5b) starts in specVP.

(5) a. Stories about herself$_i$ rarely [$_{VP}$ annoy her^i e_i profoundly]
    b. *Stories about herself$_i$ generally [$_{VP}$ e_i [$_{V'}$ describe her^i accurately]]

Since the original formulation of BG refers to the θ-position of the external argument, (5a) should be an unaccusative construction, which it is not. BG, reformulated as an external-internal case dependency relation captures (5a): The verb may license the internal structural case because there is an external structural case licensed functionally. But how can we avoid the case conflict discussed above? The answer will be: The case conflict does not arise because there is an essential difference between double objects and pych-verbs in the argument grid, indicated in (6). Transitive psych-verbs are exceptional: Subject-selection does not pick the highest argument:

(6) a. offer: ⟨A̲$_1$ ⟨A$_2$ ⟨A$_3$⟩⟩⟩
    b. annoy: ⟨A$_1$ ⟨A̲$_2$⟩⟩
    c. describe: ⟨A̲$_1$ ⟨A$_2$⟩⟩

(6) indicates the argument-grid of three verbs. The angled bracketings indicate the ranking of the arguments, which determines the order of projecting them into the V-projection structure. Underlining signals the argument with priority for external case licensing. Note that this is different from William's (1981) notion of external argument. As pointed out in Haider (1984), '*external*' should be construed as a relational notion: The case licenser of the '*external*' argument is *external* and not necessarily the argument itself. What is common in both approaches is that an argument grid with more than one structural argument[4] must designate one for external licensing.

In most cases, subject selection by designating the external argument and the ranking of arguments in the argument-grid go parallel, as for (6a) and (6c): The highest argument is the designated one. For a principled reason, this is not the case for those transitive psych-verbs for which the cause of emotion and the target of emotion is identical, if ranking and subject selection are derived from the lexical-conceptual structure, as indicated in (7):

(7)   *annoy* $\langle A_y, \underline{A_x} \rangle$ (as in: *The noise annoys me*):
        [x CAUS [BECOME [y in P-STATE (annoy) [with target x]]][5]

The exceptional argument-structure of a psych-verb like *annoy* can be captured in the following principled way: Subject selection and ranking of arguments may produce different outcomes. The *subject selection* rule, i.e. the choice of the argument in the A-structure that gets 'underlined', identifies the argument that is associated with the *highest* occurrence of a variable in the lexical-conceptual structure, whereas the *ranking of arguments* in the argument-grid is determined by the *relative embedding* of variables. It reflects the compositionality of the lexical-conceptual structure: The *lower* occurrence of a variable in the lexical-conceptual structure determines the *lower* rank of the corresponding A-position in the lexical argument structure. If, as in the case of *annoy* (or: *frighten, interest, shock*, etc.), an argument relates to more than one occurrence of a variable in the lexical-conceptual structure, subject selection and ranking may dissociate.[6] As illustrated in (7), psych-verbs like *annoy, frighten, fascinate,* etc. and its counterparts in other languages, are special in the following sense: One argument position in the A-structure is associated with two variables in the lexical-conceptual structure (viz. cause of emotion and target of emotion): The highest occurrence determines the subject selection. But there is a lower occurrence too. Since ranking follows the compositional structure, the designated argument (by subject selection) ends up as the lower ranked argument. Immediate supportive evidence comes from German.

In German, the basic word order for the corresponding verbs is accusative before nominative. This is reflected, for instance, by the contrasting focus potential of nuclear stress on the argument preceding the main verb. In (8a), stress on the Nominative is compatible with maximal focus, that is, with the whole clause being in focus. (8b) with stress on the Nominative has the same focus potential as (8c) with stress on the Nominative, namely minimal focus. For (8b) there is no stress assignment that would be compatible with maximal focus because the position that would have to host the stress exponent is the preverbal one and in (8b) this position is a trace of scrambling. Conversely, the order in (8a) cannot be a scrambling order but a base order.

(8)   a.   *Haben je   Linguisten   ODEN   interessiert?*
             have ever linguists-ACC odes-NOM   interested?
             'Have linguists ever been interested in odes'

b. *Haben Oden$_i$ je   LINGUISTEN e$_i$ interpretiert*
have   odes-ACC ever linguists-NOM   interpretiert?
'Have linguists ever interpreted odes?'
c. *Haben je   LINGUISTEN Oden interpretiert?*
have   ever linguists   odes interpreted?

The crucial difference in the argument structure between double objects and the two arguments of transitive psych-verbs is exactly the exceptional dissociation of subject selection and ranking: A transitive psych-verb has an argument designated for external licensing that is ranked lower than an undesignated argument. Since the undesignated argument is projected VP-internally, the lower-ranked argument is projected VP-internally as well. This is the origin of the VP-structure (5a).

A principle that guarantees this outcome is independently supported by the distribution of VP-internal subjects in VO-languages without the option of postverbal subjects (cf. Burzio 1986: 137). The argument marked for external licensing in the argument-structure must be licensed externally. In other words, an argument-DP that instantiates the designated argument position of the verbal head cannot be licensed VP-internally in a language in which the external argument is projected in SpecVP:

(9) a. *??Il a téléfoné trois amis*
it has telephoned three friends
'there have telephoned three friends'
b. *Il est arrivé trois amis*
it is arrived three friends
'there have arrived three friends'

In the French example (9), an expletive pronominal subject is assigned nominative and triggers singular agreement despite the presence of a plural argument that — in the absence of the expletive — would be the subject and trigger plural agreement. Consequently the postverbal DP must receive its case license VP-internally. The contrast between (9a) and (9b) is a reflex of the restriction discussed above: The designated argument cannot be licensed VP-internally. Ergative verbs as in (9b), in contrast to intransitive verbs, do not have a designated argument.

A final piece of evidence against the original version of BG can be observed in the German middle construction. Middle formation in German, like in Romance but unlike English or Dutch, employs a reflexive. The object argument appears in the nominative and the reflexive is marked accusative:

(10) a. *Du*-NOM *fühlst dich*-ACC **(kalt/wie Marmor) an*
you feel yourself cold/like marble
'you feel cold/like marble'
b. *Sie fühlte den Körper an*
'she felt/touched the body'

The fact that the object argument in (10a) is licensed for nominative implies that there is no primary subject. In terms of the determinants of BG, the subject must be θ-free. Nevertheless accusative is assigned to the reflexive in the transitive middle construction. This is a problem for BG but not for an account in terms of a dependency relation between functional and categorial licensing: The categorially licensed accusative in (10a) is in accordance with the dependency constraint because there is a functionally licensed case in the same licensing domain, too, namely the nominative on the derived subject.

2. On an economy condition for case licensing

Given, that the subject matter of BG is the interdependency of the licensing conditions of structural case, a foremost remarkable feature of BG is its restricted range of application. It applies only to verbs.[7] Structural case licensed by nouns or prepositions is not affected. In German, nouns license genitive for structural arguments. In (11a), the deverbal noun licenses the genitive NP-internally in the absence of an external one. The presence of an external argument as in (11b) is not required.[8] A preposition like in (11), licenses accusative without there being a θ-marked subject of the preposition:

(11) a. *[die Befragungen der Zeugen*-GEN *(durch den Richter)]*
questionings (of) the witnesses (by the judge)
dauerten einen Tag
took one day
b. *[Peters*-GEN *Befragungen der Zeugen*-GEN*] dauerten einen*
Peter's questionings (of) the witnesses took one
Tag
day
c. [For [*him* to arrive in time]] ...

What is the relevant property that singles out the verb? Verbs are inflected and inflection features are case licensers. What this indicates is that BG is the reflex of a constraint that guarantees deterministic licensing relations in potentially non-deterministic contexts: In a context with one structural argument and more than one licensing option — a categorial and a functional one — the BG determines the priority relation for case licensing. For arguments with structural case, external licensing overrides internal licensing. This is not necessarily confined to a specific structural positional. In English, licensing is positional: External licensing applies in Spec-positions and not VP-internally.

It is well-known that in English external licensing is confined to specific structural positions and, in addition, the nominative position must be made use of. In Chomsky (1986), this is stipulated as the EPP, the extended projection principle. German is not subject to this requirement (cf. 12a–d), so potentially conflicting licensing relations can be studied more directly.

(12) a. *daß (*es)   auf mich-*ACC *nicht gewartet wurde*
        that it/there for me   not waited was
        'that for me not waited was'
     b. *daß (*es)   mir-*DAT/**ich-*NOM *nicht geholfen wurde*
        that it/there me/*I   not helped was
        'that I was not helped'
     c. *daß (*es)   nicht geschossen wurde*
        that it/there not shot   was
     d. *daß ich-*NOM/**mich-*ACC *nicht gesehen wurde*
        that I/*me   not seen was
        'that I was not seen'

In (12a), ACC is licensed by a preposition. (12b) illustrates a passive clause with an inherently case-linked argument, namely dative, licensed by the verb. (12c) is the passive of an intransitive verb, with no argument left for licensing.[9] Eventually, (12d) is the familiar BG-dependency of internal and categorial licensing by V^0 on external licensing: Nominative-licensing has priority over accusative licensing. It is important to realize that both, nominative and accusative, can be licensed VP-internally. This can be demonstrated with VP-topicalization: (13a) is an example with a topicalized VP that contains a VP-internal nominative on the argument of an unaccusative verb. (13b) contains a nominative on the direct object, as a consequence of a passive construction.

(13) a. *[[VP] Ein Fehler   unterlaufen] ist einem Linguisten*
        a   mistake-NOM undergone is a   linguist-DAT
        dabei   schon   zweimal
        that-with already twice'
        'Already twice, a linguist happened to make a mistake in that matter'

b. *[Schwere Fehler nachgewiesen] wurden Linguisten*
bad mistakes-NOM proven were (to) linguists-DAT
schon oft
already often
'Linguists have already often been given proof of bad mistakes'

Let us recapitulate. In German, representative for a language with a NOM-ACC-system, both accusative and nominative are potentially licensed in VP-internal positions. Accusative is categorially licensed by V^0, Nominative is functionally licensed by agreement, which is spelled out in the verbal morphology. Hence, an argument without inherent case specification is generally in a conflicting licensing environment. What BG refers to is a priority condition that settles the conflict. It states that internal licensing applies only if the external licensing potential has been exploited. This implies for a finite clause that an argument cannot be licensed as accusative if a nominative license is available for this argument.

If one asks oneself why things should be as they are, it is worthwhile asking how an alternative implementation would look like. There are two alternative possibilities, in fact. One is free licensing: If there is more than one licensing option, the choice is free. In this case, the accusative would be in free alternation with nominative in unaccusative and passive structures.[10] The second possibility is the inverse of BG, that is, categorial licensing gets priority over functional licensing. For a finite clause this would mean accusative always has priority over nominative. The solution that eliminates the second possibility will eliminate the first one, too.

Even on the basis of limited crosslinguistic evidence on case systems, it is safe to conjecture that there exists no language with priority of categorial licensing over functional licensing. This would mean that a single structural argument would be licensed for accusative (as a categorial license), and nominative (as a functional license) would be found only if there is a second structural argument. The resulting system could be called anti-ergative.

(14) a. me is watching (instead of: *I am watching*)
b. I am watching her

For verbs with an optional direct object, as in (14a), this would imply that the subject is accusative (14a) unless an object is projected (14b). Only in this case the subject would be licensed as nominative. Note that (14) cannot be interpreted as an ergative case system. The ergative system would be (15):

(15) a. I *am* watching
b. Her *is* watching I (meaning: *She is watching me*)

What I propose is that the answer should be given in terms of an economy constraint on licensing: Licensing case by Agr simultaneously licenses the functional features (φ-features) of the verb. If the verb licenses the accusative and the φ-features of the verb are licensed separately, for instance by adjusting the values of the feature matrix to a default value — for licensing case by morphological paradigms the default is usually third person singular — licensing has to operate twice. So, intuitively the combinatorial licensing is more economical: Licensing the nominative simultaneously provides the feature values for the φ-features of the finite verb. This covers licensing by *functional* features. But there is also a positional implementation option for functional licensing, either with or without overt agreement.

Licensing as a purely *positional* function (in the absence of agreement, as for instance in continental Scandinavian languages) requires a unique structural position. For external arguments, this is the Spec-position of a functional head. This position is mandatory, just as the agreement inflection is mandatory in an agreement system. If there is no element for this position, an expletive element is required.

In positional implementations of licensing, the required position is part of the general and obligatory set-up of a clause. This is what the EPP-condition intends to capture. But the EPP is redundant once this is realized: The EPP redundantly postulates that for languages with positional licensing of the external argument there is a structural position in the clause in which licensing applies. Since the structural set-up for this position is a property of the general clause structure of a language with a positional licensing system, the presence of the position cannot be contingent on the presence of an argument that is in need of such a position for its licensing requirements. The EPP is the structural counterpart of licensing by agreement: In languages with agreement, agreement morphology is realized irrespective of the presence or absence of an element that it is in agreement with.

EPP, on the other hand, does not exist in a language with a non-positional licensing system, as in German. There is no unique position for licensing an argument and there is no unique position provided in the clause structure. So, no expletive is licensed in the cases illustrated in (12a–c). A language like English is representative of languages whose licensing systems combine positional licensing with licensing by agreement. Licensing by agreement takes place in a specific functional position.

Let us recapitulate: Burzio's generalization can be interpreted as the effect of an economy constraint on licensing systems: The priority of functional licensing has the effect that the licensing a DP at the same time licenses agreement morphology and/or Spec–Head configurations. Conversely, the priority of categorial checking would in many case require the insertion of an expletive and/or a separate default licensing of agreement features. The case systems found in natural languages can be characterized as those systems that pass an economy criterion:

(16)   The BG-axiom: Minimize licensing-checks

In the set of possible implementations of functional and categorial licensing given in (17), only (17a) meets (16). In the discussion above, (17b) already has been shown to be inferior to (17a) on an economy measure on the number of independent licensing checks. For monadic verbs, (17c) is equivalent to the union of (17a) and (17b). Ruling out (17b), however, reduces (17c) to (17a).

(17)   a.   Option 1:   Priority of functional licensing over categorial licensing
       b.   Option 2:   Priority of categorial licensing over functional licensing
       c.   Option 3:   Equal applicability of categorial and functional licensing

If the licensing systems for verbal and nominal features obey (16), BG is the result. It applies both to morphologically overt as well as to positional licensing. In an SVO language without functional morphology, like Chinese, there are structural licensing positions for the subject and the objects. (16) guarantees that there is a default licensing option in the core grammar for a structural argument that receives priority. The obligatory licensing of the subject position (EPP) is a reflex of a structural default in the licensing system.

(18)   *Corollary of the BG-axiom*: There are no case systems with both functional and categorial licensing of structural case in which categorial licensing has priority over functional licensing.

What (18) rules out is a NOM–ACC system in which nominative licensing is dependent on the presence of a DP marked for accusative, with the effect that accusative as a categorial license gets priority and nominative as a functional license is available only if the categorial license has been exploited. For a NOM–ERG system, (18) eliminates the option that nominative/absolutive licensing is dependent on the presence of a DP marked ergative.

(16) should be regarded as the characterization of a meta-principle, that is, a principle of UG. It guarantees that the licensing system implemented in the core grammar of a given language is organized in such a way that there is no strongly equivalent grammar with a more economic licensing system. Economy

considerations are not part of the core grammar proper. This distinction is important. Economy is valid only on the level of explanatory adequacy, that is on the UG-level. If (16) were a principle of individual grammars, the ensuing licensing system would have to embody a complex economy metric. This is neither plausible nor empirically justified. The brief crosslinguistic survey (constructions with expletive subjects in Romance and Scandinavian and impersonal construction in Slavic languages) discussed in the following paragraphs provide empirical support for this claim.

In the Italian reflexive impersonal construction (cf. Burzio 1996: 46) the object either stays in its VP-internal position or it moves to the nominative-position. If it stays, it may be licensed as accusative (19a). When it moves, it is licensed as nominative (19b) only.

(19) a. *Si **leggerà/leggeranno** volentieri alcuni articoli*
REFL will-read-3SG/3PL voluntarily several articles
'One will voluntarily read several articles'
b. *Alcuni articoli si **leggeranno** volentieri*
several articles REFL will-read-3PL voluntarily
'One will read several articles voluntarily'
c. **Alcuni articoli si **leggerà** volentieri*

At first glance (19a) with accusative seems to contradict (16) and (17a). But a comparative look at French reveals the underlying grammatical causality. Just like (20a), (19a) is a construction with an expletive subject pronoun (3SG) that triggers agreement.[11] In Italian, the expletive is a null-subject, in French it is overt. The expletive pronoun is third person singular. It is the target for the agreement values, and it receives the nominative. The object argument is licensed for accusative. If there is no expletive the object is fronted and licensed as nominative.

In a core grammar implementation of economy of licensing, (20a) with singular morphology on the finite verb should be ruled out, but as a matter of fact (20b) with plural on the verb is ungrammatical. Plural agreement with a plural expletive or movement of the argument (cf. 20c) would be the more economic way of licensing. But, as pointed out, despite the fact that the particular set-up of core grammar may be the result of an economy metric, the core grammar itself does not contain the metric. Therefore (19a) is either a construction with an expletive subject and accusative, or it is a construction with a postverbal nominative subject. The latter option is excluded for French, which does not allow postverbal subjects (20b).

(20) a. *Il **a** manqué trois enfants*
 it is missing three children
 'three children are missing'
 b. **Il **ont** manqué trois enfants*
 it-PL are missing three enfants
 c. *Trois enfants **ont** manqué*
 three children are missing

There is a parallel setting attested for Slavic. Keenan & Timberlake (1985) point out that in Polish and Russian passive constructions, ACC is assigned to the object if the verb is inflected in the impersonal form, whereas NOM is obligatory if the verb is inflected in the agreement paradigm:

(21) a. *Lipa ścięta* (Polish)
 the linden-NOM was cut-NOM.FEM.SG.PASS
 b. *Lipę ścięto*
 linden-ACC cut-NOM.NT.SG.PASS
 c. *Ja zarezal telenka* (Russian)
 I slaughter a calf-ACC
 d. *(U menja) telenok zarezan*
 By me a calf-NOM.MASC.SG slaughtered-NOM.MASC.SG.PASS
 e. *(U menja) zarezano telenka*
 By me [there was] slaughtered-NOM.N.SG.PASS a calf-ACC

A case system that produces patterns as in (21) is not excluded by BG in a core grammar selected under the maxim (16), if the inflection system of a language provides an impersonal paradigm. ACC-licensing is in fact the only option for an object DP then: ACC licensing is not in competition with functional licensing, hence there is no economy conflict. The impersonal paradigm does not admit nominative licensing. Therefore, the verb is a monadic licenser of a structural argument, much like a preposition or an adjective.

Eventually, languages without subject verb agreement, like the mainland Scandinavian languages, may employ a system of licensing that admits more than one structural option in some cases, each of which compatible with BG implemented as in (16). In Swedish and other Scandinavian languages, NP-movement in passive is in variation with an expletive subject (cf. Hedlund 1992: 137 f.).

(22) a. *Det visades honom båtar.* (Swedish)
 EXPL showed-PASS him boats

b. *Han$_i$ visades   e$_i$ båtar.*
He shows-PASS boats
'He is shown boats'

c. *Båtar$_i$ visades   honom e$_i$.*
Boates show-PASS him
'Boate are shown to him'

In English, the construction corresponding to (22a) would be ungrammatical, because of the anaphoric character of the English Agr–Head and the lack of a pronominal expletive. The adverbial expletive *there* in English cannot serve as an antecedent for Agr. The Swedish expletive is pronominal, but this is not crucial, because of the general absence of subject verb agreement in the mainland Scandinavian languages. *Der*, the Danish expletive in passives is, like the English one homophonous with the locative adverbial proform. A grammar without Subject–Verb agreement that admits the patterns in (22) is consistent with (16): Accusative is licensed categorially because the positional licensing in the Spec-position is not available. This position for functional licensing is blocked by the expletive.

Less straightforward is the Norwegian case, illustrated in (23). Clauses like (23c–e) involve at least three potentially case licensing heads, namely P, V, and a functional head. First of all, the subject DP in (23a, c) can be licensed alternatively by P in its base position. In this case, SpecI has to be filled with an expletive. This could be handled with optional incorporation of P^0. Remarkable is the alternation in (23c, d).

(23) a. *at det vart   tala   om   Jon*
that it became talked about Jon
'that Jon was talked about'
(Norwegian: Åfarli 1992: 18,20)

b. *at Jon$_i$ vart   tala   om e$_i$*
that Jon became talked about
'that Jon was talked about'

c. *at brevet$_i$ ble klisteret frimerker på e$_i$*
that letter-the was pasted   stamps   on
'the letter was pasted stamps on'
(Norwegian: Taraldsen 1979)
(Afarli 1992: 18, 20)

d. *at frimerker$_i$ ble   klisteret e$_i$ på brevet*
that stamps   were pasted   on the letter

e. *at det ble klisteret frimerker på brevet*

f. *at det var   kjøpt   ein hund*
   that it became bought a   dog
   'that a dog was bought'

From a descriptive point of view, the remarkable feature of (23c) is the optionality of P-standing in the presence of a direct object. If stranding is possible, there are several possibilities to arrive at grammatical result: The preposition is stranded (23c), or the direct object is fronted (23a), or an expletive is inserted (23e). This option exists for all cases, that is, also for dyadic verbs (23f) and for the passive of an intransitive verb. In each case, two DP-positions must be licensed. One is licensed functionally, namely the subject position, and the other, that is, the complement of the verb or the preposition, is licensed categorially. Norwegian, as all continental Scandinavian languages lacks Subject–Verb agreement. If the combined licensing of V-features and DP-features is the relevant factor for economy, movement becomes as 'costly' as the insertion of an expletive in a language without Subject–Verb agreement.

In sum, the reinterpretation of BG as the result of an economy constraint on licensing systems is on the one hand a monomodular constraint, which is a conceptual advantage, and on the other hand its empirical implications are in harmony with the recalcitrant evidence from expletive and impersonal constructions in various languages. The next section pursues the effects of (16) for ergative systems.

Under an economy account in terms of (16), BG is the effect of the priority of functional licensing over categorial licensing of an argument with structural case. The potential case licensing capacity of the verb is not exploited if there is a functional licenser available. Bittner & Hale (1996a) suggest the opposite. The verb must be activated by a case competitor in order to be able to license structural case. Under this view, the verb is equipped with a case licensing capacity only in specific contexts. The verb cannot license structural case unaided. "Any head, even one which is empty, can assign marked structural Case to an argument which it Case-binds, being activated by a visible Case competitor for that argument." (Bittner & Hale 1996a: 2). The case competitor of a nominal is defined as a caseless co-argument.

Restricting the case licensing capacity of V to contexts in which there is a DP competing for structural case may be descriptively adequate, but it does not provide an answer to the question why this should be so. Why is accusative licensing dependent on functional licensing and why could it not be the other way? A structural case would be licensed by V. In case V is unable to check, a functional head would check the case. This is what (18) rules out and what should follow from a general principle. The activation-restriction on structural case licensing is an implementation whose theoretical reason is left open. As long as this reason is missing, the proposed restriction remains an empirically motivated but theoretically accidental device.

Up to this point, the effects of the BG-axiom (16) have been discussed with reference to languages with a NOM-ACC system. In the following section it will be shown to be a general principle that applies to NOM-ERG systems as well.

3. BG-effects in NOM-ERG systems

In (24) the three types of A-structures with structural arguments are listed. The parametric split between the nominative-accusative system of licensing and the absolutive/nominative-ergative system is the choice of the argument for licensing priority. The two systems correspond to the two logical possibilities, given an argument structure with two structural arguments (cf. 24a).

(24) a. $V^0 \langle \underline{A}_1, A_2 \rangle$ transitive
b. $V^0 \langle \underline{A} \rangle$ intransitive
c. $V^0 \langle A \rangle$ unaccusative

(25) a. priority license for $\underline{A}$: nominative-accusative system
b. priority license for A: absolutive-ergative system

BG states that the non-priority argument is licensed in the same way as the priority argument if the priority argument is absent. The argument of the verbs with unaccusative argument structure (24b) or the non-designated argument of (24a) in contexts with a blocked external argument (e.g. passive) will be licensed in the same way as the priority-argument of (24a) and (24b). The morphologically or structurally visible effect is case-conversion (nominative instead of accusative, absolutive instead of ergative) or movement to the structural licensing position of the priority licensing relation.

Chomsky (1992: 13) and Bobaljik (1993: 6) favor a unified account in terms of a single parameter: For Chomsky, the differentiating property between nom-acc and erg-nom systems is the higher activity of either AgrS or AgrO. An ergative language is characterized as a language with an active AgrO and an inert AgrS, rather than an active AgrS head. Languages with an ergative case system but a nominative-accusative type of person-agreement like Georgian (cf. Harris 1981) or Warlpiri (cf. Jelinek 1984; Bittner & Hale 1996b) are unexpected under this account. Bobaljik suggests a parametric difference in terms of a choice of the obligatory case, either nominative as AgrS or absolutive as AgrO.

This is virtually equivalent with (25).[12]

(25) cannot be conceived of as a simple parametrical duality of implementing a priority relation of argument licensing, though. In the nominative-accusative systems, the dependency is in the majority of languages a dependency between functional and categorial licensing of structural case. Languages with object agreement in addition to subject agreement instantiate a different system, namely one with two functional licenses. For the ergative-nominative systems, there is reason to assume that this is the case in general. Two cases are functionally licensed. In (26), an example from Inuktitut, the finite verb agrees with both, the nominative DP and the ergative DP.

(26) Inuktitut (North Baffin)
    a. *inu-up   qimmiq taku-v-**a**-a*
        person-*up* dog-*Ø* see-INDIC-**TRANS**-3/3
        'a/the person saw the dog'
    b. *inuk   (qimmir-mik) taku-v-**uq***
        person-*Ø* dog-*mik*)   see-INDIC-**INTR**-3
        'A/the person saw (the dog)'

In (26a, b), the verbs contain a transitivizing and a detransitivizing suffix, respectively. The ergative-marked noun in (26a) appears as nominative in (26b), that is, as the unmarked form. The unmarked form of (26a) is marked with an oblique case, if it is optionally chosen to appear.

In Quiche (27), there is no nominal morphology for case. WH-extraction (cf. 27c, d), relativization and focussing, however, require a DP in the nominative relation: In (27d), the detransitivizing suffix *ow* changes the erg-relation to the abs-relation. The result is a structure like in a NOM-ACC system with subject agreement only (cf. Larsen & Norman 1979).

(27) Quiche (as representative for the Mayan family)
    a. *x-Ø-war-ik*
        COMPL-3SG.ABS-sleep-PHRASEFINAL SUFF
        'He slept'
    b. *x-Ø-a-ch'ay-oh*
        COMPL-3SG.ABS-2SG.ERG-hit-PHRASEFINAL SUFF
        'You hit him'   (Larsen & Norman 1979: 347)
    c. *jachin x-Ø-u-ch'ay lee ixoq*
        who COMPL-3SG.ABS-3SG.ERG-hit the woman
        'Who did the woman hit?' [*Who hit the woman]

d. *jachin x-Ø-ch'ay-**ow** lee ixoq*
    who COMP-3SG.ABS-hit-**intr**. the woman
    'Who hit the woman?'   (Larsen & Norman 1979: 357)

Another systematic difference is the distribution across word order types: NOM-ACC systems are found in all the Greenbergian word order types. This does not seem to hold true for ergative systems. Inuktitut is an XV-language, Quiche is VX. According to Trask (1979: 385), ergative languages are SOV, occasionally VSO, but virtually never SVO. This seems to indicate that the differentiation between a VP-external positional functional mode of licensing and a VP-internal categorial licensing mode for arguments in situ does generally not apply to ergative systems. What this implies is that ergative systems are pure functional licensing systems. Functional licensing is uniform with respect to the directionality of licensing. So, the verb as the exponent of functional licensing features either remains in situ, following all arguments, or is fronted and precedes all arguments. In an SVO-language like English, the functional licenser AgrS follows the nominative while the verb as the categorial licenser precedes the objects. The directionality of functional and categorial licensing, therefore, cannot be uniform in English.

As for the order of inflection morphemes on the verb, Bittner & Hale (1996b: 569) point out for Inuit that the agreement marker construed with the ergative argument is closer to the verb stem or auxiliary base, while the marker construed with the nominative/absolutive is more peripheral in the inflected verb. This serialization pattern of morphemes is a consequence of the priority asymmetry (25b): The least embedded form in terms of the morphological structure is the form of the priority agreement slot of the finite verb. Both in ergative and in accusative languages, the priority slot is the slot for nominative-agreement. The dependence of ergative on nominative resembles the accusative-nominative dependence, but it is not a dependence between categorial and functional licensing, since both cases, nominative as well as ergative are functional cases. As the example of Quiche illustrates, the ergative agreement system is subject to the same priority dependency between the cases, and it is a functional licensing system.

What is the role of the BG-axiom (16) in an ergative case system in comparison to a NOM-ACC system? The role is the same, only the implementation of the priority dependency is different. In the discussion of typical NOM-ACC systems, economy was claimed to favor the priority of functional licensing over categorial licensing because of simultaneous feature checking. Functional licensing combines the licensing of agreement and case features and thus reduces the number of independent licensing operations per clause. The same kind of reasoning can be applied to NOM-ACC systems with object agreement and to NOM-ERG systems with functional licensing for both cases. The premises that lead to BG as a conclusion are:

First, a licensing system with a default functional case is more economic than a system without. Languages without a licensing priority (3-way case systems) are rare: Bittner and Hale (1996a: 51) cite Antekerrepenhe (Arandic, Australia) and Nez Perce (Penuitan, Oregon), languages in which subjects of monadic verbs are in the unmarked nominative/absolutive, while transitive subjects and objects are marked with specific case forms (ergative and accusative). The default licensing reduces the system from three to two licensing values for structural arguments: The argument of a monadic verb and the designated argument of the dyadic verb is each licensed in the priority case.

Second, a licensing configuration that is a default licensing option is part of the general clause structure. What this means is, that the licensing constellation is independent of the argument structure of the verb that happens to be the main verb. Third, the economy metrics favors systems with default licensing. If the default is ignored this implies that an additional licensing mechanism must be invoked while the default option applies vacuously.

Third, BG amounts to the statement that the default option cannot be the dependent partner in a priority relation of licensing. In an accusative-system, the nominative cannot be dependent of the accusative assignment, and in an ergative system, the absolutive cannot be dependent on ergative assignment. In each case, the dependent licensing relation is dependent on the default licensing relation, that is, the nominative/absolutive. In structural terms, the dependency amounts to a reduced structure. The default case being absolutive, the ergative-absolutive dependency covered by BG amounts to the effect that (28b) is sufficient for licensing the second argument of a dyadic verb in the absence of the designated one (antipassive and related contexts).

(28) a. ... $[_{FP} F^0_{abs} [_{FP} F^0_{erg} [_{VP} DP_{erg} DP_{abs} V^0 ...]]]$
     b. ... $[_{FP} F^0_{abs} [_{VP} DP_{abs} V^0]]$

The parametric difference between accusative and ergative systems is the designation of the argument for the default licensing relation (cf. 25): In the accusative-system, it is the highest ranking structural argument, in the ergative system, it is the lowest ranking argument (cf. Wunderlich 1997: 49)

4. Summary

UG guarantees default licensing environments for structural case. The functionally licensed default in a finite clause is the nominative or absolutive. Functional licensing requires either a Spec–Head relation or overt agreement. The difference between the nom-acc type and the erg-nom type is the result of the parametric alternative on the choice of the argument for the functional default licensing: Either the highest or the lowest ranking structural argument gets priority. BG is the result of an economy constraint on licensing systems. There is a priority relation among the licensing options for structural case. The priority relation is the dependency relation between the default licensing relation and the remaining option, either a categorial or a functional one.

Notes

1. Burzio's Generalization is: $\theta_s \leftrightarrow$ Acc (Burzio 1986: 185). "All and only the verbs that can assign θ-role to the subject can assign (accusative) case to an object." (Burzio 1986:178).
2. Uncontroversial evidence for functional licensing of object case by means of AgrO on the PF-relevant structure is wanting for languages without overt object agreement, and there are several reasons for not adopting the hypothesis that case-licensing requires a functional head in general. First, languages like English exemplify that a clause obligatorily provides a subject position. Object positions, however, are a function of the A-structure of the verb. If a clause were to provide functional heads for objects outside VP, every clause would have to contain structural positions for objects which remain empty if the verb does not provide arguments, since heads are insensitive to the internal structure of their complements. Second, structurally mandatory positions trigger expletives (cf. obligatory expletives with impersonal passive in the mainland Scandinavian languages). There are no object expletives in intransitive VPs, however, neither in an OV-language like German nor in a VO-language like English. Third, the morphological form of a structural case depends on the category of the element that checks it. In German, verbs license the accusative as a structural case while nouns license the genitive as the structural case:

    a. einen Baum-ACC pflanzen — to plant a tree
    b. das Pflanzen eines Baumes-GEN–the planting (of) a tree

    AgrO, therefore, is a morphologically typed feature. The distinction between genitive and accusative is irrelevant at LF, however. Hence the case for the object should be licensed before spell out. The NP-internal complement does not seem to have been moved to a functional position, however. In addition, it is unclear how the required AgrO position should be integrated in the structure of the N-projection.

3. For double object constructions in head-inital VPs, I assume a kind of Larsonian VP-shell structure: The V-projection consists of stacked [XP [V^0 [YP]]]-structures, with raising of the verbal head to the top-most head-position in the stacked VP. The positions of the arguments in the stacked VP are base positions.

THE LICENSE TO LICENSE 53

4. 'Structural argument' is short for: Argument in the argument-grid of a lexical entry not specified for inherent case and therefore in need of structural case licensing.

5. Roughly: x causes y to be in a psychological state P (= being annoyed) targeted at x. So, „the noise annoys me" would roughly translates into: The noise makes me be annoyed at the noise. The noise is both cause of emotion and target of emotion.

6. The dissociation is conditioned by the fact that there is also a causative-agentive conceptualization for these verbs with independent instantiations of agentive cause, experiencer and instrument/target:
    a. He annoyed me with the noise he produced
    b. He frightened me with the noise he produced

    Note that the interpretation is not necessarily agentive, since the noise can be unintended. If the instrument is simultaneously the cause, the result is a lexical-conceptual structure with two variables that are related to one argument in the argument structure of the verb.

7.` The applicability of BG to AP-internal case licensing is less easy to decide in full generality. With respect to German the answer is easy, however. German adjectives do not license accusative. This unaccusativity-property indicates that BG is at work: Adjectives are bound to be unaccusative predicates because they are selected by an unaccusative auxiliary, the copular verb *be*.

8. Nouns do not tolerate inherently case marked complements, which is easy to check with deverbal nouns: Inherently case marked arguments (dative and verbal genitve) do not occur as objects of (deverbal) nouns. Only arguments that surface as direct objects or subjects in a clause may occur as arguments of nouns.
    a. *das Helfen dem Freund-DAT — the helping the friend
    b. *das Anklagen des Mordes-GEN — the accusing (of) murder

9. It is not justified to assume an expletive *pro* (cf. Haider 1997, Section 3: 90–92): First, in German, *es* is a suitable expletive element for a Spec-position, namely SpecC. Second, *es* cannot be dropped freely (e.g. in middle or in extraposition constructions). Third, in Dutch an expletive is obligatory in the construction corresponding to (12c):
    a. *daß *(es) heute peinlich war daß niemand zum Vortrag kam*
        'that it today embarrassing was that nonone attended the lecture'
    b. *Meestal werd *(er)   gelachen*
        mostly was   there laughed

    The Dutch-German difference is not a difference in terms of pro-drop but rather in terms of the EPP proper.

10. If there are two structurally licensed arguments, that is, if the verb is transitive, there is no choice. One will be accusative and one nominative. This is guaranteed by a uniqueness requirement: Each licensing relation can be applied only once. This exludes at least double nominatives. The condition that singles out the designated argument for external licensing guarantees that there is at least one nominative.

11. Zaenen & Maling (1994: 145) note the following contrast for Icelandic:
    a. *Stormurinn*-ACC *blés strompinn   af húsinu*
        the-storm   blew the-chimney off the-house
    b. *Strompinn   blés af húsinu*
        the-chimney blew off the-house

c. *Strompurinn*-NOM *var blásinn af húsinu*
the-chimney was blown off the-house

In the passive, nominative is obligatory, while in (b), which Zaenen & Maling call unaccusative, the accusative is conserved. In fact (b) is an impersonal construction, like (4b), without an overt expletive. In Icelandic, subject expletives in the form of quasi-arguments (cf. weather verbs) are missing. In the corresponding German version (*daß es den Schornstein vom Dach blies*), the subject is the expletive quasi-argument *es*.

12. Interpreted literally, Bobaljik's statement does not admit constructions without structural case altogether, which do occur in Icelandic or German, however.

References

Belletti, A. and Rizzi, L. 1988. "Psych-verbs and theta-theory". *Natural Language and Linguistic Theory* 6: 292–352.
Bittner, M. and Hale, K. 1996a. "The structural determination of case and agreement". *Linguistic Inquiry* 27: 1–68.
Bittner, M. and Hale, K. 1996b. "Ergativity: Toward a theory of a heterogeneous class". *Linguistic Inquiry* 27: 531–604.
Bobaljik, J. 1993. "On ergativity and ergative unergatives". *MIT Working Papers* 19: 45–88.
Burzio, L. 1986. *Italian Syntax*. Dordrecht: Kluwer Academic Publishers.
Chomsky, N. 1992. "A minimalist program for linguistic theory". In *MIT Occasional Papers in Linguistics 1*. [1993 in *The View from Building 20: Essays in Honor of Sylvain Bromberger*, K. Hale and S.J. Keyser (eds), 1–51, Cambridge, MA: MIT Press].
Haider, H. 1984. "The case of German". In *Studies in German Grammar*, J. Toman (ed.), 65–101. Dordrecht: Foris.
Haider, H. 1985. "A unified account of case and θ-marking: The case of German". *Papiere zur Linguistik* 32: 3–36.
Haider, H. 1997. "Projective economy and the minimal functional structure of the German clause". In *German: Syntactic problems problematic syntax*, W. Abraham and E. van Gelderen (eds), 83–103. Tübingen: Niemeyer.
Harris, A. 1981. *Georgian Syntax*. Cambridge: CUP.
Hedlund, C. 1992. On Participles. PhD Dissertation, University of Lund.
Jelinek, E. 1984. "Empty categories, case, and configurationality". *Natural Language and Linguistic Theory* 2:39–76.
Keenan, E. and Timberlake, A. 1985. "Valency affecting rules in extended categorial grammar". *Language Research* 21:415–434.
Koch-Christensen, K. and Taraldsen, T. 1989. "Expletive chain formation and past participle agreement in Scandinavian dialects". In *Dialect Variation and the Theory of Grammar*, P. Benincà (ed.), 53–83. Dordrecht: Foris.

Laka, I. 1993. "Unergatives that assign ergative, unaccusatives that assign accusative". *MIT Working Papers* 19:149–172.
Larson, T. and Norman, W. 1979. "Correlates of ergativity in Mayan grammar". In *Ergativity*, F. Plank (ed.), 347–370. New York: Academic Press.
Marantz, A. 1991. "Case and licensing". *Proceedings of ESCOL* 8: 234–53. [reprinted in this volume].
Taraldsen, T. 1979. "Remarks on some central problems of Norwegian syntax". *Nordic Journal of Linguistics* 2:23–54.
Trask, R. 1979. "On the origins of ergativity". In *Ergativity*, F. Plank (ed.), 385–404, New York: Academic Press.
Williams, E. 1981. "Argument structure and morphology". *The Linguistic Review* 1: 81–144.
Wunderlich, D. 1997. "Cause and the structure of verbs". *Linguistic Inquiry* 28:1–25.
Zaenen, A. and Maling, J. 1994. "Unaccusative, passive and quirky case". In *Modern Icelandic Syntax*, J. Maling and A. Zaenen (eds), 137–152. New York: Academic Press [Syntax and Semantics 24].

The Nature of Verbs
and Burzio's Generalization

Teun Hoekstra[†]
Leiden University/HIL

Introduction

Burzio's generalization concerns a relationship between licensing structure (Case marking) and argument structure, a correlation which is conceptually unclear. In this paper I put forth a specific proposal concerning argument structure and licensing which explains Burzio's generalization.

In Section 1, I argue that Burzio's generalization should be traced to parameters involving the availability of Accusative Case. In Section 2, it is shown that Accusative Case results from the incorporation of a prepositional element associated with the external argument. This claim yields a different view on the relationship between Actives and Passives. It is argued that the notion of transitivity is derivative. In Section 3 I further develop this idea, by considering the nature of the category verb, where I argue that lexical verbs are also derived elements. I compare my approach to the theory of argument structure developed by Hale & Keyser. In Section 4, finally, a more global discussion of parameters of variation with respect to the availability of Accusative Case is presented.

1. Burzio's generalization and Case marking

Let us start with a brief look at Burzio's generalization, which states a correlation between the availability of Accusative Case and External argument. Subdividing the class of intransitives in unergatives, which possess an external argument, but no internal (accusative) argument, and ergatives, which have an internal argument, but lack an external one, Burzio's generalization comes down to stating that an argument structure distinction gets suppressed at the level of licensing. Apparently, the licensing potential of Nominative case takes precedence, which can be formulated in several ways. Let's call it the NOM-first property (cf. Hoekstra 1984: 298; Hoekstra & Mulder 1989: 36; as well more recent proposals to that effect).

We may then wonder why the NOM-first property would hold. An immediate answer is provided once we realize the asymmetry that exists between NOM and ACC: the former is T(ense)-Case, and T is a property of all sentences, while the latter is V(erb)-Case, and hence depends on properties of V, i.e. not for all verbs, and for some verbs not always is ACC available. We need to ask the question as to what the parameters of ACC-availability are, but it is in any event clear that they differ from NOM-availability.

Turning to languages with ergative case systems, we are led to identify Absolutive Case as a T-related Case, as, like Nominative, Absolutive Case is always available, independent of verb-type. In fact, even in copular sentences, the subject is marked with Absolutive Case. This conclusion is quite different from Chomsky's (1992: 13) suggestion on this matter: distinguishing between AgrS and ArgO, Chomsky maintains that in intransitive sentences only one is required, but both are in principle available. The choice between the two is formulated in terms of "activity" of one of them. In Nom-Acc languages AgrS is active, giving the subject the properties of a transitive subject; in Erg-Abs languages AgrO is active, giving the subject the properties of a transitive object. He stresses that AgrS and AgrO are not different inherently, but only configurationally. Specifically, AgrS is linked up with Tense, i.e. AgrS checks the Case made available (selected) by Tense, while AgrO is linked up with V. On this basis, then, we are led to conclude that Absolutive, being Tense dependent, is checked by AgrS. The difference between Nom-Acc and Erg-Abs languages can thus not be captured by a choice as to which Agr is active.

A further similarity of Nominative and Absolutive (although there are (apparent) exceptions to this generalization) is that Absolutive must be assigned, even where one might argue that ergative case is likewise available. A case in point is the anti-passive construction in West-Greenlandic Eskimo. As (2a) shows, if an Absolutive-marked object is available, the external argument is rendered with Ergative Case. In (2b), the object may be said to have been put "en chomage", to borrow a term from Relational Grammar: it is shunted from a primary grammatical relation by what is adequately called anti-passive, here morphologically manifested by the suffix *-si*. Assuming that anti-passivization affects the notional object, but not the external argument, it is surprising to note that the Case of the external argument nevertheless changes from Ergative to Absolutive. We might account for this by assuming that Absolutive takes precedence over Ergative. With respect to this situation, then, it seems if a distinction at the level of licensing does not correspond to a distinction at the level of argument structure.

(2) anti-passive in Eskimo.
    a. *Jaani-up tuktu-Ø   tuqut-vaa*
       John-ERG caribou-ABS kill-IND.3SG3SG
       'John killed the caribou'
    b. *Jaani-Ø tuktu-mik   tuqut-si-vuq*
       John-ABS caribou-INSTR kill-ANTI-3SG
       'John killed caribous'

If ABS = NOM, it seems that the difference between NOM–ACC and ERG–ABS languages involves AgrO, as the Case associated with it (Accusative) appears to be unavailable in the latter. Indeed, we might think of a purely ergative case system as lacking Accusative Case[1]. Imagine that the Accusative in "John read a book" were missing. How could the semantic transitivity of *read* be realized? In English there are two ways available: the conative construction "John is reading in a book" or a passive construction "The book is read (by John)". The former is inherently imperfective, i.e. while "read the book" is an accomplishment (or telic predicate), the conative construction is atelic, and therefore falls in the class of simple activities. The well-known use of time-modification can be used to show this: "John read the book in an hour", "John read in the book for/*in an hour". While perfectivity is lost in the conative construction, it may be maintained under passivization: "The book was read in an hour". The antipassive construction in Eskimo has precisely this feature with the conative construction in common: the logical object appears in an oblique case, and is preferably indefinite, and the Aktionsart is that of an imperfective activity predicate. The ergative construction is in many respects similar to the passive. This is evident if we compare (3a) with (3b), its passive counterpart.

(3) a. *nanuq-Ø   Piita-p   tuqu-ta-a*
      polar.bear-ABS Peter-ERG kill-PART-3SG
      'Peter killed the polar bear'
   b. *nanuq-Ø   Piita-mit   tuqu-ta-q*
      polar.bear-ABS Peter-ABL kill-PART-3SG
      'The polar bear was killed by Peter'

In either case, the logical object is in the Absolute Case (=Nom), while the logical subject is in an oblique Case, ergative in (3a), ablative in (3b). The verb forms are also rather similar: both in (3a) and (3b) we find a participial form of the verb. This form can also be used as a nominal predicate. In addition, the verb form shows agreement inflection. But, there is a difference: in (3a), the agreement is taken from the nominal agreement paradigm, and it agrees with the ergative DP, while (3b) shows verbal inflection, this time with the Absolutive DP. The sentences in (3) can therefore be paraphrased with "The polar bear is Peter's killed one" and "The polar bear is the one stabbed by Peter" (cf. Johns 1992 for discussion). The situation in Maya, as described by Seler (1887 [1960]) is entirely identical: "Sie kennen nur Nomina und absolute Verba, die einen Zustand des Seins, eine Eigenschaft oder eine Thätigkeit bezeichnen, die als Prädikate zu einem Personalpronomen oder einer dritten Person als Subjekt konstruirt werden, aber kein direktes Objekt zu sich nehmen können" (p. 89). "... dass den transitiven Verbal Ausdrücken nominale Themata zu Grunde liegen, denen die Possessiva präfigirt werden" (p. 85). "Die Mayaphrasen *a cimzah in yum, a Bibah uuh* heissen also eigentlich: "dein Getödteter ist mein Vater", "dein Geschriebenes ist das Buch", — Ausdrücke, die allerdings dem Sinn nach vollkommen dasselbe bedeuten wie unser "du hast meinen Vater getödtet", "du hast das Buch geschrieben". (p. 86)[2] In both Eskimo and Maya, then, a nominal (participial) form is either used in a kind of copular construction of which the underlying object is the subject, with oblique rendering of the agent internal to this nominal predicate, or this entire construct relates to the agent as a possessive structure, the latter functionally equivalent to a transitive rendering with a nominative agent and an accusative object. As in the case of passive, perfectivity can be obtained, as the object is in the absolute case.

If we are correct in assuming that the Ergative Case patterning results from absence of Accusative Case, the question is why this is lacking in some but not in all languages. In the minimalist framework, Accusative is licensed in the Spec of AgrO. Lacking Accusative Case, then, might be thought of as resulting from the absence of AgrO. Such an assumption would be consistent with a theoretical position which holds that presence or absence of particular functional categories is a language particular matter. So, Nom-Acc languages, under such a view, would have AgrS, T and AgrO, but Erg-Abs languages would only have AgrS and T. Such a view is clearly much weaker than the alternative view that all languages are "identical" in a fundamental sense. This is particularly true as the option that the child would have to determine which functional categories are available in the adult language places a heavy burden on the acquisition task. However, a more subtle version of the same idea is possible. Instead of assuming that the absence or presence of AgrO itself is a primitive parameter, we may take the view that the presence or absence[3] relates to the presence of the element on which it is dependent for its licensing function. In the case of AgrS the element on which its Case-licensing function is dependent is, as we saw above, Tense. For AgrO, on the other hand, its Case licensing potential is dependent on the verb. Hence, if there is no verb, AgrO will not derive Case-licensing potential from it. Such a view easily relates to Seler's statement in the above quote "..dass den transitiven Verbal ausdrücken nominale Themata zu Grunde liegen" (o.c. p. 85, emphasis added). Lack of AgrO (or its activity), as well as the ergative Case pattern, may then be traced to the nominal status of the (semantically) transitive predicate, in fact an old hypothesis on the nature of ergative systems.

2. Passives and transitives

2.1 *The passive nature of participles*

Before going into this any further, I would now like to turn to passivization in Nom-Acc languages. Disregarding the Ergative Case for now, it is clear, as already indicated in the discussion above, that these have properties similar to constructions in ergative languages. I would like to restrict my attention here to participial passives. The traditional view that participles are nominal forms of the verb fits in well with one of the ingredients of passives, viz. absence of Accusative, now regarded as a consequence of the nominal status of the predicate head. Participles are indeed inherently passive, as argued for in Hoekstra (1984)[4]. Their passive nature is evident when they occur in isolation, as in (4), as modifying adjunct:

(4) a. *de gelezen boeken*
        the read   books
     b. *de man zat geslagen in een hoek*
        the man sat beaten   in a   corner
     c. *Read all of Marx John could not claim any naïvety

The subject of predication of these adjunct predicates corresponds to the deep object argument of the participles. If one tries to construct an independent participle with the subject argument, as in (4c), the result is ungrammatical. The verb BE (or its counterparts in other languages) is neutral as regards the argument structure of its complement: via its functional structure it is capable of licensing one argument of the complement, but it neither removes nor adds an argument. Hence, the combination of BE plus a participle retains the passive nature of the participle, the surface subject of BE again corresponding to the object of the participle. Put differently, while BE provides a site for licensing a

Nominative argument, in terms of a AgrS+Tense relationship, it does not contribute an AgrO with Case licensing potential. We now proceed to analyze the participial structure itself as in (5), as a first approximation:

(5) Spec AgrS T [DP$_i$ stem DP$_j$]

DP$_j$, the object, raises out to SpecAgrS, a movement which is possible under Chomsky's (1992) minimal chain link condition if the stem raises out, via T to AgrS, making SpecTP (if there is one) equidistant to the Spec of the projection headed by the stem. I shall later modify this structure. For now, let us concentrate on its motivation. The claim made by (5) is that AgrO is lacking (or inactive). This may cause surprise in view of the agreement which participles may show with the object, as in Romance languages (cf. Kayne 1985, 1989). However, I maintain that such participial agreement constitutes AgrS, rather than AgrO. It should be borne in mind that there is no inherent distinction between AgrS and AgrO: their differentiation is based on their relative position in the structure: AgrS dominating Tense, AgrO being lower than Tense (note that in passives, AgrS normally agrees with the deep object). So, the correctness of identifying this agreement as AgrS depends on two considerations: a. can we identify Tense in participial constructions?; b. is the agreement peripheral to Tense or not? Indeed, we may identify Tense in participles. In fact, the same morpheme that expresses Past Tense in simple Past constructions occurs on participles, in English -*ed*, in Dutch/German -*t/d*. The meaning of the relevant morpheme is also equivalent, i.e. Past vis-à-vis an anchoring point. In the case of a simple sentence in Past Tense, this anchoring point is the speech-time, so that the eventuality linked up with Tense is placed prior to speech time. In complex tenses, involving participles, the past of the participle is relative to the anchoring provided by the governing auxiliary, placing the eventuality in the Past relative to that anchoring point (cf. Guéron & Hoekstra 1993 for discussion). Having established the identification of Tense, it is clear that the agreement displayed by participles in e.g. French is morpho-syntactically peripheral to this Tense-morpheme. If we assume the relevance of Baker's (1985) mirror principle, this leads us to equate the relevant agreement with AgrS, rather than with AgrO. I note on the side that this conclusion is the more natural one, as French normally has no visible effects of AgrO, while it does for AgrS.

In BE-participle constructions, the structure in (5) occurs in the complement of BE, a verb which itself likewise does not license an AgrO. Hence, the structure of "John was captured" is as in (6):

(6) John$_i$ AgrS PAST [was [AgrSP t_i AgrS ed$_T$ [DP$_j$ capture t_i]]]

Movement of *John* from the embedded SpecAgrS to the matrix SpecAgrS does not violate greed, as no Case-licensing takes place in the embedded SpecAgrS position. This is so, despite the presence of Tense. We are therefore led to the conclusion that the embedded Tense does not provide the embedded AgrS with (Nominative) Case licensing potential.[5]

2.2 *The transitivity of HAVE*

Let us now proceed to active perfect tense constructions, equally involving a participial complement. The basic idea in Hoekstra (1984) was that the auxiliary verb HAVE restores the transitivity of the participle, a feature that was lost in the formation of the participle. This line of reasoning appealed to the inherent transitivity of main verb HAVE. I want to adapt this approach to some recent developments, while still maintaining some of its basic features. This requires a discussion of two aspects: first, the notion of the inherent transitivity of HAVE, and second the idea that participle formation involves detransitivization. Note that this latter assumption has always been somewhat cumbersome in that it leads us to say that participial formation affects argument structure in some cases, viz. if the verb has an external argument participle formation somehow removes or suppresses this external argument, while it is void in this respect in other cases, viz. with verbs that don't have an external argument, i.e. ergative verbs. This goes against the idea of a uniformity in the role of functional or derivational morphemes. But let us turn to HAVE first.

As is well-known, HAVE-constructions often alternate with BE-constructions, not only in their role of aspectual auxiliaries, but also as so-called main verbs. Several languages lack a verb HAVE altogether, and rather express possessive predications with BE. Choice of HAVE and BE also determines the Case-patterns of the possessor and the possessed. Typically we find the following pattern:

(7)   BE DP$_i$ DP$_j$ ⇔   HAVE DP$_i$ DP$_j$
      OBL NOM   NOM ACC

We may say, then, that BE is a genuine intransitive verb. The Nominative Case is available in function of Tense. The oblique Case of DPi in (7) is equally not determined by BE, as we see no sign of such an oblique Case e.g. on adjectival predicates,[6] as in "John is ill". Rather, in these copular sentences, the general assumption is that [John ill] is the complement of BE, from which *John* raises to the matrix SpecAgrS to be licensed for Nominative Case, as in (8):

(8) [AgrS John$_i$ AgrS TNS BE [SC t_i ill]]

BE seems to be involved merely as carrier of functional features, then. We may likewise model the analysis of the possessive BE-pattern in (7) on this analysis, assuming now that the two DPs equally form a SC-complement to BE, whatever the exact nature of this SC (clearly, SC itself is not a category-label). We may think of this possessive construction as an instance of a locative construction: "the book is to me" conveys that the book's location is with me (cf. Guéron 1985; Hoekstra & Mulder 1989; Freeze 1992). Clearly, the locative relation is considered to be of a special kind, interpreted as possession or part-whole or something similar. I shall not at this point elaborate on this. The point is that "thematically" as well as in terms of Case, BEs contribution to the structure is nihil, or rather indirect in as far as BE supports the functional features of Tense and Agreement.[7]

Unlike BE, possessive or main verb HAVE seems to clearly contribute to structures in which it occurs: it makes Accusative Case available, i.e. it caters for syntactic transitivity, and it seems to express the thematic structure relevant to the two DPs with which it is construed. However, this may be just a matter of appearances, at least when viewed from the underlying structure. Kayne (1993) implements Benveniste's (1960) hypothesis that "avoir" (HAVE) is just an inversed "être à" (BE TO), arguing that the P of the possessor incorporates into BE, yielding a lexicalization with HAVE. Under this "HAVE=BE+P" view, it is not HAVE, but rather the incorporated P that contributes the thematic nature of the two DPs in the structure. HAVE, then, does not contribute any semantic transitivity to the structure. How about its alleged contribution of syntactic transitivity, or, phrased differently, where does the Accusative Case come from? The most obvious answer would seem to be that it also comes from the incorporated P. Let us make these suggestions concrete and propose the structure in (9):

(9) [$_{AgrSP}$ AgrS TNS [$_{AgrOP}$ AgrO [$_{FP}$ F [$_{SC}$ DP$_1$ P DP$_2$]]]]

F here stands for "functional". We shall come back to its nature later on. For now, we will say that F is lexicalized with a form of BE as the most neutral candidate. There are two ways in which the structure can have a convergent derivation. One is for DP$_1$ to raise, successively, to SpecAgrSP, to be licensed there with Nominative Case. DP$_2$ could not bear Nominative Case, independently of whatever Case DP$_1$ bears, as it is not allowed to leave its position by the Minimal Chain Link condition (MCL). Hence DP$_2$ is Case-licensed by P. However, as Chomsky (1992) proposes, the locality effect of the MCL can be suspended as a result of head-movement. Under these assumptions a second derivation is possible: movement of DP$_2$ is allowed once P head-moves to F, as now SpecFP and SpecSC become equidistant. Incorporation of P into F yields HAVE. Subsequent head movement of HAVE to AgrO makes SpecAgrOP and pecFP equidistant to DP$_1$, which may therefore move to SpecAgrOP, where it may check Accusative Case, for which HAVE inherits the licensing potential from the incorporated P. DP$_2$ is obviously allowed to raise further to SpecAgrSP in the normal manner, to check its Nominative Case.

We see, then, that the Case distribution in (7) is entirely compatible with a derivation in conformity with the minimalist assumptions on economy, without the need for any semantic or syntactic distribution of either HAVE or BE. Both may be regarded carriers of functional information, the transitivity of HAVE ultimately stemming from an incorporated preposition. Languages without HAVE apparently cannot create HAVE for whatever reason. This is an important result in the present context. HAVE and BE structures alternate in a way that is in conformity with Burzio's generalization if we attributed a θ-structure to HAVE: HAVE could then be said to assign both an external argument role and a Case for an internal argument, whereas BE would lack both. We see here that this conformity with Burzio's generalization can be explained without reference to argument structure differences of HAVE and BE, but by appealing solely to properties of licensing structures.

2.3 *Have plus participle*

Obviously, this analysis of HAVE/BE should preferably be extended to their auxiliary use, appealing to the same principles. We already established that BE leaves the passive nature of the participial complement intact, allowing the deep object to move to its SpecAgrSP, and lacking the possibility of Case-licensing the deep subject, cf. the structure in (6). The rise of HAVE and the concomitant availability of Accusative as a licenser of the deep object can now be modeled in a similar fashion if we assume that some P incorporates into BE, yielding HAVE plus its Case-licensing potential. As we already concluded that HAVE does not make a "thematic" contribution, its auxiliary nature in perfect tense constructions requires no further comment, as it is fully consistent with this claim. The question, however, is where the relevant P comes from. In order to make the parallel with the patterns in (7) complete, the P should originate in the combination with the DP that bears the Nominative in the HAVE-pattern. We may think of the P as *by* in passives. The structure of "the enemy has destroyed the city" would then be as in (10), on first approximation:

(10) $[_{\text{AgrSP}}$ AgrS TNS $[_{\text{AgrOP}}$ AgrO $[_{\text{FP}}$ F [[P DP$_1$] Part DP$_2$]]]]

Again, F is lexicalized as BE in the passive construction "the city was destroyed by the enemy", and as HAVE if P incorporates, allowing DP$_1$ to bear Nominative Case. The perspective in (10) is reminiscent of e.g. Fillmore's (1968) approach, in which all arguments of a predicate bear a role-marker, which gets suppressed if the argument is either "subjectivized" or "objectivized", all other arguments retaining their "deep" case. While such a conception is not inherently at odds with the current framework, the structure in (10) is not compatible with the economy considerations we appealed to earlier in the derivation of main verb HAVE. Specifically, the relationship between P and its superstructure is different, P now not being the head of F's complement. It is unclear how DP$_2$ could be moved from its position to SpecAgrOP to be licensed with Accusative Case. Head movement of the participle (Part) to F is not possible, as F is the site where HAVE arises.[8] DP$_2$ is therefore stuck in its position. The problem would immediately be solved if the structure in (10) were more parallel to (9), viz. as in (11):

(11) $[_{\text{AgrSP}}$ AgrS TNS $[_{\text{AgrOP}}$ AgrO $[_{\text{FP}}$ F [[$_{\text{PartP}}$ DP$_2$ Part] P DP$_1$]]]]

If this were the correct structure, the derivation can proceed as in (10): P incorporates into F, yielding HAVE and allowing DP$_1$, the "external" argument to move to SpecFP, which has become equidistant as a result of P's head movement. DP$_2$, sitting in the highest specifier position within the participial domain, as in (6), may move further on to SpecAgrOP where its Accusative Case may be checked.

This representation makes the claim that the "external" argument resides outside the participial structure, a claim which may be supported by the observation that the "by"-phrase is indeed independent of the participial construct per se, as in "the destruction of the city was by the enemy" (cf. "*the destruction by the enemy was of the city"). If this view is correct, HAVE does not so much restore the transitivity of the participle, but rather gives it its transitive appearance by integrating into one complex a predicate and its argument (the participle and its "object") as well as a second predicate, i.e. the relator of the external argument.

2.4   *Transitivity as a derived property*

If the analysis in (11) is correct for perfect tense forms, specifically, if it is correct that the "external" argument is not an argument of the participle itself, the next step is to make the same claim with respect to the stem-form on which the participle is based, i.e. the verb itself. Having an external argument, then, is not an inherent property of a lexical primitive, but rather a compositional property. In order to briefly make this idea somewhat precise, let us look at the pair in (12):

(12)   a.   the screen clears
         b.   John clears the screen

The representation of (12a) seems rather straightforward: the structure is essentially as in (13), with again F representing the functional information relevant to the structure, let's say ingression. It is dominated by Tense and AgrS, which in conjunction make Nominative licensing of the subject of *clear* possible. *Clear* itself incorporates into F, thereby becoming a verb, i.e. an element that is inflected for Tense and Agreement.

(13)   AgrS TNS F [$_{AP}$ [the screen] clear]]

The analysis of (12b) runs parallel to the derivations we have seen sofar. The structure is as in (14), with the AP [*the screen clear*] in subject position of P-*by*. The P incorporates into F, as does *clear*. The complement of P *John* may move in the manner already discussed via SpecFP to SpecAgrS, while *the screen* is licensed with Accusative Case in AgrO's SpecF inheriting the relevant potential from the incorporated P. Both the syntactic and the semantic transitivity of *clear* in (12b) are thus derivative.

(14)   AgrS TNS AgrO F [$_{PP}$ [$_{AP}$ [the screen] clear] P [John]]

This approach is not as novel as it may seem. It extends Kayne's analysis of HAVE to transitive verbs in general. It is also similar to Pesetsky's (1992) analysis of causative psych verbs of the type "This worried me". In Pesetsky's analysis the surface subject originates in an underlying Cause adjunct, headed by a preposition CAUS, taking *this* as its complement. This preposition incorporates into a non-causative form *worry*, represented as √*worry*. While Pesetsky limits this proposal to causative psych verbs, I extend it to transitive verbs in general. Also, the structure I argue for deviates less dramatically from standard X' structures than his cascade structures. Specifically, the assumption that the Cause-prepositional phrase is an adjunct or modifier vis-à-vis the verb is at odds with assumptions about legitimate incorporation. In my proposal, it is the head of a complement, in X' theoretic sense, which incorporates.

Let me summarize the main features of the analysis in this section. The most important results are the following:

a. transitivity is a combinatorial property, i.e. results from the incorporation of a P-relator into another head, making the complement of P seemingly an argument of this complex derived head.
b. lexical verbs are equally derived complex elements, being composed out of functional material and a lexical basis which is incorporated into a functional head.

The second result requires further comments. These are provided in the next section.

3. Verbs

3.1 *Functional and lexical features*

The category V is a heterogenous one: on the one hand, there are elements which are called auxiliaries, but which nevertheless are verbal, whereas on the other hand, there are lexical verbs. Their commonality is not so much a matter of shared semantics, but rather of inflectional properties, specifically inflection for Tense. Nouns and Adjectives normally do not inflect for Tense, and when they do, they are considered verbs. So, in (12) we see a tensed-inflected adjective, and therefore say that the relevant element is a verb. This may be accounted for by assuming that there is a lexical rule or word formation rule transposing (members of the class of) adjectives to the class of verbs, i.e. a mapping from one lexical category to another lexical category. A question to be asked is what makes something into a lexical category.

It would seem that there is a growing consensus on how to answer this question. The division of labour between functional categories and lexical categories primarily seems to be that lexical elements have an argument structure or θ-grid, while functional categories constitute the licensing features for these argument structures. So, if we take a transitive verb, i.e. a verb with two arguments, AgrS and AgrO serve to formally license the DPs that bear the argument roles, but do not themselves contribute any argument roles. Agr-projections function to Case-check the DP-arguments, where Case may be thought of as a formal licensing of the referential content of DPs. The functional category D itself may be thought of as being associated with the referential potential of the nominal phrase, where again the noun supplies the "argument" role of the referent, i.e. *the dog* can be thought of as the object which bears the "dog" role supplied by *dog*. Tense may be said to play the same role vis-à-vis the VP (or V),

THE NATURE OF VERBS AND BURZIO'S GENERALIZATION 69

as in Higginbotham's (1985) view on Tense and D. Another way of putting this is that lexical categories have descriptive content, i.e. denote properties of classes of referents. Functional categories, on the other hand, are not descriptive, as they do not denote properties of classes of referents. Let us formulate this as in (15):

(15) *Strict separation hypothesis*
Lexical primitives denote properties of ontological classes of individuals, Functional primitives do not.

It will be clear that (15) needs further research to determine what is and what is not a property of an ontological class of individuals, but it is sufficient for the present discussion. Consider pronominals such as *he* and *she*, in contrast with a determiner such as *the*. Postal (1969) and Abney (1986) a.o. have proposed that pronouns instantiate D, lumping all three elements in the same functional category. If (15) is correct, such a step cannot be accepted, as clearly *he* and *she* do denote a property that corresponds to ontological classes of individuals, viz. male vs. female. By (15) this denotational value must be expressed by a lexical primitive. At the same time, *he* and *she*, like *the*, are functional in the sense that they involve denotation of a non-descriptive nature (let's say, definiteness). Hence, *he* and *she* cannot be primitive members of the category D, nor of N, but must be composite elements. I shall not at this point elaborate on the exact way in which this compositionality obtains, but refer to Koopman (1994) and Zwarts (1994) for relevant discussion, which supports this conclusion.

3.2 *Lexical verbs as composite elements*

Verbs have a cumbersome status vis-à-vis (15). Auxiliaries, while not meaningless, do not refer to ontological classes of individuals, and hence are functional. This comes hardly as a surprise for English modals and also perhaps not for aspectual auxiliaries, but it might be more surprising for other "auxiliary verbs", e.g. the modals in Romance or non-English Germanic, which do not seem to behave much different from "normal" verbs. But it is precisely the "normal" verbs that are problematic for (15). Consider again *clear*. In its adjectival status it is unproblematic for (15): it denotes the property shared by things which are 'clear', and hence it may be thought of as a lexical primitive. On the other hand, the intransitive verb *clear* does not denote a class of clear things, but rather denotes a process by which things become clear, i.e. it is semantically complex in denoting both ingression, which is not descriptive, and clearness, which is. This is also evident from the paraphrase of "the screen clears" with "the screen gets clear", where *get* is a functional or auxiliary verb: it only expresses the non-descriptive feature of ingression. Under the analysis proposed in the previous section, this semantic complexity finds a syntactic account, the verb being a complex element with a lexical primitive incorporated into a functional head. Consonant with (15), there is no syntactically primitive verb *clear*.

The analysis of the intransitive verb *clear* is very similar to the one proposed by Hale & Keyser in a number of papers (Hale & Keyser 1991, 1992, 1994). In their analysis, however, the category verb is taken to be lexical. They reject Stowell's (1981) proposal according to which all lexical categories may have a subject. In retrospect, Stowell's proposal may be regarded as a precursor of the general idea underlying (15) and the discussion preceding it, viz. the idea that thematic marking takes place in the domain of the lexical head. In Hale & Keyser's analysis of change of state verbs like *clear*, the complement of an abstract verb is said to be a predicate which passes its predication requirement on to the abstract verb. Their analysis is represented in (16):

(16)   F [$_{VP}$ DP V [$_{AP}$ clear]]

Here again, F stands for functional material, not relevant to Hale & Keyser's discussion, as they take the formation of the verb *clear* to be a lexical matter. The DP subject of the VP does not originate internal to the AP, but is an argument of the verb, which itself is generated by head movement of the adjective in the lexicon. My analysis differs, in terms of configuration, only minimally: F and V in (16) fall together under F, and the DP originates inside AP. Conceptually, the differences are more principled. My analysis is based on Stowell's internal subject hypothesis, now as a consequence of the principled division of labour between F-categories and L-categories. While both analyses agree on the derived nature of the verb *clear*, this is a matter of syntax rather than the lexicon in my analysis, and the status of the derived element is a complex F-head, rather than a lexical element.

3.3 *Argument structure*

The enterprise of Hale & Keyser is motivated by a concern about available argument structures. They note that the number of distinct argument structures is rather limited, for which they seek an explanation in terms of a lexical syntax, which has all the main properties of what they call Big Syntax. In particular, argument structures are represented by binary branching structures defined in terms of the Spec–Head and the Head, Complement relations. Incorporation is constrained by the ECP (the Head Movement Constraint). Furthermore, each lexical category (N,A,V and P) has its specific interpretation, as in (17):

(17) A is a predicate
P takes a complement and forms a predicate
N denotes a thing
V takes a complement and denotes an event

The notion predicate is to be understood as explained above: while AP and PP are predicates, their predication requirement can only be satisfied through the subject of a V of which they are the complement. N and V, on the other hand, are not predicates. The importance of this distinction is that potential recursion of the system is extremely limited. As verbs must take a complement, there are two possibilities.

a. its complement is a predicate, i.e. an AP or a PP. This gives VPs of the type (18a), with a subject at the level of lexical argument structure. This subject is required by the predicative nature of the complement. VPs of the type in (18a) are functionally complete, and may therefore occur as complements themselves.
b. its complement is not a predicate, but a VP or a NP. This gives VPs of the type in (18b), without a subject at the level of lexical argument structure. Their subject is supplied in Big Syntax. VPs of the type in (18b) are functionally incomplete, and may therefore not themselves occur as complements to other verbs.

Hence, only VPs of the type (18a) may take the complement VP-position in a VP of the type (18b), as in (18c):

(18) a. [$_{VP}$ DP V$_2$ AP/PP]   change of state or location
     b. [$_{VP}$ V$_1$ NP/VP]
     c. [$_{VP}$ V$_1$ [$_{VP}$ DP V$_2$ AP/PP]]

The interpretation of a V-VP structure is a causative predicate. Such causative predicates may not themselves be embedded. Broadly speaking, this system generates argument structures with an agent/cause external argument (subject of V$_1$) and a theme internal argument (subject of V$_2$), or only a theme argument, if embedding under V$_1$ does not take place. In addition to an optional agent and a theme, there may be one more argument, viz. the complement of P. I refer to Hale and Keyser's papers for further discussion and illustration of the merits of their system.

I already looked at the difference between the analysis I proposed and Hale & Keyser's in as far as structures of the type in (18a) are concerned. Let us therefore look at structures of the type in (18b). The V$_1$ shell represents the transitivity of the predicate. Its subject is an external argument, i.e. an agent or a cause. Yet, the external argument is not represented at the level of argument structure. This is achieved by making a distinction between two types of predication: predication as imposed by the predicate nature of AP/PP and predication as imposed by Big Syntax. However, the Big Syntax predication requirement is a formal requirement, ultimately the so-called Extended Projection Principle of Chomsky (1981), and does not in itself relate to the external argument requirement. The stipulated absence of the external argument at the level of argument structure, then, is solely intended to stop the recursion of the system in order to obtain the result that the number of distinct argument structure types is severely limited. However, the same result is obtained under the analysis that I propose. Under that analysis, there is no V_1. Rather, the external argument is genuinely external as it originates in a prepositional phrase which combines with what corresponds to a VP of the type in (18a). For clarity sake I give Hale and Keyser's representation of the transitive verb *clear* in (19a) and my analysis in (19b):

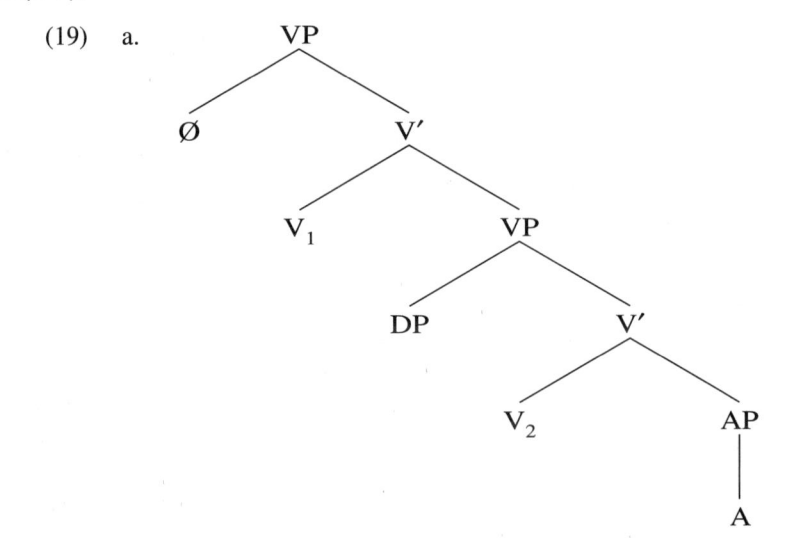

(19) a.

```
        VP
       /  \
      Ø    V'
          /  \
        V₁    VP
             /  \
           DP    V'
                /  \
              V₂    AP
                    |
                    A
```

b.
```
         F         PP
                 /    \
              AP       P'
             /  \     /  \
            DP   A   P    DP
```

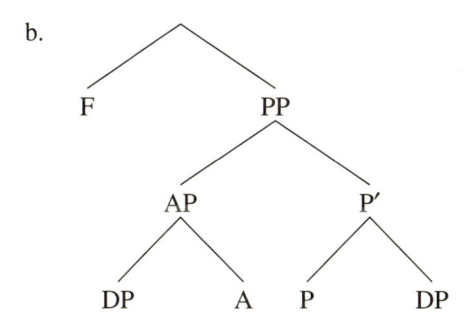

In (19a), the AP predicate is dominated by two VP-shells. The lowest verb denotes ingression and its subject satisfies the predication requirement of the AP-complement, headed by *clear*. Head-movement of *clear* creates the intransitive verb. The upper shell represents the causative layer. The abstract verb again serves as a receptacle for incorporation of the embedded verb. There is no subject.

In (19b), the AP is the subject of a prepositional phrase. The DP subject of *clear* originates in the specifier of the AP, while the Agent or Cause argument is external to this AP, as it occurs in the complement of P. The derivation is as described above: head movement of P into F, as well as incorporation of A yield a derived transitive structure, headed by the verb *clear*. This derivation is entirely compatible with the minimalist assumptions of Chomsky (1992), and can therefore be considered fully syntactic rather than lexical.

We have sofar been silent about unergative intransitives. In this respect I follow much current literature (a.o. Hale & Keyser 1992; Kayne 1993) in assuming that they are basically transitive verbs that result from the incorporation of a (cognate) noun. So, the verb *dance* is generated by noun incorporation of a noun *dance* into "do a dance". Again, of course, the "do"-part itself is generated via incorporation of a P which hosts the external argument in underlying structure. A paraphrase of "John danced" that brings out the structure assigned to it under the current proposal is "there arose a dance by John", where the "arose" part is ingressive aspect, a functional category, the lexical base is the noun *dance* which is incorporated into F from the specifier of "by John"[9].

3.4 *A verb typology*

As in Hale & Keyser's system, then, possible argument structures of verbs are extremely limited. Whether the limitations imposed by the analysis can be upheld is a matter of further research. In my analysis, lexical verbs are never primitive, but always the result of incorporation of a lexical primitive into functional material. If no such incorporation takes place, the verb is a functional element. This captures the fact, argued for by Menuzzi (1994), that verbs, like other functional heads, can have zero-form. Such zero-verbs are never lexical, obviously, but functional. We can set up a verb typology as in (20):

(20)　　　F (+N/A) (+P)
　　　a.　only F:　　auxiliary verbs
　　　b.　F+P:　　　HAVE-type auxiliaries
　　　c.　F+N/A:　　ergative lexical verbs
　　　d.　F+N/A+P:　transitive lexical verbs

4. Case marking

Let us summarize the conclusions from the previous sections. We have argued that Tense makes Nominative available. Constructions and languages vary with respect to the availability of Accusative. Accusative results from the incorporation of the oblique preposition of the external argument. This captures Burzio's generalization in a straightforward fashion: only if there is an external argument that can be Nominative-licensed is Accusative available. This availability thus depends on the possibilities of incorporating the oblique element. Where this is impossible, the external argument retains its oblique marking (or is absent). Apparently, this is what happens in languages (or constructions) with an ergative Case pattern. Mahajan (1993) claims that there is a typological correlation of ergative Case patterns and Verb final order and absence of HAVE-auxiliaries in complex tenses. He explains this be extending Kayne's (1993) proposal on the rise of HAVE as resulting from BE plus an incorporated preposition, much like in my proposal above, although the details are quite different. In brief, he assumes that BE takes some XP-complement, containing the ergative DP, as in (21a). This XP-complement may move to the specifier of BE, as in (21b).

(21)　a.　BE [$_{XP}$ ..DP$_{erg}$...V...]　　　VO
　　　b.　[$_{XP}$ ..DP$_{erg}$... V...]$_i$ BE t_i　　OV

The ergative feature may be incorporated from inside XP to BE in (21a), yielding VO order and HAVE, but such incorporation is blocked in (21b), as it would require downward movement into BE. Thus OV correlates with absence of HAVE and retention of ergative marking.

Whether this explanation can be upheld is not easy to evaluate. There clearly are VO languages with an ergative Case system, just as much as there are

OV-languages with HAVE, but the tendency might exist, and Mahajan's account may be one of the possibilities to explain absence of a NOM-ACC pattern, in fact, a very interesting one.

Other factors may trigger the same effect, though. To just mention one case, in nominal constructions English and French appear to differ in a way parallel to the way in which clausal constructions in English differ from those in Eskimo. Consider the contrast in (22) and (23):

(22) a. the destruction of the city by the enemy "passive"
     b. the enemy's destruction of the city   "active transitive"
(23) a. la déstruction de la ville par l'ennemi "passive"
     b. la déstruction de l'ennemi de la ville "ergative active"

While much more needs to be said about the Romance alternation in (23) (cf. Picallo 1991 for relevant discussion on Catalan), the case patterning difference is similar to the NOM–ACC vs. ERG–ABS distinction. To see this, let us take (22a) first, with a passive oblique rendering of the external argument. This is parallelled by (23a) in Romance. Hence, both English and French have "passive nominals", just like both English and Eskimo have "passive" clauses (cf. (3b) above). Romance has, in addition, a different oblique rendering of the external argument, similar to the ergative Case in Eskimo, but English allows such obliqueness to be incorporated, and have the external argument in morphologically unmarked Case checked by Agreement. Apparently, such incorporation is excluded in Romance.

If my hypothesis on transitivity as a derived property is correct, we expect a variety of factors to come into play in the determination of transitivity. One is the option of incorporating the obliqueness of the external argument. If such incorporation is not possible at all in a language, we expect a consistent ergative marking of the external argument. Another factor is the possibility of incorporating a lexical head into dominating functional structure. If this is impossible in general, no lexical verbs will be generated in the language. These two factors may interact: one might have systems where a lexical head may be incorporated, but not if P is also incorporated. That would yield ergative lexical verbs, but no transitive lexical verbs. Yet another factor may be involved, yielding a Tense or Aspect split. This is the situation discussed most extensively above, viz. when participial forms are involved. If a language does not create HAVE, for instance for reasons as discussed by Mahajan (1993), participial structures will always yield an ergative or a passive pattern. The nominal basis, i.e. the participle, cannot be incorporated into the dominating functional element, i.e. nominal participles cannot be "verbalized". The reason for this cannot be that nominal elements themselves may not be incorporated in general. Rather, participial structures constitute their own functional domain, or extended projection in Grimshaw's (1991) terms. On the assumption that lexical heads can, but functionally satisfied complexes cannot incorporate, this property of participles is explained.

Notes

1. The hypothesis that lack of accusative Case assignment is the proper characterization of ergative case systems was also put forth in Bok-Bennema & Groos (1984). For them, this was a primitive property of such systems, i.e. accusative case assignment was itself regarded as a parameter.
2. "They [i.e. Mayan languages, T.H.] only know nouns and absolute verbs, which denote a condition of being, a property or an activity, which are construed as predicates to a personal pronoun or a third person as its subject, but which cannot combine with a direct object" (p. 89). "... that transitive verbal expressions are based on nominal themes prefixed with possessive prefixes" (p. 85). "The Mayan phrases .... really say: "your killed one is my father", "your written one is the book", — expressions which in their meaning are fully identical to our "you have killed my father", "you have written the book". (p. 86).
3. Alternatively, we may think of this in terms of a functional category being active or inactive.
4. Haider (1985) arrived at almost identical conclusions in this respect.
5. The lack of Nom licensing potential of the AgrS+Tense combination might be due, as in Guéron & Hoekstra (1993), to lack of an independent operator to which Tense is related. We may then think of "finite" Tense as a Tense which is related to C, and only through the operator head-feature of C does Tense get Nominative-licensing potential. As the participle is not bound from C by an independent operator, it lacks Nom-licensing potential.
6. There are situations where a predicative complement bears some inherent Case, e.g. dative or instrumental as in Japanese and Russian respectively. However, also in those situations it doesn't seem likely that this Case is assigned by BE. More problematic is the Accusative that shows up on predicative complements to the (overt) verb BE in Arabic. I have no proposal as to where this accusative comes from.
7. This is not to say that absence or presence of BE will not have an effect on the meaning of the construction as a whole. Various cases are known from the literature where this is clearly not the case. An example is Williams' (1983) discussion of BE in "John seems (to be) absent". However, this meaning difference is a consequence of the functional structure represented (since borne) by BE.
8. We might assume that the participle does raise to HAVE, adjoining to it, and to allow HAVE to escape from this position by way of excorporation. However, as we will see, such a manoevre is not required.
9. Khalayli (1994 and work in progress) argues that verbs quite generally arise through noun-incorporation, for which he provides empirical evidence from Arabic.

References

Abney, S. 1986. The English noun phrase in its sentential aspect. PhD Dissertation, MIT.
Baker, M. 1985. "The mirror principle and morphosyntactic explanation". *Linguistic Inquiry* 16(3): 373–415
Benvéniste, E. 1960. "Être" et "avoir" dans leur fonctions linguistiques. *Bulletin de la Société Linguistique de Paris LV*.
Bok-Bennema, R. and A. Groos. 1984. Ergativiteit. *GLOT* 71–49.
Burzio, L. 1981. Intransitive Verbs and Italian Auxiliaries. PhD Dissertation, MIT.
Chomsky, N. A. 1991. *Lectures on government and binding*. Dordrecht: Foris Publications.
Chomsky, N. A. 1992. "A minimalist program for linguistic theory". In *The View from Building 20*, K. Hale and J. Keyser (eds), 1–52. Cambridge, MA: MIT Press.
Fillmore, C. 1968. "The case for case". In *Universals in Linguistic Theory*, E. Bach and R. T. Harms (eds). New York: Holt, Rinehart and Winston.
Freeze, R. 1992. "Existentials and other locatives". *Language* 68: 553–595.
Grimshaw, J. 1991. Extended projections. Ms., Rutgers University.
Guéron, J. 1985. "Le verbe *avoir*". *Recherches linguistiques* 14. Paris: Presses Universitaires de Vincennes.
Guéron, J. and Hoekstra, T. 1993. "The temporal interpretation of predication". To appear in *Small Clauses*, A. Cardinaletti and M. T. Guasti (eds). New York: Academic Press.
Haider, H. 1985. "Von *sein* oder nicht *sein*". In *Erklärende syntax des Deutschen*, W. Abraham (ed.). Tübingen: Gunter Narr.
Hale, K. and Keyser, J. 1991. "The syntactic character of thematic structure". In *Thematic Structure: Its role in grammar*, I. Roca (ed.). Berlin: Mouton.
Hale, K. and Keyser, J. 1993. "On argument structure and the lexical expression of syntactic relations". In *The View From Building 20*, K. Hale and J. Keyser (eds), 1–52. Cambridge, MA.: MIT Press.
Hale, K. and Keyser, J. 1994. "On the complex nature of simple predicators". Ms., MIT.
Higginbotham, J. 1985. "On semantics". *Linguistic Inquiry* 16(4): 547–594.
Hoekstra, T. 1984. *Transitivity*. Dordrecht: Foris Publications.
Hoekstra, T. and Mulder, R. 1989. "Unergatives as copular verbs". *The Linguistic Review* 7: 1–79.
Johns, A. 1992. "Deriving ergativity". *Linguistic Inquiry* 23: 57–88.
Kayne, R. 1985. "L'accord du participe passé en français et en italien". *Modèles linguistiques* 7: 73–90
Kayne, R. 1989. "Facets of Romance past participle agreement". In *Dialect Variation and the Theory of Grammar*, P. Benincà (ed.), 85–103. Dordrecht: Foris Publications.
Kayne, R. 1993. "Toward a modular theory of auxiliary selection". *Studia Linguistica* 47: 3–31
Khalaily, S. 1994. "A syntax of verbs from a nominal point of view". In *Linguistics in the Netherlands 1994*, R. Bok-Bennema and C. Cremers (eds). Amsterdam: John Benjamins.

Koopman, H. 1994. "The internal and external diustribution of pronominal DPs". Ms., UCLA.
Mahajan, A. 1993. "The ergativity parameter". *NELS* 23.
Menuzzi, S. 1994. "Double objectc constructions in Icelandic". HIL manuscripts 2.1.
Pesetsky, D. 1992. "Zero syntax", part 1. Ms., MIT.
Picallo, C. 1991. "Nominals and nominalization in Catalan". *Probus* 3: 279–316.
Postal, P. M. 1969. "On so-called 'pronouns' in English". In *Modern Studies in English: Readings in transformational grammar,* D. A. Reidel and S. A. Shane (eds), 201–224. Englewood Cliffs: Prentice-Hall.
Seler, E. 1887. "Das Konjugationssystem der Maya-Sprachen". PhD Dissertation, Leipzig. In *Gesammelte Abhandlungen zur Amerikanischen Sprach- und Altertumskunde,* vol. I, E.Seler. Graz: Akademische Druck- und Verlagsanstalt. 1960: 65–126.
Stowell, T. 1981. "Origins of phrase structure". PhD Dissertation, MIT.
Williams, E. 1983. "Against small clauses". *Linguistic Inquiry* 14(2): 287–308.
Zwarts, J. 1994. "Pronouns and N-to-D movement". In *OTS Year Book 1993*, M. Everaert, B. Schouten and W. Zonneveld (eds). University of Utrecht.

Oblique Subjects
and Burzio's Generalization

Anoop Mahajan
UCLA

1. Introduction

Burzio's Generalization (BG) is a somewhat of a puzzle within theoretical linguistics since it relates two rather distinct properties of a predicate: the inability of a predicate to assign an external θ-role and its inability to assign a structural accusative Case to its object. While the empirical consequences of this correlation are fairly well understood (as detailed in Burzio 1986 and going back to the influential discussion of this topic in Perlmutter 1978), there is no clear perspective on why there should be such a correlation between thematic licensing and Case licensing.

In this paper, I will concentrate on a comparison between two types of languages, the languages in which the effects associated with BG are readily observable (as is the case in English, many other Germanic languages and many Romance languages) and the languages that apparently do not display BG effects in many construction types (for instance Hindi and many other Indic Indo-European languages).[1] In particular, I will argue that Hindi has a number of oblique subject constructions (constructions with a non-nominative subject followed by an adposition) including a passive construction (with instrumental subjects) and an ergative construction (with an ergative marking on the subject) which appear to be inconsistent with Burzio's Generalization. These constructions have predicates that are arguably unable to assign a structural accusative Case but still license structural thematic subjects. It should be noted that these construction types violate the version of BG that takes the inability of licensing of external θ-role and inability of assigning structural accusative Case to be a bi-directional relationship (i.e., if no external θ-role then no structural accusative AND if no structural accusative then no external θ-role). I will explicate the properties of the relevant construction types using a variety of tests to confirm that these constructions are indeed inconsistent with BG. I will then outline a theory that accounts for the properties of these construction types in Hindi without making any reference to BG. Since the parallel constructions in English type languages have somewhat different properties (one of these cases being a classical example of BG), I will argue that the essential properties of these construction types also follow within the theory outlined without making any reference to BG. The effects of BG, wherever apparent, follow from well-known and independently motivated principles of UG interacting with certain language particular properties. In a sense then, Burzio's Generalization is not a true generalization. Its effects, whenever they appear in certain construction types, are due to a number of independent factors.

The paper is organized as follows: in Section 2, I present two constructions from Hindi and show that while both of these constructions employ an arguably non Case-assigning verb, they do allow for the presence of the external argument in the subject position. These construction types therefore are inconsistent with BG. The non Case-assigning property of these verbs will be apparent from the fact that the object in these constructions has to move higher up in the clause to seek (nominative) Case which is reflected by its agreement with a higher auxiliary. In Section 3, I will present an analysis of these construction types by elaborating an approach to the assignment of instrumental/ergative marker to the subject in perfect participle constructions. I will then suggest that given this approach and some independent properties of Hindi (concerning word order and agreement), Hindi (and other Hindi type languages) will always have construction types that are inconsistent with BG. In Section 4, I will argue that the reason that we see effects of BG in parallel construction types in English is related to an independent fact that English type languages lack oblique subject constructions in general. The conclusion will be that BG is just an epiphenomenon that is observed only in certain language types for well defined reasons.

2. The ACTIVE Passive and the ergative constructions in Hindi

In this section, I present two construction types in Hindi that are inconsistent with BG. The essential property that these construction types share is that they allow for the presence of an external argument in configurations in which they fail to license an accusative Case. The object in these construction types is licensed in a position higher up in the clause (as shown by the facts of object agreement). The construction types that I examine in this paper are the ACTIVE

Passive construction and the ergative subject construction. I will present data that justifies the claim that the instrumental subjects of the ACTIVE Passives and of the ergative subjects of the ergative constructions are in fact structural subjects (that have not been demoted). I also argue that the objects in these constructions are structural objects (that have not been promoted). In that sense, these two construction types are 'active' and the external argument is in fact licensed in both of these construction types despite the non assignment of the accusative Case. The two construction types that are relevant are exemplified in (1) and (2) below. (1) is a normal active construction with a nominative Case subject (this construction will be used as a test case for the relevant comparisons).

NOMINATIVE SUBJECT CONSTRUCTION: The verb is a non perfect participle and the subject agrees with the verb. The subject is unmarked.

(1) *siitaa vah ghar khariidegii*
Sita-FEM-NOM that house buy-FUT-FEM
'Sita will buy that house.'

ERGATIVE SUBJECT CONSTRUCTION: The verb is a perfect participle and the object agrees with the participle as well as the auxiliary *be* (if there is one). The subject is followed by the ergative marker *ne*.

(2) *siitaa ne vah ghar khariidaa (thaa)*
Sita-FEM-ERG that house-MASC buy-PERF-MASC be-PAST-MASC
'Sita had bought that house.'

dwaaraa INSTRUMENTAL SUBJECT CONSTRUCTION (ACTIVE Passives): The verb is a perfect participle and is followed by the (passive) auxiliary *go*. The object agrees with the participle and the auxiliary. The subject has the instrumental marker *dwaaraa*.[2]

(3) *siitaa dwaaraa vah ghar khariidaa gayaa*
Sita-FEM by that house-MASC buy-PERF-MASC go-PERF-MASC
= 'By Sita was bought that house.'

2.1 *Tests for the subjecthood of the external argument*[3]

2.1.1 *Anaphor binding*
Agentive phrases in the ACTIVE Passive (example (5)) and ergative (example (6)) constructions can bind anaphors the same way that nominative subjects can (example (4)).[4]

(4) salmaa$_i$ apne$_i$ ghar kaa niriikshan karegii
Salma self's house GEN examination do-FUT-FEM
'Salma will examine self's house.'

(5) salmaa$_i$ ne apne$_i$ ghar kaa niriikshan kiyaa
Salma-ERG self's house GEN examination do-PERF-MASC
'Salma examined self's house.'

(6) salmaa$_i$ dwaaraa apne$_i$ ghar kaa niriikshan kiyaa
Salma by selfs home GEN examination do-PERF-MASC
gayaa
go-PERF-MASC
= 'Self's house was examined by Salma.'

2.1.2 Antisubject Orientation of pronouns

Possessive pronouns in Hindi have an anti-subject orientation (cf. Gurtu 1985; Mohanan 1990). They may corefer with an object of the same clause but not with the subject. Ergative and ACTIVE passive subjects behave like nominative subjects with respect to antisubject orientation of pronouns.

(7) salmaa$_i$ uske*$_i$ ghar kaa niriikshan karegii
Salma her house GEN examination do-FUT-FEM
'Salma$_i$ will examine her*$_i$ house.'

(8) salmaa$_i$ ne uske*$_i$ ghar kaa niriikshan kiyaa
Salma-ERG her house GEN examination do-PERF-MASC
'Salma$_i$ examined her*$_i$ house.'

(9) salmaa$_i$ dwaaraa uske*$_i$ ghar kaa niriikshan kiyaa
Salma by her home GEN examination do-PERF-MASC
gayaa
go-PERF-MASC
= 'Her*$_i$ house was examined by Salma$_i$.'

According to a theory of antisubject orientation such as that of Hestvik (1992), pronouns have a disjoint reference to subjects in sentences like (7) (actually the parallel cases in some Scandinavian languages) because they move at LF to I. Principle B, applying at LF, ensures that the subject and the pronouns cannot corefer. This being the case, the position occupied by the ergative phrase in (8) and the *dwaaraa* phrase in (9) must be structurally the same as that of the nominative subject in (7).[5,6]

2.1.3 *Control into argument clauses*
The behavior of agent phrases in ergative constructions and ACTIVE Passives in subject control constructions (examples (11) and (12) respectively) indicates that they have the same control properties in a corresponding active construction as in (10):

(10) *salmaa$_i$ [PRO$_i$ ghar jaanaa] caahtii thii*
Salma home go-INF want-IMP-FEM be-PAST-FEM
'Salma wanted to go home.'

(11) *salmaa$_i$ ne [PRO$_i$ ghar jaanaa] caahaa*
Salma ERG home go-INF want-PERF-MASC
'Salma wanted to go home.'

(12) *salmaa$_i$ dwaaraa [PRO$_i$ ghar jaanaa] caahaa gayaa*
Salma by home go-INF want-PERF-MASC
go-PERF-MASC
= 'It was wanted by Salma to go home.'

2.1.4 *Control into adverbial clauses*
As noted by Kachru, Kachru and Bhatia (1976) and Mohanan (1990), control into conjunctive participle (*kar*) adverbial clauses can be used as a test for subjecthood. Agentive phrases of ergative and ACTIVE Passive constructions (examples (14) and (15) below) behave like nominative subjects (13).

(13) *salmaa$_i$ [PRO$_i$ ghar jaa kar] mohan ko dāāṭegii*
Salma home go do Mohan ko scold-FUT-FEM
= 'Salma will scold Mohan after going home.'

(14) *salmaa$_i$ ne [PRO$_i$ ghar jaa kar] mohan ko dāāṭaa*
Salma ERG home go do Mohan ko scold-PERF-MASC
'Salma scolded Mohan after going home.'

(15) *salmaa$_i$ dwaaraa [PRO$_i$ ghar jaa kar] mohan ko dāāṭaa gayaa*
Salma by home go do Mohan ko scold-PERF
go-PERF-MASC
= 'Mohan was scolded by Salma after she went home.'

2.1.5 *Extraction out of an extraposed clause*
This test can be used to show that the agent phrases of ACTIVE Passive and ergative constructions are arguments and have not been demoted to an adjunct

status (this test does not distinguish between subjects and objects since they behave alike with respect to extraction in Hindi). In Hindi, extraposed argument clauses may co-occur with an expletive *yah* in the object position as shown in (16) below.

(16)   salmaa ne   yah socaa   ki   mohan raam ko maaregaa
       Salmaa ERG it   thought that Mohan Ram ko hit-FUT-MASC
       = 'Salma thought *it* that Mohan will hit Ram.'

Extractions out of the extraposed clauses yield the familiar argument/adjunct asymmetries. Argument extraction from extraposed *yah* clauses yields a weaker (subjacency) violation as exemplified in (17) (where a nominative subject is extracted) while adjunct extractions yield stronger (ECP) violation as exemplified in (19) below (cf. Mahajan 1990, 1993; and Srivastav 1991).

Nominative subject extraction
(17)   ???*mohan, salmaa ne   yah socaa ki   raam ko maaregaa*
       Mohan Salmaa ERG it   think that Ram ko hit-FUT-MASC
       = 'Mohan, Salma thought *it* that (he) will hit Ram.'

Adjunct *in situ*
(18)   salmaa yah soctii   thii   ki   mohan ne   raam ko ghar
       Salmaa it   think-IMP be-PAST that Mohan ERG Ram ko home
       me maaraa
       at hit-PERF
       'Salma thinks that Mohan hit Ram at home.'

Adjunct extraction
(19)   **ghar me, salmaa yah soctii*   thii   ki   mohan ne   raam
       home in, Salma it   think-IMP be-PAST that Mohan ERG Ram
       ko__maaraa
       ko hit
       = 'At home, Salma thinks that Mohan hit Ram.'

It should be noted that adjunct extractions are allowed if the expletive *yah* is absent (i.e., there is no overall restriction on adjunct movement). This is shown by (20) below.

(20)   *ghar me, salmaa soctii*   thii   ki   mohan ne   raam
       home in, Salma think-IMP be-PAST that Mohan ERG Ram
       ko__ maaraa
       ko hit
       = 'At home, Salma thinks that Mohan hit Ram.'

Ergative phrases behave like arguments *and not like adjuncts* with respect to extraction out of such clauses, indicating that they have not been demoted to the syntactic status of adjuncts. (21) and (22) below illustrate this fact with respect to ergative NP extraction and ergative wh-extraction.

Ergative NP extraction
(21) ???*mohan ne, salmaa yah soctii thii ki__ raam ko maaraa*
Mohan ERG Salma it think-IMP be-PAST that Ram ko hit-PERF
= 'Mohan, Salma thinks that (he) hit Ram.'

Ergative wh extraction
(22) ???*kis ne, salmaa yah soctii thii ki__ raam ko maaraa*
who ERG Salma it think-IMP be-PAST that Ram ko hit-PERF.
= 'Who does Salmaa think that (he) hit Ram?'

dwaaraa agentive phrases of active Passives behave in a manner similar to the ergative phrases as shown below.

dwaaraa phrase extraction
(23) ???*mohan dwaaraa, salmaa yah soctii thii ki__ raam ko*
Mohan by Salmaa it think-IMP be-PAST that Ram ko
maaraa gayaa
hit-PERF go-PERF
= 'By Mohan, Salma thinks that Ram was hit.'

dwaaraa wh-phrase extraction
(24) ???*kis ke dwaaraa, salmaa yah soctii thii ki__ raam ko*
who GEN by Salmaa it think-IMP be-PAST that Ram ko
maaraa gayaa
hit-PERF go-PERF
= 'By whom does Salma thinks that Ram was hit?'

2.1.6 *Summary*
The syntactic behavior of the external arguments in ergative and ACTIVE Passives constructions indicates that they are in the subject position and have not been syntactically demoted. The last test indicates that the ergative and the *dwaaraa* phrases are arguments with respect to movement and cannot be viewed as adjuncts for the purposes of extraction out of *yah* islands.

2.2 Objects of Ergative and ACTIVE Passive constructions

We show now that the object in the ergative and ACTIVE Passive constructions behaves like a normal object and appears not to be either promoted or demoted. This will further confirm that these construction types are in fact 'active'.

2.2.1 Morphological Case

Objects in Hindi can be marked with a *-ko* ending that denotes specificity. The examples below indicate that in that respect objects in nominative, ergative and ACTIVE Passive constructions do not differ.[7]

(25) raajaa saare šerõ ko maar degaa
king NOM all tigers ko kill give-FUT-MASC-SG
'The king will kill all the tigers in the jungle.'

(26) raajaa ne saare šero kõ maar diyaa
king ERG all tigers ko kill give-PERF-MASC-SG (default AGR)
'The king killed all the tigers in the jungle.'

(27) raajaa dwaaraa saare šerõ ko maar diyaa
king by all tigers ko kill give-PERF-MASC-SG
gayaa
go-PERF-MASC-SG (default agr)
'All the tigers in the jungle were killed by the king.'

2.2.2 Pronominal coreference

Unlike subject non-coreference, pronouns in Hindi can corefer with objects as shown in a normal active construction exemplified by (28). The objects in ergative and ACTIVE Passive constructions ((29) and (30) below) can corefer with the object indicating that the object has not moved to the subject position.

(28) siitaa$_j$ salmaa$_i$ ko uske$_{i/*j}$ ghar bhej degii
Sita Salma ko her home send give-FUT
'Sita will send Salma to her home.'

(29) siitaa$_j$ ne salmaa$_i$ ko uske$_{i/*j}$ ghar bhej diyaa
Sita ERG Salma ko her home send give-PERF
'Sita sent Salma to her home.'

(30) siitaa$_j$ dwaaraa salmaa$_i$ ko uske$_{i/*j}$ ghar bhej diyaa gaya
Sita by Salma ko her home send give-PERF go-PERF
'Salma was sent to her home by Sita.'

2.2.3 Object Control

The object in ergative as well as active Passive constructions ((32) and (33) below) has the ability to control into argument clauses in the same way as the object in a normal active construction as in (31).

(31) *raam$_i$ mohan ko [PRO$_i$ ghar jaane ke liye] kahegaa*
Ram Mohan ko home go-INF GEN for tell-FUT
'Ram will tell Mohan to go home.'

(32) *raam$_i$ ne mohan ko [PRO$_i$ ghar jaane ke liye] kahaa*
Ram ERG Mohan ko home go-INF GEN for told
'Ram told Mohan to go home.'

(33) *raam$_i$ dwaaraa mohan ko [PRO$_i$ ghar jaane ke liye] kahaa*
Ram by Mohan ko home go-INF GEN for tell-PERF
gayaa
go-PERF
'Ram told Mohan to go home.'

2.2.4 Object Control into adverbial clauses

Object control into adverbial clauses also treats the objects in ergative and ACTIVE Passive constructions at a par with the object in nominative subject constructions. This is illustrated by the examples given below.

(34) *raam$_i$ mohan$_j$ ko [PRO$_{i/j}$ ghar se aaane ke baad] baazaar*
Ram Mohan ko home from come-INF after market
bhejegaa
send-FUT
= 'Ram will send Mohan to the market after coming back from home.'

(35) *raam$_i$ ne mohan$_j$ ko [PRO$_{i/j}$ ghar se aaane ke baad] baazaar*
Ram ERG Mohan ko home from come-INF after market
bhejaa
send-PERF
= 'Ram sent Mohan to the market after coming back from home.'

(36) *raam$_i$ dwaaraa mohan$_j$ ko [PRO$_{i/j}$ ghar se aaane ke baad]*
Ram by Mohan ko home from come-INF after
baazaar bhejaa gayaa
market send-PERF go-PERF
= 'Ram sent Mohan to the market after he coming back from home.'

2.2.5 Object Extraction out of a *yah* extraposed clause

This test shows that the underlying object of ergatives and ACTIVE Passives remains an argument and is not demoted to an adjunct status (though this test does not show whether or not the object has been promoted). (37) below illustrates that object extraction out of *yah* extraposed clauses (as discussed above for subject extraction) patterns alike for the object of a normal active sentence (37), an ergative sentence (38), as well as for an ACTIVE Passive sentence (39). In all cases, the extraction of the object yields a subjacency violation indicating that the object in all of these cases retains its argument status with respect to extraction out of these islands.

(37) ???*mohan ko, salmaa yah soctii   thii   ki   raam___ maarega*
Mohan ko Salmaa it   think-IMP be-PAST that Ram   hit-FUT-MASC
= 'Mohan, Salma thinks that Ram will hit.'

(38) ???*mohan ko, salmaa yah soctii   thii   ki   raam ne___ maaraa*
who   ko Salmaa it   think-IMP be-PAST that Ram ERG hit-PERF
= 'Mohan, Salma thinks that Ram hit?'

(39) ???*mohan ko, salmaa yah soctii   thii   ki   raam dwaaraa___*
Mohan ko Salmaa it   think-IMP be-PAST that Ram by
maaraa gayaa
hit-PERF go-PERF
= 'Mohan, Salma thinks that (he) was hit by Ram?'

2.2.6 Object agreement

This is one respect in which ergative and ACTIVE passive constructions differ from the nominative construction. Objects in ergative and ACTIVE Passive constructions show agreement with the participle and the auxiliaries. This is illustrated in (40) and (41) below. The object in a normal active construction can never agree with the object.

(40) *raajaa ne   jangal ke   saaree šer   maar*
king   ERG jungle GEN all   tiger-MASC-PL kill
diye   the
give-PERF-MASC-PL be-PAST-PL
'The king had killed all the tigers in the jungle.'

(41) *raajaa dwaaraa jangal ke   saaree šer   maar*
king   by   jungle GEN all   tiger-MASC-PL kill
diye   gaye   the
give-PERF-MASC go-PERF-MASC-PL be-PAST-PL
'All the tigers in the jungle had been killed by the king.'

We will argue below that this indicates that the object in ergative and ACTIVE Passive constructions may occupy a position different from that of a normal active sentence. However, this position must be distinguished from the subject position that is occupied by the external argument.

2.2.7 Summary
We have seen that the object in the ergative and the active Passive construction displays all the normal object properties (except for object agreement). This, in conjunction with the subject properties displayed by the agentive phrases (as seen in the previous subsection), indicates that the ergative as well as the ACTIVE Passive constructions are in fact 'active' constructions in which the external argument has not been demoted in the same sense that it is argued to be demoted in English Passives. Furthermore, the object in these construction types cannot be argued to have moved to the subject position (or to have been demoted). One crucial link between the object in the ergative and ACTIVE passive constructions and the normal subject of the active constructions is the property of agreement. The verb and auxiliary agreement is controlled by the subject in the normal active constructions while it passes on to the object in the ergative and ACTIVE Passive constructions.

3. Analysis of ACTIVE Passive and ergative constructions

3.1 Object agreement and Case

As shown in (40) and (41) above (these examples are repeated below for convenience), a key property of the constructions that we are dealing with is the fact that these constructions involve a form of object agreement that is not typical of normal active clauses in Hindi.

(40) *raajaa ne jangal ke saaree šer maar*
king ERG jungle GEN all tiger-MASC-PL kill
diye the
give-PERF-MASC-PL be-PAST-PL
'The king had killed all the tigers in the jungle.'

(41) *raajaa dwaaraa jangal ke saaree šer maar*
king by jungle gen all tiger-MASC-PL kill
diye gaye the
give-PERF-MASC go-PERF-MASC-PL be-PAST-PL
'All the tigers in the jungle had been killed by the king.'

As seen in these examples, the auxiliaries as well as the perfect participle in these construction types agree with the object and not with the subject. We follow here an analysis of object agreement under which agreement is a relationship mediated through a Spec–Head relationship (cf. Mahajan 1989 for Hindi; for a general proposal along these lines, see Chomsky 1989 and Sportiche 1991). Under this approach, the agreement between the auxiliary and the object indicates that the object has moved to the Spec-position of the auxiliary.[8] Given this theoretical assumption, we want to know why perfect participle constructions demonstrate this kind of object movement while, for example, a non perfect participle construction has subject agreement. The subject agreement property of non perfect participle constructions is illustrated below in (42):

(42) raajaa jangal ke   saaree šer   maar
     king jungle GEN all tiger-MASC-PL kill
     detaa   thaa
     give-IMP-MASC-SG   be-PAST-SG
     'The king used to all the tigers in the jungle.'

Following Hoekstra (1984) and Haider (1985), I will assume that perfect participles are not Case-assigners (cf. Mahajan, 1989), therefore the object has to move for Case reasons.[9] This leads to object agreement in perfect participle constructions in Hindi. In Section 2, we observed that this movement is not to the subject position, so the target of movement should be lower than wherever the subjects are, but high enough to trigger agreement with auxiliaries.[10] If the locus of the structural (nominative) Case received by the object is the highest finite auxiliary in these cases (cf. Mahajan 1989), we can straightforwardly explain why the object has to move so high. In moving through the lower (available) Spec-positions, the object triggers agreement with the perfect participle as well as the intermediate (nonfinite) auxiliaries.

The fact that non perfect participle constructions like (42) do not show object agreement can now follow from the fact that these types of verbs can assign accusative Case and therefore the object need not move.[11] In these cases, the subject can (and does) move through the intermediate Spec-positions, thereby agreeing with the imperfect participle (in (42)) as well as the higher auxiliaries.

This relatively simple approach relies on four independently proposed and relatively uncontroversial ideas: NP movement can be triggered for Case reasons, agreement is mediated through a Spec–Head relationship, the source of structural Case is either a finite head or a certain type of verbal form (I ignore prepositions here), and the Hoekstra/Haider proposal that perfect participles are non Case-assigners. The last idea is rather crucial since it distinguishes perfect participles from other verbal forms in Hindi that must be treated as bearers of a structural accusative Case.

3.2 *The 'Case' of subjects*

It is apparent from our examples so far that the presence of object agreement is somehow directly related to the fact that the subject in ACTIVE Passives and ergative constructions is marked with a special postpositional marker; *dwaaraa* in ACTIVE Passives and *ne* in ergative constructions. In this subsection, I develop an idea presented in Marantz (1991) which will account for this fact. The exact proposal that I outline below differs in some respects from Marantz's original proposal. Furthermore, I elaborate Marantz's idea as it applies to the origin of ergative Case to other type of oblique subject Cases found in Hindi and in many other languages.

The core of the idea is that subjects of transitive verbs can receive a special kind of Case ('dependent' Case for Marantz) if the verbs themselves are not structural Case-assigners. The specific mechanism of dependent Case assignment to subjects that I propose is as follows:[12]

(43) Dependent Case assignment:
  $[_{XP}$ YP $[_{X'}$ X ZP]]
  Assign a dependent lexical Case to YP (in SpecXP) if ZP (a complement of X) does not receive a structural Case from X.

While this mechanism of Case assignment has the peculiar property that the assignment of a dependent Case to the subject is contingent on its inability to discharge a structural accusative to the object by the verb, this mechanism could be understood as an extension of the standard idea regarding the assignment of genitive within nominals[13] (where X is a non structural Case assigning (nominal) head and it licenses a genitive in its Spec). In fact, with respect to ergative assignment, this proposal is similar to proposals like Bok-Bennema (1991) and Johns (1992) where ergative assignment is explicitly comparable to genitive assignment.

Within the context of the two construction types that we are considering, we need to say that the form of the dependent Case assigned to the subject varies with the choice of X. If X is a simple perfect participle, the dependent Case assigned is ergative (*ne*) while if the choice of X is a complex predicate composed of a perfect participle and the passive auxiliary, then the Case assigned is instrumental (*dwaaraa*).[14] This dependent Case assignment rule can further handle other types of so called quirky Case-marked subjects such as dative subjects and locative subjects that are not discussed in this paper.[15]

Assuming that XP in (43) corresponds to the highest VP shell, the dependent Case is assigned internal to the VP. The subject later moves to the higher subject position within the functional projection system external to the VP. Since there is no evidence for subject demotion in Hindi in the ergative and the ACTIVE Passive constructions, it is evident that this dependent Case marked VP internal (thematic) subject is mapped onto a VP external A-position. As is evident from our earlier discussion, this position has to be higher than the position from which the object agrees with the highest (finite) auxiliary, though it is unclear what this position is.[16]

The main implication of this analysis is that the ergative and the ACTIVE Passive constructions in Hindi are inconsistent with BG since the subject is not dethematized in the contexts in which the verb fails to assign a structural accusative Case.[17]

This analysis of the ergative and ACTIVE Passive constructions of Hindi leaves open the question as to why such construction types do not arise in English type languages. Related to this is the issue of why the effects of BG are readily observable in English type languages. I discuss this problem in the next section.

4. BG and English Type languages

Let us first investigate why English type languages do not have direct counterparts of the construction types that we have discussed from Hindi. That is, why do English type languages lack the ergative and ACTIVE Passive constructions? This will provide us with a further clue about the nature of the BG effects in these types of languages.

The closest counterparts of the Hindi ergative and the ACTIVE Passive constructions types in English would be the regular past participle construction (*Mary has bought a house.*) and the regular syntactic passive construction (*The book was stolen by John*) respectively. Both of these construction types are consistent with BG. If the past participle in English can be argued to be an accusative Case assigner, then one needs to say nothing additional about the active past participle constructions in English. It is straightforwardly compatible with BG (assignment of accusative Case and the presence of the thematic subject). Furthermore, the fact that the logical subject in English passives is demoted in the Passive construction in English where the passive participle is a non Case assigner is also consistent with BG. This approach distinguishes between the participles in the active and the passive constructions with respect to their Case assigning properties (even though they look morphologically identical on the surface).

I would like to pursue an idea here that makes Hindi and English virtually identical in their VP internal syntax. This would be based on the assumption that the perfect participle of Hindi and the past participle of English are also identical in their Case assigning properties, both are non Case assigners (cf. Hoekstra 1984; Haider 1985). Pursuing this further, I would like to suggest that the dependent Case assignment mechanism is applicable not only in Hindi (or other such rich Case languages) but it is applicable in languages like English. Thus, in the relevant construction types, the ergative and the instrumental Case is also assigned in English. However, the VP external syntax of English differs from that of Hindi for principled reasons and this is the part of syntax that yields the differences between Hindi and English (i.e., the relevant morphological Case disappears during the course of the derivation in English but not in Hindi). Furthermore, this is the part of the derivation that makes the English constructions compatible with BG.

4.1 *English ergative construction*

Given the assumptions that I have outlined above, English would have an ergative construction internal to the VP. Since the verb is a non Case assigner, the subject is assigned a dependent Case, indicated below as a preposition (which is consistent with the prepositional nature of English as compared to the postpositional nature of Hindi) (the VP external structure has been simplified):

(44) Spec Aux [$_{VP}$ P$_{erg}$ Sub V$_{past\ participle}$ Obj]

Following a proposal developed in Mahajan (1994), which in turn is based on Kayne's (1993) treatment of auxiliary selection, let us assume that the ergative marker (a type of preposition) incorporates into the Aux and the subject (without P) moves into the SpecAux position. This will have the consequence that the Aux would be *have* (= *be* + *P*) and we will have an unmarked subject. Since the object is still Caseless, we have to provide a source for Case for the object. I assume that the subject gets NOM in a normal fashion, i.e., in SpecAgrS position. I assume that the P incorporation into Aux makes ACC available for the object, that is, while the verb is still a non Case assigner, *have* provides an accusative Case for the object in the English counterpart of the Hindi ergative construction (cf. Hoekstra 1984, 1994). Modifying (44) somewhat, we can say that the accusative Case is assigned to the object in the SpecAux position by Aux+P (=*have*) while the subject moves to the SpecAgrS position and receives a structural nominative Case. The relevant modification of (44) needed to implement this idea is given in (45):[18]

(45)   SpecAgrS [SpecAux [$_{VP}$ P$_{erg}$ Sub V$_{past\ participle}$ Obj]]

Alternatively, as suggested by Hoekstra (1994), accusative Case to the object is assigned in SpecAgrPO above the AuxP. Both our approach here and Hoekstra's approach have the problem that the Aux (*have*) assigns Case to the object while it actually agrees with the subject (presumably after it raises to AgrSP). This may indicate the disassociation between Case and agreement contrary to Chomsky (1992). However, the question why the auxiliary *cannot* agree with the object remains unanswered for English even if there is an AgrOP projection mediating Case assignment between the Aux and the object. If both Case assignment and agreement are checked in a SpecHead configuration, it is unclear why the object does not agree with the Aux. One way to handle this would be to allow for Case assignment under government. One could then modify (45) above as:

(46)   SpecAgrS [SpecAux [$_{XP}$ X [$_{VP}$ P$_{erg}$ SUB V$_{past\ participle}$ OBJ]]]

where X could be viewed as a layer of the VP above the original VP. P would incorporate into Aux after it moves into X (possibly substituting into it first). The object gets its accusative Case in SpecXP from the Aux that incorporates the raised P. The subject moves into the SpecAux and further into the SpecAgrS position to receive NOM. The configuaration (46) can in fact be compared to Kayne's (1993) idea if we view XP as Kayne's DP except for the fact that the P originates within the participial phrase (with the subject, as a dependent Case) and then moves into X (=Kayne's D) and further into Aux.[19]

The important consequence of this approach is that while VP internally English is like Hindi, VP externally, P incorporation into Aux makes it different in that an ACC is made available for the object (which would have had to move higher to seek Case if that was not made possible) and the subject ends up as a nominative Case marked NP. The crucial point is that the non Case-assigning nature of the verb does not lead to subject dethematization since other factors take over in providing a Case for both the object and the subject.[20]

Hindi is obviously different from English. As discussed in Mahajan (1994a), if we make a simple assumption regarding P incorporation, that it is contingent upon linear adjacency in addition to simple government, then the facts follow since the subject adposition (postposition in Hindi) and the Aux would not be linearly adjacent in Hindi, a language which is head (Aux) final.[21]

This would have the consequence that the P would not be incorporated into the Aux and the Aux (in the ergative constructions for instance) will surface as *be.* Furthermore, simple *be,* as opposed to *have,* cannot provide an accusative Case for the object (cf. Hoekstra 1984, 1994), therefore the object has to move to a higher position in the clause to seek a structural Case. As is apparent from the agreement facts discussed earlier, the object ends up receiving the NOM Case from the finite auxiliary (possibly transmitted through T). The subject has a dependent Case (which has not been absorbed since incorporation is not possible in Hindi) and it is apparent from our earlier discussion that it moves to a position higher than the object.

To summarize the results of this subsection, under the Hoekstra/Haider assumption about the non-Case-assigning nature of perfect participles, English past participle constructions like *Mary has bought a house* (which are counterparts to the Hindi ergative construction) would be exceptions to BG except for the fact that the P incorporation into *be* yields a source for the accusative Case in English. This makes these construction types compatible with BG. The parallel Hindi construction (the ergative construction) disallows P incorporation for independent syntactic reasons and therefore the object has to move higher to receive a structural nominative Case. The resulting configuration is inconsistent with BG.

4.2 *The English Passive Construction*

It is obvious that the English Passive construction is not similar to the Hindi ACTIVE Passive construction in a crucial respect. The subject in the English passives is demoted. Let us consider the derivation of the English passives from the perspective of our discussion of the Hindi ACTIVE Passive construction. Assume that the instrumental agent in English passives originates in the same position as the instrumental agent in the Hindi ACTIVE Passive sentences. That is, the instrumental in English Passives is a kind of dependent Case and the configuration in which it arises is similar to (43) above. The question then is: why is this P not incorporated into Aux to yield *have*? If this incorporation was indeed possible in English, English passive should contain the auxiliary *have* and the construction should in fact have a non-demoted subject. One of the reasons why this is not the case is related to our discussion of Hindi ACTIVE Passives in Section 3.2. The choice of the instrumental dependent Case is determined not by the participle alone but by the combination of the participle and the passive auxiliary *be*. This implies that the auxiliary is lower than the subject in the passive constructions ruling out the possibility of incorporation. This idea is in fact supported by Baker, Johnson and Roberts' (1989: 241) suggestion that the auxiliary *be* in passives is generated lower than the I position heading a VP of its own, i.e., the d-structure for passive clauses according to them is somewhat like (47) below:

(47)   [$_s$ [Infl [$_{VP}$ be [$_S$ en [$_{VP}$ V]]]]]

We could modify this structure by adopting the VP internal subject hypothesis (and by conflating the V+en projection, though one could build in a participial projection along within the verbal phrase). The modified structure combined with our idea that the subject is generated in the Spec-position of the *be* would look like:

(48)   SpecAgrS [T [AgrO [P$_{inst}$ SUB be+V$_{part}$ OBJ]]]

Alternatively if the subject simply originates in the Spec-position of Aux *be* that selects a participial phrase as its complement, the structure would be:

(49)   SpecAgrS [T [AgrO [P$_{inst}$ SUB [be [V$_{part}$ OBJ]]]]]

In either of these configurations, P cannot incorporate into *be*. At this stage of the derivation, we are stuck with an instrumental (agentive) subject and a Caseless object (in English Passives), a state of affairs that parallels the ACTIVE Passive construction in Hindi. The derivation proceeds as it does in Hindi. The Caseless object moves higher to some position where it could obtain the Case associated with T. The problem in this derivation is the status of the agentive *by* phrase. If it was possible to license this phrase in English the same way as Hindi does (in some A-position higher than the final position of the underlying object) then English and Hindi should be identical. However, it is clear that the Hindi type derivation does not go through in English and the *by* phrase is demoted and appears (optionally) as an adjunct. For Hindi, we have already seen evidence for the 'active' nature of the agentive phrases in this type of Passive construction. Why does the status of the agentive phrases in Hindi and English differ in this respect? One possibility is that this relates to a general property of English type languages in that such languages do not allow PP subjects. This would be an independent parameter that distinguishes Hindi type languages that allow PP subjects and English type languages that do not.[22]

Given the inability of English to license VP external PP subjects, and given the fact that the preposition associated with the subject cannot be absorbed away from the subject, English simply demotes the VP internal subject (with its P).

The resulting configuration in English (and other similar languages) has the properties that makes it compatible with the properties associated with BG. The VP internal subject is dethematized just in the case where the verb is a non accusative assigner. We have seen, however, that these properties arise not because of any inherent connection between subject dethematization and accusative Case assignment but because of a general dependent Case assignment procedure (common both to Hindi and English) and the inability of English to license a dependent Case marked nominal (a PP) in the clausal subject position.

5. Conclusion

Under the analysis sketched out here, there is *no correlation between Case and θ-roles*, a desirable consequence. However, there seems to be a correlation between the inability of a verb to assign a structural Case and the ability of its subject to acquire a morphological Case (as in the rule of dependent Case assignment above). One way to derive this effect would be to generalize the genitive rule of LGB (only X′ assigns a constructional Case; in a sense this relates to Marantz's idea of dependent Case being an oppositional Case) making it sensitive to the nature of the predicate involved such that depending on the predicate involved we can get dative subjects, genitive subjects, ergative subjects, instrumental subjects etc. If these Case markers can be absorbed into some head during the course of the derivation, we will have nominative subjects licensed in the normal fashion, i.e., subject Case assignment in SpecAgrS. This is one of the sources of *have* in English type languages. The absorption of these Case markers makes possible accusative Case assignment along the lines suggested by Hoekstra (1994). Such configurations are actually not compatible with BG since we have assumed that the assignment of the dependent Case is contingent upon the non-Case assignment by the predicate. However, they appear to be compatible with BG since accusative Case is made available in an alternative fashion. In languages like Hindi, where this strategy fails due to the adjacency requirement on incorporation, dependent Case marked subjects are licensed as surface PP subjects. Since an accusative Case is not made available in the relevant construction types in Hindi, the object receives the only Case available, the nominative Case. Since there is an alternative way of realizing PP subjects in Hindi, the resulting configurations are incompatible with BG.

To conclude, BG is not really a valid generalization since there are systematic exceptions to it in many language types. The effects often associated with BG arise due to the interplay of other factors, some of which were examined in this paper.

Notes

1. The fact the ergative languages do not display BG effects is fairly well known (see many contributions in this volume). However, it appears that examples inconsistent with BG are also readily found in non ergative languages that possess other type of oblique (or PP) subject constructions. For example, Kannada (Sridhar 1976), a non ergative language, appears to have oblique subject constructions that are inconsistent with BG. Exceptions to BG are also found in many other languages as discussed in Maratz (1991) (e.g., Japanese (Kubo 1989), Kichaga (Bresnan and Moshi 1990)).

2. This construction is discussed in detail in Mahajan (1994b) where it is labelled ACTIVE Passive to distinguish it from the regular capability Passives discussed extensively in literature in Hindi syntax (as in Saksena 1978; Pandharipande 1981; Davison 1982,1988; Mohanan 1990; among others.) I will retain the label ACTIVE Passive for our discussion here. Mohanan (1990) discusses a construction type that has somewhat similar properties to this construction.

3. Some of these tests, which are originally based on Keenan (1976), have been used for identifying subjects in a variety of construction types in South Asian languages (cf. Verma 1976; Kachru 1980; Kachru, Kachru and Bhatia 1976).

4. For a number of Hindi speakers, a reflexive like *apnaa* have a subject orientation (cf. Srivastav-Dayal 1994) while many others allow non subjects as possible antecedents (cf. Gurtu 1985; Mahajan 1990). However adjunct PPs, even if they are human and precede *apnaa*, cannot serve as antecedents for it:

    (i) *raam par apnaa baccaa   beṭhaa   thaa
        Ram on self's child-MASC-NOM sat-PERF-MASC be-PAST-MASC
        = 'Self's child was sitting on Ram.'

5. An adjunct PP such as the one discussed in the previous footnote does not enforce disjoint reference for the pronoun.

    (ii) raam$_i$ par uskaa$_i$ baccaa   beṭhaa   thaa
         Ram on his   child-MASC-NOM sat-PERF-MASC be-PAST-MASC
         = 'His child was sitting on Ram.'

6. This test appears to be somewhat more reliable than the anaphor binding test since pronominal obviation appears to test the clause external subjecthood much more reliably. Interestingly, this test distinguishes between the ergative subject and the ACTIVE Passive constructions discussed here and the dative subject construction which is often taken to be a prototypical oblique subject construction. The so called dative subjects do not enforce pronominal obviation as shown below:

    (i) raam-ko$_i$ uskii$_i$ kitaab pasand hɛ
        Ram DAT his   book   like   be-PRES
        'Ram likes his book.'

   This may indicate that the dative subjects are not VP external subjects but are inverted arguments moved into a position higher than the normal subject position (cf. Jayaseelan 1990). It appears, however, that this higher position (whether the Spec-position of a higher head or an adjoined position) does have properties of an A-position with respect to tests of A-positions.

7. It is sometimes claimed that *-ko* is an accusative marker in Hindi. Since the presence or absence of *-ko* is related to the specificity of the object rather than any relevant property of the verb, it is not entirely clear how it can be construed as an accusative marker. For the purposes of this paper, *-ko* can simply be treated as an object marker denoting specificity.

8. To keep the discussion simple, I will abstract away from the possibility that auxiliaries themselves project agreement projections.

9. There is some evidence that the objects in sentences like (40) are indeed in a position higher than the object in sentences like (42). The relevant evidence comes from the interpretation of certain adverbs in such constructions. For details, see Mahajan (1990; Chapter 2).

10. The exact location of the clausal subject in these construction types is not important for our purposes here. One possibility is that the subjects in these construction types occupy an A-position higher than the SpecAuxP. This position could be the Spec-position of one of the functional heads associated with the Aux (i.e., AgrSP of dominating AuxP for instance)..

11. This analysis is not inconsistent with the idea that accusative Case is assigned through a functional projection as long as the source of the structural accusative is the verb itself (as assumed in Chomsky 1992; Laka 1991). To build in the idea of assignment of the structural accusative Case through a functional projection, we will need to posit a functional head lower than the auxiliary and lower than the position through which object agreement is mediated. This could possibly be implemented through a functional head internal to the VP. An alternative to this would be to assign the structural accusative directly under Spec–Head relationship internal to a layered VP (cf. Koopman and Sportiche 1991). These issues are however not directly relevant here.

12. Note that if a predicate is a structural Case assigner (e.g., active verb *hit* in *John hit Bill*) then the mechanism of dependent Case assignment does not come into play. That is, dependent Case assignment will take place only in restrictive environments where a transitive verb lacks the ability to assign a structural accusative. In normal non-dependent Case environments as in *John hit Bill*, nothing needs to be added to the standard Case theory (the nominative comes from the inflection and the accusative comes from the verb; they could be assigned/checked through AgrS and AgrO projections as is standardly assumed (also see the previous footnote)). In that sense, the mechanism of dependent Case assignment is an addition to the standard Case theory (in roughly the same way as genitive assignment is an addition to the standard Case theory). I should note that in this paper (as reflected in my formulation of (43)), I am only concerned with dependent Case assignment to subjects and not to other arguments. I should also note that unlike Marantz (1991), I do not treat accusative Case as a dependent Case. In this paper, I treat accusative as a structural Case.

13. The intuition behind this idea is that non structural Case assigning verbal forms are not truly verbal. Thus, perfect participles are, in that sense, non verbal categories that would trigger a genitive type rule under appropriate conditions.

14. Alternatively, the *dwaara* dependent case is assigned by the passive auxiliary which takes a phrase headed by the perfect participle as its complement.

15. In fact, genitive assignment can now also be covered under this rule by simply stating that if X is an N, the dependent case assigned is genitive. This would incorporate the insight of approaches such as Bok-Bennema (1991) and Johns (1992).

16. As indicated earlier, one possibility is that the higher position in question is the SpecAgrS position that is above the auxiliary. Another possibility is that this position is the same position as the one occupied by the locative subjects in the locative inversion constructions as discussed in Branigan (1993). However, the tests given above indicate that this position has the properties normally associated with an A-position; therefore it cannot be straightforwardly equated with the SpecAgrC position argued to be occupied by the locative subjects in English which Branigan argues to be an A-bar position (see also, Bresnan 1994). Given the fact that dative subjects differ from the ergative and active Passive subjects with respect to the pronominal

obviation test, one may be tempted to equate the surface position of the dative in the so called dative subject constructions in Hindi with that of the locative in the locative inversion construction. However, it appears that this cannot be so since dative subjects can be extracted out of the extraposed clauses (with *yah*, as discussed above) with a relatively a lower level of ungrammaticality as opposed to the extraction of real adjuncts.

(i) ???*raam ko,   siitaa ne   yah socaa   ki__ vah kitaab pasand thii*
     Ram DAT Sita ERG it   thought that that book like   be-PAST
     = 'Ram, Sita thought that liked that book.'

This indicates that different oblique subjects *may* occupy different structural (A) positions outside the VP and that these positions can sometimes be distinguished using tests such as pronominal obviation.

17. Nothing special needs to be said about the Hindi imperfectives like (42) (repeated below as (i)):

    (i)   *raajaa jangal ke   saaree ser   maar detaa   thaa*
          king   jungle GEN all   tiger-MASC-PL kill   give-IMPERF-MASC-SG be-PAST-SG
          'The king used to all the tigers in the jungle.'

In these "active" sentences with imperfect participles, the verb can assign an accusative; therefore dependent Case assignment is not triggered. The subject therefore ends up receiving a structural nominative Case in a normal fashion (in SpecAgrS or SpecAux) and shows agreement with the Aux (and the verb).

18. A reviewer raises the issue of whether preposition incorporation into a verb from the specifier of a complement of that verb should be permitted. That is, whether incorporation of P into Aux in (45) is legitimate. I do not know any reason why this movement should be excluded. Under a theory of incorporation such as that of Baker (1988), such configurations of incorporation are clearly allowed (and are not violations of the Head Movement Constraint). See Baker's (1988: 170–179) discussion of causatives for the relevant discussion.

19. One may assume that the participle itself later raises to X (more properly, trace of P now incorporated into Aux) and possibly to Aux itself (LF restructuring as suggested in Mahajan 1989; also Hoekstra,1994).

20. I will not discuss here the complications having to do with the difference between English and other Germanic (and Romance) languages with respect to auxiliary selection. One of the obvious problems has to do with the lack of unaccusative-unergative distinction with respect to auxiliary selection in English. Some of these complications are discussed in Mahajan (1994).

21. As it stands, the adjacency requirement on incorporation appears somewhat ad hoc. While we know of syntactic constraints on incorporation (for instance, the government requirement of Baker 1988), the adjacency requirement appears somewhat less motivated. However, a quick review of the data on preposition incorporation across several languages as presented in Baker (1988) shows that the arguments out of which a preposition has been incorporated typically appear adjacent to the verb into which the preposition has been incorporated. Baker (1988: 248) clearly notes this restriction with respect to the Chamorro double object constructions. See also Bok-Bennema and Groos (1988) who argue for an adjacency requirement on incorporation in a somewhat different context.

22. As pointed out by a reviewer, this difference between Hindi and English remains a stipulation. Whether or not this parametric difference could be related to some deeper property of the languages in question remains an open issue. For instance, it is plausible that there is a general tendency in languages towards having unmarked (nominative) subjects at the final point in the syntactic derivation, PP subjects being a marked option. Thus while PP subjects are generated

within the VP (via dependent case marking where dependent case is realized as P) in all languages, the adpositional element is absorbed (via incorporation) in as many cases as possible. In some language types however, such incorporation is excluded on independent grounds (for instance, because of the lack of the adjacency requirement on incorporation that we discussed earlier). In such cases, these languages simply allow such PPs to surface as surface subjects. However, languages in which such incorporation is possible at least in some cases simply disallow the option PP subjects. It is not clear how to formalize this idea within the domain of present syntactic theory.

References

Baker, M., Johnson, K. and Roberts, I. 1989. "Passive arguments raised". *Linguistic Inquiry* 20 : 219–251.
Baker, M. 1988. *Incorporation: A theory of grammatical function changing*. Chicago: University of Chicago Press.
Bok-Bennema, R. 1991. *Case and Agreement in Inuit*. Dordrecht: Foris.
Bok-Bennema, R. and Groos, A. 1988. "Adjacency and incorporation". In *Morphology and Modularity*, M. Everaert, A. Evers, R. Huybreghts and M. Trommelen (eds), 33–56. Dordrecht : Foris.
Branigan, P. 1993. "Locative inversion and the extended projection principle". Ms., Memorial University of Newfoundland.
Bresnan, J. 1994. "Locative inversion and the architecture of Universal Grammar". *Language* 70: 72–131.
Bresnan, J. and Moshi, L. 1990. "Object asymmetries in comparative Bantu syntax". *Linguistic Inquiry* 21 : 147–85.
Burzio, L. 1986. *Italian Syntax*. Dordrecht : Reidel.
Chomsky, N. 1989. "Some notes on economy of derivation and representation". *MIT Working Papers in Linguistics* 10 : 43–74.
Chomsky, N. 1992. *A Minimalist Program for Linguistic Theory*. MIT Occasional Papers in Linguistics 1.
Davison, A. 1982. "On the form and meaning of Hindi passive sentences". *Lingua* 58: 149–179.
Davison, A. 1988. "The case filter as motivation for move alpha". *Cornell Working Papers in Linguistics* 8 : 17–38.
Gurtu, M. 1985. Anaphoric relations in Hindi and English. PhD dissertation, Central Institute of English and Foreign Languages, Hyderabad.
Haider, H. 1985. "Von *sein* oder nicht *sein*". In *Erklarende syntax des Deutschen*, W. Abraham (ed.). Tubingen: Gunter Narr.
Hestvik, A. 1992. "LF movement of pronouns and antisubject orientation". *Linguistic Inquiry* 23: 557–594.
Hoekstra,T. 1984. *Transitivity*. Dordrecht : Foris.
Hoekstra, T. 1994. "Possession and Transitivity". Ms. HIL, Leiden University.

Jayaseelan, K. A. 1990. "The dative subject construction and the pro-drop parameter". In *Experiencer Subjects in South Asian Languages*, M. K. Verma and K. P. Mohanan (eds), 269–283. Stanford : CSLI.
Johns, A. 1992. "Deriving ergativity". *Linguistic Inquiry* 23: 57–88.
Kachu, Y. 1980. *Aspects of Hindi Grammar*. New Delhi: Manohar publications.
Kachru, Y., Kachru, B. and Bhatia, T. 1976. "The notion 'subject': A note on Hindi-Urdu, Kashmiri and Panjabi". In *The Notion of Subject in South Asian Languages*, M. K. Verma (ed.), 79–108. South Asian Studies, University of Wisconsin, Madison.
Kayne, R. 1993. "Toward a modular theory of auxiliary selection". *Studia Linguistica* 47: 3–31.
Keenan, E. 1976. "Towards a universal definition of subject". In *Subject and Topic*, C. Li (ed.), 247–302. New York: Academic Press.
Koopman, H. and Sportiche, D. 1991. "The position of subjects". *Lingua* 85 : 211–258.
Kubo, M. 1989. "Japanese passives". Ms., MIT.
Mahajan, A. 1989. "Agreement and agreement phrases". *MIT Working papers in Linguistics* 10 : 217–252.
Mahajan, A. 1990. The A-A-bar Distinction and Movement Theory. PhD Dissertation, MIT.
Mahajan, A. 1993. "On Gamma marking adjunct traces in Hindi". *UCLA Occasional Papers in Syntax* 11: 55–64.
Mahajan, A. 1994a. "The ergativity parameter: *Have-be* alternation, word order and split ergativity". *NELS* 23: 317–331.
Mahajan, A. 1994b. "ACTIVE passives". *WCCFL* 13: 286–301.
Marantz, A. 1991. "Case and licensing". *ESCOL* 8: 234–253. [reprinted in this volume].
Mohanan, T. 1990. Arguments in Hindi. PhD Dissertation, Stanford University.
Pandharipande, R. 1981. Passives in Selected South Asian Languages. PhD Dissertation, University of Illinois, Urbana-Champaign.
Perlmutter, D. 1978. "Impersonal passives and the unaccusative hypothesis". *BLS* 4: 157–189.
Saksena, A. 1978. "A reanalysis of the passive in Hindi". *Lingua* 46: 339–353.
Sportiche, D. 1991. "Movement, Agreement and Case". Ms., UCLA.
Sridhar, S. N. 1976. "The notion of 'subject' in Kannada". In *The Notion of Subject in South Asian Languages*, M. K. Verma (ed.). Madison, WI: South Asian Studies, University of Wisconsin.
Srivastav, V. 1991. Wh-dependencies in Hindi and the Theory of Grammar. PhD Dissertation, Cornell University.
Srivastav-Dayal, V. 1994. "Binding facts in Hindi and the scrambling phenomena". In *Theoretical Perspectives on Word Order in South Asian Languages*, M. Butt, T. King and G. Ramchand (eds), 237–261. Stanford : CSLI Lecture Notes.
Verma, M. 1976. "The notion of subject in South Asian languages". In *The Notion of Subject in South Asian Languages*, M. K. Verma (ed.), 79–108. Madison, WI: South Asian Studies, University of Wisconsin

Thetablind Case
Burzio's Generalization
and its Image in the Mirror

Itziar Laka
University of the Basque Country

Introduction

In this paper, it is argued that the effects of Burzio's Generalization (henceforth BG) can be shown to follow from Case Theoretic issues alone, without appeal to thematic relations. This argument is outlined in Laka (1993b); the present paper is an extension of that argument, with further refinements regarding Case Theory, the nature of Case assigning categories, and a broader look into cross-linguistic data.

The puzzle posed by BG is: 'why should thematic demotion affect Case assignment if they are independent processes?' Here, a view of Case Theory is presented which is indeed blind to thematic relations, and thus requires no reference to the assignment of an external θ-role by the predicate to account for a given Case assignment pattern.

There is a different question, related in some sense to BG, which inquires about the nature of unaccusativity and processes of argument demotion in predicates. This issue will not be explored in this paper;[1] the concern here is to provide an account for the apparent correlation between θ-relations and Case, by showing that there is no inherent, necessary connection between external θ-role assignment and Accusative Case assignment. The paper therefore concentrates on the Case theoretic aspects of BG, and argues that Case Theory alone provides for an explanation of the empirical effects covered by this influential generalization.

The paper is divided into seven sections. Section 1 introduces BG and the challenge it presents to a modular view of the Grammar. Section 2 presents Case Theory as assumed in this paper; Section 3 discusses the notion of *active feature*, which plays a crucial role in the derivation of BG; Section 4 puts forward the derivation of BG and illustrates the parametric nature of this generalization;

Section 5 discusses in more detail the independence of Case Theory from thematic relations, the various consequences of this independence, and it illustrates the Case Theoretic results of various thematic operations. Section 6 discusses the nature of Aspect as a Case assigner and its implication in split Case systems. Section 7 summarizes the conclusions arrived at in the paper.

1. Burzio's Generalization

Since Perlmutter's (1978) pioneering work, it is widely accepted that the set of predicates traditionally described as intransitives divides into two natural classes: *unergative predicates* and *unaccusative predicates*. The examples in (1) illustrate the two types in English and Spanish:

(1) a. *a woman spoke clearly*
    b. *a woman arrived on time*
    c. *una mujer habló claramente*
    d. *una mujer llegó a tiempo*

Although the sentences in (1) appear identical in the surface, Perlmutter (1978) argued that sentences containing unergative predicates like (1a) and (1c), differ significantly from sentences containing unaccusative predicates like (1b) and (1d). These differences are due to the fact that two distinct initial syntactic representations are involved: specifically, Perlmutter argued that the initial relation born by 'a woman' or 'una mujer' with respect to the predicate 'speak' or 'hablar' is that of *subject*, whereas the initial relation born by 'a woman' or 'una mujer' with respect to 'arrive' or 'llegar' is that of *object*. In subsequent representations (or *strata*, in Relational Grammar terms), both predicate types converge in a representation where 'a woman' or 'una mujer' bears the relation *subject* with respect to the predicate, yielding the surface forms in (1).

This research project, concerned with the original syntactic representation of predicates and the transformations that these original representations undergo, is pursued in Burzio (1986), within the Theory of Government and Binding (Chomsky (1981) and subsequent work). Burzio's account of the surface similarity of (1a) and (1b) relies crucially on what has come to be known as *Burzio's Generalization*, stated in (2):

(2) $[-A] \leftrightarrow [-T]$

BG claims that if a verb does not assign an external θ-role, then it does not assign Case. Consider some of the phenomena covered by this generalization:

arguments of unaccusative predicates do not surface bearing Accusative Case, even though they originally sit in the canonical position where this Case is assigned (3a), (3b); passive participles may not assign Accusative Case to their complements because no external argument is assigned (3c), (3d).

(3)   a. *arrived her
        b. she_i arrived t_i
        c. *was appointed her
        d. she_i was appointed t_i

BG has been a powerful drive in the understanding of the similarities between unaccusative predicates and various types of constructions, such as passives, causative alternations, middles and raising predicates. BG has thus brought together a number of apparently disparate phenomena, and has facilitated the conception of the Grammar as the interplay of various modules that give rise to seemingly unrelated grammatical constructions.

BG has also presented a problem for the Theory of Syntax as outlined in the Government and Binding framework: how can thematic relations condition Case relations in such a direct fashion, if these are two independent sub-theories of the grammar? Where exactly does the connection between the two ends of the correlation lie? In other words, it is not clear what principle or principles could derive BG, because there is no explicit connection between external θ-role assignment and Accusative Case assignment besides the very one stated by the generalization itself. Thus, BG appears to cover a wide range of phenomena, but it poses a challenge to the idea that human grammars are designed in a strictly modular way, an idea put forward by Chomsky (1981), which lies at the very core of the articulation of the Government and Binding Theory, and subsequent developments within this framework (Chomsky 1989, 1993).

BG is intended as a generalization about Universal Grammar. However, here it will be argued that it concerns only a subpart of the possible human grammars: BG effects surface only in Nominative Case systems, and not in Ergative Case systems. This will provide the basis for the derivation of BG argued for in this paper; but before turning to it, a few considerations regarding Case Theory are in order. They are presented in the following two sections.

2. On Case Theory

Following the framework for Case Theory presented in Chomsky (1989), where Case is argued to be a Spec–Head relation involving AgrS and AgrO, Bobaljik

(1992) argues that the crucial factor determining the differences between Nominative and Ergative Case systems is the choice of Case when only one Case is required: (a) if the Case chosen is assigned by AgrS and Tense, the resulting Case system is Nominative; (b) if the Case chosen is assigned by AgrO and Verb, the resulting system is Ergative.[2] More specifically, Bobaljik argues that the choice of Case is determined by the 'activation' of either AgrS or AgrO. This paper follows the basic insight of Bobaljik's approach to the Ergative/Nominative distinction.

In Laka (1993b), based on the behavior of unergative predicates in Basque (as well as Georgian and Hindi), it is argued that the 'activation' of the relevant Case does not depend on the choice of Agr, but rather, on the Case feature borne by the Case assigner (Tns or V): Nominative systems activate the Case feature born by Tense (C_T), whereas Ergative systems activate the Case feature born by the Verb (C_V).

Here, the claim that Agreement is not a Case assigner will be maintained (see also Marantz (1991), Bittner & Hale (1996a), den Dikken (1993) and Holloway King (1994), among others for different approaches to Case Theory that share this view). A modification of Laka (1993b) will be pursued: in particular, the paper argues that the set of Case assigning categories does not include lexical elements such as the Verb. Instead, the set of Case assigners is argued to include functional categories such as Tense and Aspect, and possibly Prepositions and Determiners.[3] Evidence supporting the role and relevance of Aspect in Case assignment is discussed in Section 6.

I adopt the idea put forward in Bittner & Hale (1996a), following a proposal by Lamontagne & Travis (1987), that Case on the argument DP is a functional head which dominates DP, call it K, and which projects a KP. Support for this view is found in the consistency in which Case particles (that is, K heads in this approach) abide by the head parameter: head final languages display head final K elements, while head initial languages display initial K elements. Some examples are illustrated in (4), which are taken from Bittner & Hale (1996a) except for the Basque data. Examples (4a,b) correspond to head final languages, and (4c,d) to head initial languages:

(4)   a. $[_{KP} [_{DP} [_{NP}$ *sula*$]$ *ba*$]$ *ra*$]$ Miskitu
            deer   DET   ACC

       b. $[_{KP} [_{DP} [_{NP}$ *orein*$]$ *a*$]$ *k*$]$ Basque
            deer   DET   ERG

       c. $[_{KP}$ *ya* $[_{DP}$ *'u* $[_{NP}$ *khlaa*$]]]$ Khasi
            ACC   DET   tiger

d. [_KP e [_DP le [_NP teine]]]   Samoan
         ERG DET   girl

It will be assumed here that all Case marked arguments are KPs, including Nominative/Absolutive bearing arguments, which tend to display a phonologically empty K. From this perspective, Case assignment is the discharge of the Case feature borne by a Case assigning head to the K head of the argument, as shown in (5).[4] For the sake of consistency in the notation, the C_T and C_A features will be renamed as K_T and K_A, and this notation will also be used in glosses, to indicate what type of Case has been assigned to a particular KP. The feature-bearing Tense and Aspect heads are represented as T_K and A_K.

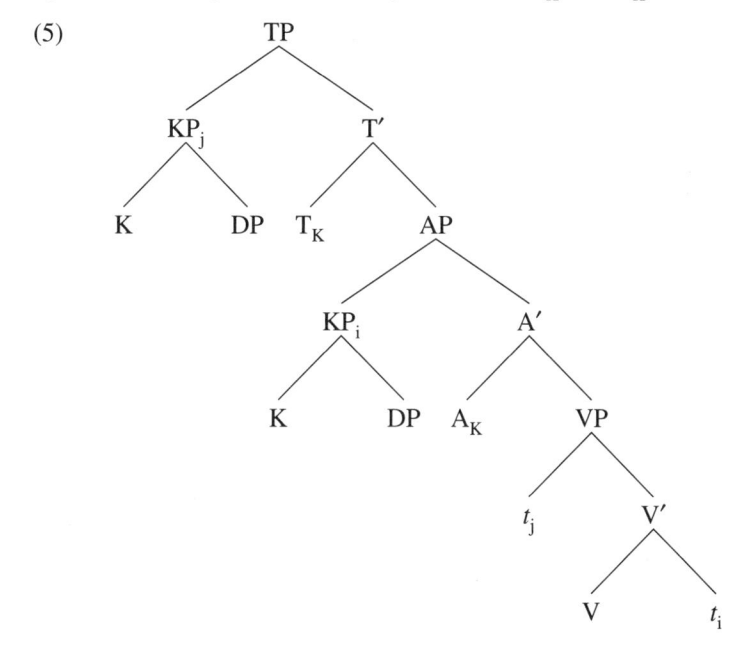

(5)
```
              TP
             /  \
          KP_j   T'
          /  \   / \
         K   DP T_K  AP
                    /  \
                  KP_i  A'
                  / \   / \
                 K  DP A_K  VP
                           /  \
                          t_j  V'
                              / \
                             V   t_i
```

From this perspective, then, the difference between Nominative/Accusative Case systems and Ergative/Absolutive Case systems depends on whether the Case feature of Tense (K_T) or Aspect (K_A) is active, since that will be the feature discharged when only one Case is required. This is schematically illustrated in (6):

(6)   a. $K_T \rightarrow K_A$ primary Case assigner Tns: Nominative system
      b. $K_A \rightarrow K_T$ primary Case assigner Asp: Ergative system

As (6) illustrates, a Nominative system is one where the Case feature borne by Aspect (K_A) can only be activated if the Case feature borne by Tense (K_T) has been discharged. In an Ergative system, the Case feature borne by Tense can only be activated if the Case borne by Aspect has been discharged. This approach to Case Theory is conceptually compatible with the notion of 'dependent case' developed in Marantz (1991, this volume), and also with the notion of 'Case-competitor' in Bittner & Hale (1996a, b), although the actual analyses differ significantly. What is shared is the insight that Ergative or Accusative are only assigned if the conditions for the assignment of Absolutive or Nominative are satisfied.

3. On the notion of 'active feature'

The implementation of the parametric distinction between K_T active versus K_A active systems does not pose any extra burden on the Theory of Grammar. It is encoded in the specifications of the functional elements in the lexicon. The parametric difference between the two systems reduces to varying properties of the items in the functional part of the lexicon, following the view on language variation put forward in Chomsky (1989).

Assume that, if a functional item is specified as containing an *active* Case feature, then this feature must be discharged or a violation ensues. There are several ways to implement this basic notion, and the details will vary depending on the particular theoretical assumptions made.

For instance, within the Minimalist approach developed in Chomsky (1992), all features must be checked by LF. If we are to incorporate the notion of *active* feature into this system, we must somehow distinguish it from the notions of *strong* and *weak* features.

To illustrate this, assume that an *active* feature is a feature that must be checked prior to Spell Out. Under this characterization, an *active* feature would be identical to a *strong* feature, which is not desirable: there are systems where both Case features are strong in the sense of Chomsky (1992): they force overt raising to the specifier positions of inflectional heads. An example of such a language is Basque, argued in Laka (1988), (1993a), to involve S-Structure representations like (7) (for the purpose of the argument, AuxP correlates with AP):

(7)
```
                TP
               /  \
             ERG   T'
                  /  \
                AuxP  T
               /   \
             ABS   Aux'
                  /   \
                 VP   Aux
```

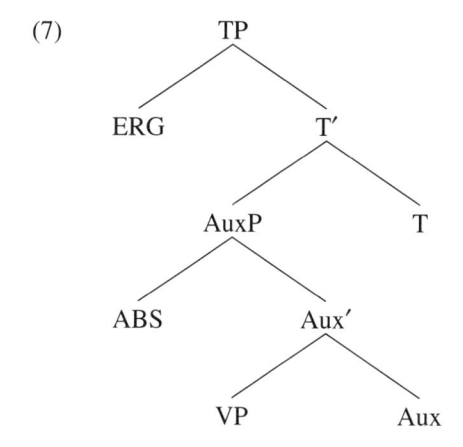

A complete identification of the notions *active* and *strong* yields the unwanted result that both K_T and K_A would require to be assigned whenever Tense and Aspect are involved in the derivation, contrary to fact. In monadic predicates only K_A is checked.

Consider the following approach: an *active* feature is one that must be checked prior to PF or Spell Out. A *strong* feature, if checked, is checked prior to Spell Out. A *weak* feature is checked after Spell Out. The consequences of this modification of Chomsky's (1993) typology of features are the following: an *active* feature is always *strong*, in the sense that it must be discharged prior to Spell Out or the derivation crashes. A *strong* feature is not available after Spell Out, therefore it must be checked, if required, prior to it. A *weak* feature is available at LF. In this typology, the assumption is that features that are not active are available but need not be checked.[5]

Thus, an Ergative system involves an *active* K_A and it may involve a strong K_T or a weak one. This entails that the argument assigned K_A will have to raise to [SpecAsp] prior to Spell Out (8):

(8)
```
        AP
       /  \
     KPᵢ   A'
          /  \
         Aₖ   VP
             /  \
            V    tᵢ
```

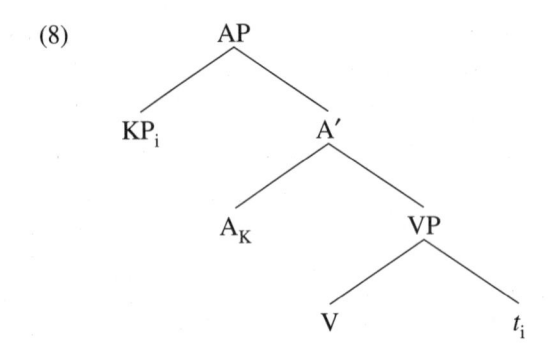

Consequently, it is predicted that all Ergative systems will display a basic OV order, a generalization noted in Mahajan (1993): ergative systems do not display rigid VO order.

This generalization must be distinguished from another typological generalization, attributed to Keenan by Woodbury (1977), which claims that there are no verb-medial ergative languages. A look at cross linguistic data suggest that there are in fact verb medial ergative languages, although the ones found involve an OVS order (that is, an ABS-V-ERG order). Among these languages we find Päri, a Nilotic language, one of the few African languages to display ergativity, (Andersen (1988), and also the following, noted by Dixon (1994): Kuikuró (Brazil), Macushi (Carib family), Huastec (Mexico), Tolai (Austronesian) and Waurá (Brazil).[6]

As for the K_T feature, two choices are available: if K_T is strong, movement of the Ergative argument will be overt, as in Basque, Hindi, and Georgian (9a). Levin (1983), Ortiz de Urbina (1986), Mahajan (1990), Marantz (1991), Bobaljik (1992), Holloway King (1994) and others have provided evidence from these languages that the Ergative argument is higher than the Absolutive argument in transitive predicates.

If K_T is weak, movement of the argument will not be overt, yielding a Spell Out representation where the Absolutive argument is higher than the Ergative argument. The latter is the S-structure configuration argued for by Bittner & Hale (1996a) for Dyirbal and Inuit (9b).[7] Within the present approach, the Spell Out placement of the Ergative Case marked argument in these languages follows from the weakness of the K_T Case feature. Verb medial ergative languages such as the ones mentioned above, would also result from a derivation where the ergative case is assigned by means of a weak feature.

(9) a.
```
         TP
        /  \
      KPᵢ   T'
           /  \
          Tₖ   AP
              /  \
            KPⱼ   A'
                 /  \
                Aₖ   VP
                    /  \
                   tᵢ   V'
                       /  \
                      V    tⱼ
```

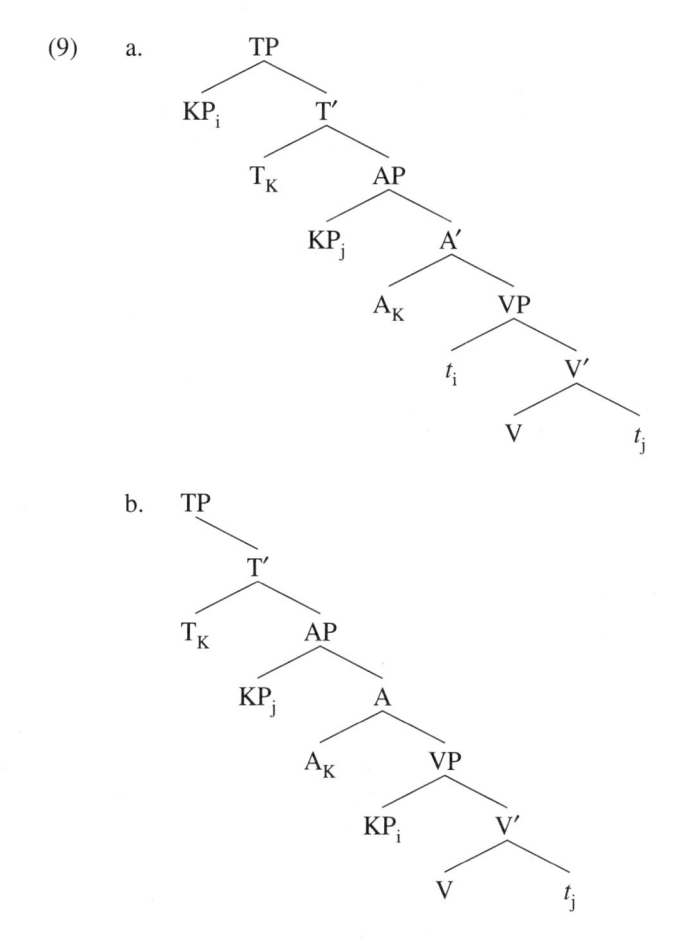

b.
```
       TP
        \
         T'
        /  \
       Tₖ   AP
           /  \
         KPⱼ   A
              /  \
             Aₖ   VP
                 /  \
               KPᵢ   V'
                    /  \
                   V    tⱼ
```

Functional categories may or may not contain an *active* feature in their lexical specifications. The distinction between an Ergative and a Nominative system depends on what functional elements, those belonging to the categories Tense or Aspect, contain an active Case feature. As will be discussed in Section 6, the specification for an active feature is a property of particular lexical items, rather than syntactic categories. This in turn lends further support to the claim that the source of language variation rests solely on the properties of particular functional elements.

Without an approach in terms of active Case features, a number of fundamental problems remain unexplained in Case Theory. Consider the better studied Nominative systems. More specifically, consider how it is standardly determined that in monadic predicates Nominative Case will necessarily be assigned instead of Accusative.[8]

In the case of the argument of unergative predicates, the answer may vary depending on whether the VP internal hypothesis is assumed. If this hypothesis is not assumed (Williams (1994)), then the external argument of the unergative predicate is generated in the structural position where Nominative is assigned, and that answers the question of why it cannot receive Accusative.[9] If the VP internal hypothesis is assumed (Kitagawa (1986), Fukui & Speas (1986), Koopman & Sportiche (1987)), then the answer is not so straightforward, especially if we give up the idea that V assigns Accusative Case to its sister under strict adjacency (see Stowell (1981), Kayne (1984), Chomsky (1989)). Under a picture of Accusative Case assignment that involves either government by V or movement to SpecAgrO (or some structurally equivalent functional projection), it is unclear what prevents the external argument of the unergative predicate from moving into that position.

Consider now the single argument of unaccusative predicates. In this case, we encounter BG as the account for why that argument must receive Nominative Case instead of Accusative. But if the attempt is to derive BG, theoretical scenarios must be entertained where BG does not exist as an independent axiom of the theory.

As an alternative, assume now that a given grammar (the one underlying English, for instance) has Tense specified to contain an active Case feature, K_T, and that the Case feature borne by Aspect, K_A, is only discharged or checked when K_T has been employed and more Case relations need to be established, because there are more KPs to be licensed.[10] Within these assumptions, the question of why Nominative surfaces when only one Case is licensed receives a straightforward answer, given a Nominative system: it is the only possible outcome. Moreover, we can do that without appeal to BG.

This is the core of the derivation of BG that will be offered in more detail in the following section.

From this perspective, then, it is not only the need to account for Ergative versus Nominative Case systems that forces us to conclude there is such a thing as an active Case feature. This is independently motivated in order to arrive at a Theory of Case that contains no reference to Thematic relations, a Theory of Grammar that does not need to state BG as an independent axiom.

In sum, the Case Theory defended here is basically the one argued for in Bobaljik (1992), adopted in Chomsky (1992), and it incorporates the claim that Case is a functional category, (Bittner & Hale (1996a). It should be noted, however, that this proposal departs from Bobaljik (1992) in the following respects: (a) Case is not a compositional relation, consisting both of a functional head with a Case feature and an Agreement Projection. Rather, it is a relation of specification to a single Case assigning head; (b) the assigner of Accusative/ Absolutive is Aspect and not the Verb or AgrO. The proposal is sketched in (10):

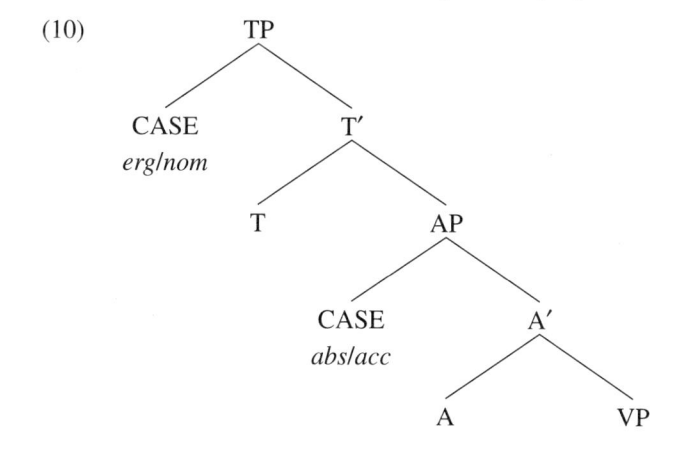

(10)
```
            TP
           /  \
        CASE   T'
       erg/nom /  \
              T    AP
                  /  \
               CASE   A'
              abs/acc /  \
                     A    VP
```

4. BG and its image in the mirror

In this section, it is argued in detail how BG follows directly from Case Theory, without appeal to any accessory principle. It is also shown how Case Theory predicts that BG effects do not surface in Ergative Case systems. Instead, Ergative Case systems display effects that mirror those covered by BG.

Consider first a K_T active system. Consider Case assignment in the case of unergative predicates (11a). In this system, unergative predicates result in the assignment of Nominative Case to the external argument. In a K_T grammar, the one argument that requires to be Case-licensed will have to find itself in a configuration of Nominative Case assignment, necessarily, because otherwise K_T would remain unassigned.

(11) a.
```
        TP
       /  \
     XPᵢ    T'
           /  \
          T    AP
              /  \
             A    VP
             |   /  \
             tᵢ     V'
                    |
                    V
```

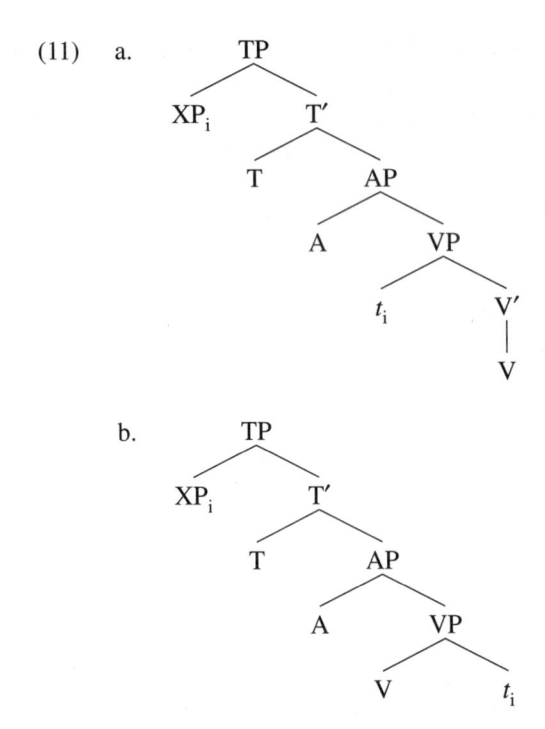

b.
```
        TP
       /  \
     XPᵢ    T'
           /  \
          T    AP
              /  \
             A    VP
                 /  \
                V    tᵢ
```

Now consider the case of the unaccusative predicate, shown in (11b). Following Perlmutter (1978) and Burzio (1986), the argument of the verb is born as a complement. Again, the only choice for the argument is to move to Spec of TP, to receive Nominative. Any other choice would leave the active Case feature of Tense unassigned. This follows without any special mention of the fact that the predicate is unaccusative. Even though (11a) and (11b) differ regarding the structure of their VPs, the are identical as far as Case Theory is concerned: only one argument requires Case. This entails that only one Case is required. The only possibility for a K_T active system is to assign Nominative. Therefore, the effects covered by BG follow necessarily, but they are not due to the thematic properties of the predicate. They obtain because unaccusative predicates are monadic.

It also follows from this Case assignment mechanism that BG effects will only surface in K_T active configurations. In K_A active configurations, the system predicts no BG effects. Consider the derivation of an unergative and unaccusative predicate in a K_A active configuration, as illustrated in (12a) and (12b) respectively.

(12) a.
```
         TP
         |
         T'
        / \
       T   AP
          /  \
        XPᵢ   A'
             / \
            Aₖ  VP
            |   \
            tᵢ   V'
                  \
                   V
```

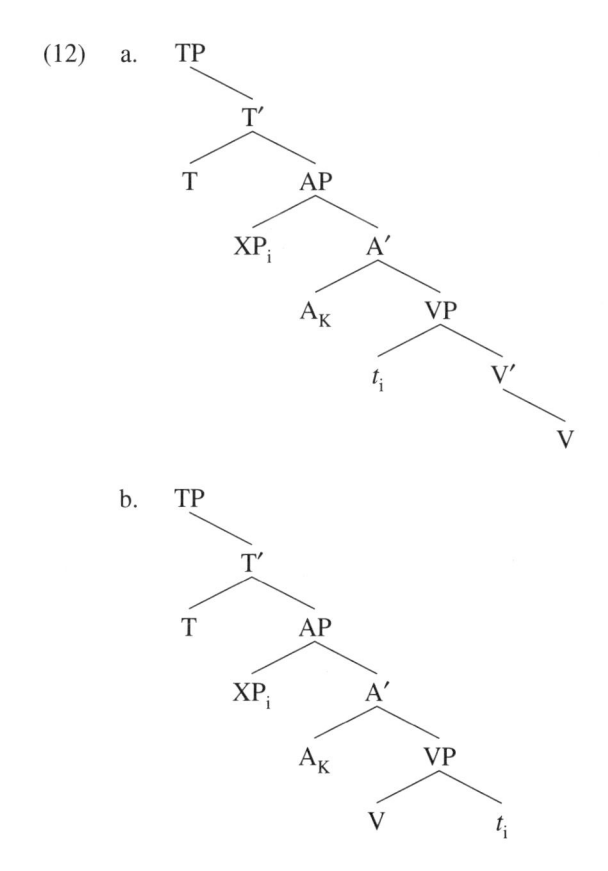

b.
```
         TP
         |
         T'
        / \
       T   AP
          /  \
        XPᵢ   A'
             / \
            Aₖ  VP
               / \
              V   tᵢ
```

The representation in (12a) involves the same type of predicate as (11a). In this case, the active Case feature is the one borne by Aspect, and therefore the only argument requiring it receives it. This result is the mirror image of BG: a predicate that does not have an internal argument cannot assign Ergative Case. The 'subject' of the unergative predicate displays the same Case as the 'object' of a transitive predicate, mirroring the fact that in Nominative languages the 'object' of the unaccusative predicate receives the same case as the 'subject' of the transitive predicate. Again, this 'mirror image BG' follows directly from Case Theory, without reference to the nature of the predicate. The Case effects follow from the fact that the unergative predicate is syntactically monadic and requires only one Case relation.

The representation in (12b) involves an unaccusative predicate. There being only one argument again, only the Case feature of Aspect is assigned. This results in an unaccusative assigning the same Case that is assigned to 'objects' of transitive clauses (cf. (10)). That is, this results in lack of BG effects, since an external θ-role is not assigned, and yet Accusative Case (that is, K_A) is assigned.

The derivations illustrated in (11) and (12) are instantiated by Nominative and Ergative Case systems. The data in (13) and (14) provide examples of the derivations discussed: (13) illustrates sentences from Inuit (from Bobaljik (1992)) a K_A system, and (14) illustrates sentences form Latin, a K_T system.

(13) a. *Jaani-up natsiq kapi-jana*
Jaani-K_T seal-K_A stab-trans
'Jaani stabbed a seal'
b. *inuk tiki-tuq*
person-K_A arrived
'The person arrived'
c. *iliniaqtitsiji uqaq-tuq*
teacher-K_A spoke
'The teacher spoke'

(14) a. *mulier mulierem videt*
woman-K_T woman-K_A sees
'a woman saw a woman'
b. *mulier cadet*
woman-K_T falls
'a woman falls'
c. *mulier ridet*
woman-K_T laughs
'a woman laughs'

Sentences (13a) and (14a) illustrate transitive sentences, where both Cases have been assigned. Sentences (13b) and (14b) illustrate unaccusative predicates, where the discrepancy in Case assignment between Inuit and Latin can be observed. Latin displays BG effects, in that it does not assign Accusative Case, whereas Inuit does not. Finally, (13c) and (14c) illustrate unergative predicates, where the Case discrepancy still obtains: Inuit assigns Accusative to its argument, whereas Latin assigns Nominative. Note the contrast between (13a) and (13c), where a 'mirror BG' effect obtains.

In what follows, this general argument will be pursued more exhaustively. Various thematic configurations will be presented, and their Case consequences in the two systems will be considered. It will be argued that all the derivations predicted to be possible are instantiated by particular grammars, whereas those that are not permitted are not attested.

5. Thetablind Case: Thematic configurations and Case patterns

The Case Theory argued for in this paper is highly modular; it is blind to the particular operations that take place in the predicate, where thematic relations are configured (Hale & Keyser (1993)). In this sense, it is a 'thetablind' theory of Case. The type of predicate determines the number of arguments that require Case licensing; this is the only condition that thematic operations impose on Case Theory. It is only this factor that Case Theory is sensitive to: whether one or more arguments require to be licensed by Case. The type of thematic relations that the arguments bear with respect to the predicate is irrelevant to Case assignment. This is not information Case Theory is sensitive to.[11]

Following Hale & Keyser (1993), I assume that thematic roles are configurationally determined, and not primitives of the Grammar. I will also follow these authors in the idea that Incorporation, a variety of X^0 movement (Baker (1988)), is involved in processes of thematic conflation. Consider the two main configurations that are found in the predicate structure, illustrated in (14): (14a) contains no external argument, either because it has been demoted or because the predicate does not assign it; the type of VP in (14a) corresponds to unaccusatives and passive type predicates. The configuration in (14b) illustrates a predicate where the internal argument has been incorporated onto the predicate, yielding a single argument in need for Case.

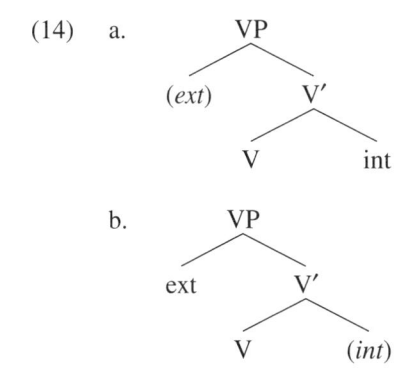

(14) a. VP
         / \
      (ext) V'
            / \
           V   int

    b. VP
        / \
      ext V'
           / \
          V (int)

The VPs illustrated in (14) have been simplified for ease of exposition. The details of VP structure are not crucial for the argument developed here (see Larson (1988), Hale & Keyser (1993)). What is crucial is that both in (14a) and in (14b) only one argument requires Case. This accounts for why Case Theory treats both (14a) and (14b) similarly: in K_T systems both predicates result in the assignment of K_T, whereas in K_A systems both predicates result in the assignment of K_A. The same predicate configuration results in different Case patterns in Nominative and Ergative systems, whenever the predicate yields one argument to be Case licensed, regardless of the nature of the thematic relation borne by the argument with respect to the predicate.

The paradigm in (15) illustrates the various constructions that arise from the combination of the predicates in (14) and the two types of Case systems:

(15)

		ARGUMENT STRUCTURE VP[−ext][+int]	ARGUMENT STRUCTURE VP[+ext][−int]
ACTIVE CASE K_A		no BG effects lack of passive impersonals	"mirror BG" effects (in unergatives) antipassives
ACTIVE CASE K_T		BG unaccusatives passive	lack of antipassive indefinite object deletion

Within this approach, all construction specific-processes derive from the general mechanisms, including BG. Constructions turn out to be epiphenomena, resulting from the interaction of grammatical modules, in the spirit of Chomsky (1989).

Thus, for instance, a predicate with no external argument, combined with an Aspect head containing and active Case feature, yields a sentence with an argument Case marked by Aspect. These are instances of unaccusative predicates that do not abide by BG; (13b) illustrated an example from Inuit, and (16b) illustrates an example from Basque, another K_A active system:

(16)   a.   *emakume-a-k emakume-a   ikus-i du*
                woman-D-K_T woman-D-K_A see-A has
                'the woman saw the woman'
      b.   *emakume-a   etorr-i   da*
                woman-D-K_A arrive-A is
                'the woman arrived'

The same predicate configuration yields a different effect in a K_T system such as English, as shown in (17b) as opposed to (17a):

(17)   a.   *she-K_T saw her-K_A*
      b.   *she- K_T arrived*

A well known instance of predicates displaying an alternation in the licensing of an external argument is found in 'causative-alternation' predicates. Once again, a K_T system will display BG effects, whereas a K_A system will not. Assuming the Nominative Case system to be familiar to the reader, (18) provides data from two Ergative systems, illustrating the consistent assignment of K_A to the internal argument of the predicate.

(18) a. *emakume-a-k emakume-a   hil du*
    woman-D-K_T woman-D-K_A kill has
    'the woman killed the woman'
  b. *emakume-a   hil da*
    woman-D-K_A die is
    'the woman died'
  c. pro *piniartoq   toquppaa*
    K_T hunter-K_A kill-IND-3SG3SG
    '(he) killed the hunter'
  d. *piniartoq   toquppoq*
    hunter-K_A kill-IND-3SG
    'The hunter died'
  e. *emakume-a-k leiho-a   ireki du*
    woman-D-K_T window-D-K_A open has
    'the woman openened the window'
  f. *leiho-a   ireki da*
    woman-D-K_A open is
    'the opened the window'

Examples (18a–d) are parallel in their Case marking, and they correspond to K_A systems: (18a, b) are from Basque; examples (18c, d) are taken from Marantz (1984), and belong to Greenlandic Eskimo. (18e, f) illustrate one more instance of unaccusative alternation in Basque. From data like (16) and (18) we can conclude that K_A systems do indeed not display any observable effects corresponding to Burzio's Generalization; this observation was made by Levin (1983) for Basque. It can now be shown to be a necessary consequence of Case Theory.

Consider now two more instances of alternation in the assignment of an external argument: one results in the construction named 'passive', and it surfaces in Nominative grammars. The other one results in the construction named 'impersonal' and it is pervasive in Ergative systems. within this view of Case theory, both consist of a predicate where an external θ-role has not been assigned. They depart in the resulting Case pattern in the usual manner seen so far. Assuming the first construction to be familiar, (19) illustrates the second one, which turns out to be the equivalent of the passive construction in a Nominative system. The predicate configuration is the same, but there is no difference in the Case assigned to the internal argument that requires licensing.

(19) a. *emakume-a-k etxe-a saldu du*
 woman-D-K_T house-D-K_A sold has
 'the woman sold the house'
 b. *etxe-a saldu da*
 house-D-K_A sold is
 'the hose has been sold'

(19a) is a transitive sentence, where both Cases have been discharged. (19b) contains the same verb, but the predicate contains no external argument. While in a Nominative system this yields a 'passive' (K_T being active), in an Ergative system no significant Case alternation obtains, and the resulting construction is labelled 'impersonal' (Ortiz de Urbina (1986)). The 'passive' is standardly understood to be a composite of (a) a predicate where the external argument has been demoted (or 'absorbed') and (b) the assignment of Nominative Case to the internal argument. Given the proposal put forward here, it follows that Ergative grammars do not display 'passives' of the sort Nominative grammars do: (a) is in principle available, but not (b). Moreover, it also follows that Nominative Case (K_T) must be assigned to the only argument of the passive predicate, without any stipulation about the Case assigning properties of the past participle being required.

So far, given the paradigm in (15), we have considered the constructions resulting from the combination of a predicate with no external argument and the two Case systems available. Let us now turn our attention to the combination of predicates where the internal argument has incorporated onto the predicate, leaving only the external argument in need of Case licensing.

In a K_A system, two constructions result from this combination. The best known one is the 'antipassive'. As argued by Baker (1988), antipassives involve transitive predicates where the internal argument has incorporated onto the predicate. Given this, only the external argument needs Case. In a K_A system, it follows necessarily that this Case is K_A (Accusative/Absolutive), the same Case assigned to the internal argument of a transitive construction. The incorporated argument can be 'doubled' by an adjunct, in the same fashion in which the 'by phrase' doubles the demoted external argument in a passive. Examples of the 'antipassive' construction are illustrated in (20):

(20) a. *Jaani-up tuktu tuqut-vaa*
 Jaani-K_T caribou-K_A kill-3SG-3SG
 'Jaani killed a caribou'
 b. *Jaani tuktu-mik tuqut-si-vuq*
 Jaani-K_A caribou-P_{ins} kill-ANTP-3SG
 'Jaani killed caribous'

It has been widely noted in the literature that the antipassive construction is characteristic of Ergative systems, and does not surface in Nominative grammars. Here, the antipassive construction turns to be the mirror image of the passive in a very specific sense. The antipassive construction, like the passive, consists of two components: (a) a predicate where the internal argument has been incorporated, (b) assignment of Absolutive Case to the external argument (which in the transitive version is assigned Ergative). Note that (b) now follows given (a), but it will only in a K_A system, not in a K_T one.

A Nominative system will display no Case alternation given a predicate with an incorporated internal argument and its unincorporated transitive version. As argued by Postal (1977), the 'Indefinite object deletion' construction can be considered the Nominative system equivalent of the antipassive:

(21) *this woman writes*

The antipassive cases and the Indefinite object deletion in (21) share the same predicate structure, in that an internal argument is incorporated onto the predicate (a). However, they differ necessarily in the Case theoretic consequences of this incorporation.

The 'mirror BG' effects displayed by unergative predicates in Ergative and Nominative systems also follows within the current proposal: in K_A systems the external argument of the unergative is prevented from receiving K_T Case, as illustrated in the derivation (12a), and instantiated in the Inuit example in (13). In K_T systems, however, this is the only Case available for the only argument in need of Case (11a), (14c). As argued in Laka (1993b), lack of incorporation of the internal argument of the unergative predicate in the syntax yields a transitive pattern, and thus both K_A and K_T are discharged, regardless of which category bears the active Case feature. This yields languages like Basque, which have been described as a special type of Ergative system. See Section 6 for further discussion.

It has been argued so far that the only information Case Theory is sensitive to is the number of arguments that require Case in a given sentence. The nature of the thematic relation born by the argument with respect to the predicate is not relevant for Case purposes. In this sense, Case is 'thetablind'. This picture emerges rather simply given the structural configuration os the sentence assumed throughout this paper: As argued by the proponents of the VP internal hypothesis, thematic relations are established in the predicate, the projection of the lexical category V. As argued by Chomsky (1989), Case licensing takes place in a configurationally higher domain, which involves specifier positions of inflectional categories. Therefore, the relation between thematic operations and Case is mediated by movement (or any equivalent chain-creating device), and thus the relation between thematic relations and Case is configurationally determined, not inherently specified by the thematic relation itself.

From this perspective, consider the data in (22), from the Australian language Dyirbal (taken from Marantz (1984)): (22a) illustrates a transitive sentence, containing the predicate 'hide', where both Ergative (K_T) and Absolutive (K_A) have been assigned. In (22b), one of the arguments of the predicate 'hide' is missing, or rather it is encoded in the morpheme *yirnu*, glossed as a 'reflexive'.

(22) a. *bala yugu bangul yarangu buyyban*
    stick-ABS man-ERG   hides
    'Man hides stick'
  b. *bayi yara buybayirnu*
    man-ABS hides-REFL
    'Man hides' (himself or something)

As reported in Marantz (1984), the meaning of (22b) can either be the unaccusative version of (22a), 'a man hides', or the antipassive version of (22a), 'a man hides (something or other)'. The difference between the two readings depends on whether *yirnu* reflects the absorption of an external argument, in which case the unaccusative reading obtains, or whether *yirnu* reflects the incorporation of an internal argument, in which case the antipassive or 'indefinite object deletion' reading obtains. Crucially, though, Case treats both instances identically, because as far as Case is concerned they are identical: both involve *one* argument in need of Case, so both result in assignment of K_A to that argument, given the fact that Dyirbal is an Ergative grammar.

6. Aspect as a Case assigner

It is a well known fact that a given grammar can display both an Ergative Case system and a Nominative Case system, depending on a number of factors. Dixon (1994), in his extensive discussion of Ergativity, considers various types of split Case systems. According to Dixon's description, there are three main factors that can trigger an alternation of Ergative and Nominative Case systems in a given grammar: (I) The semantic nature of the verb. (II) The semantic nature of the NPs. (III) Aspect, Tense, Mood alternations.[12]

The group in (I) contains Ergative Case systems that distinguish unergative predicates from unaccusatives: The subject of the unergative predicate receives the same Case as the subject of a transitive predicate (K_T; S_A in Dixon's notation); The subject of the unaccusative predicate receives the same Case as the object of the transitive (K_A; S_O in Dixon's notation). Dixon refers to this type as *Split-S System*. As argued in Laka (1993b), this distinct Case marking of unergative and unaccusative predicates need not reflect a change from a K_A active system to a K_T active system. Rather, it can be accounted for by assuming that the unergative predicates, which involve a transitive frame (Hale & Keyser (1993)), have not undergone incorporation of the complement, and are therefore forced to assign both K_A and K_T. Unaccusative predicates, on the other hand, only discharge K_A.

The group in (II) contains grammars where pronouns differ in their marking from NPs, and where within NPs there might also be differences in marking depending on factors such as [± human], [± animate] etc. This type will not be discussed here, see Jelinek (1993) and Phillips (1993) for discussions and proposals regarding these phenomena.

The type of split in (III) is widespread, although of course not present in all Case systems. Thus, some systems are exhaustively K_T active, like English, and others are exhaustively K_A active, like Basque, regardless of the particular Tense and Aspect heads involved. These are systems where (a) all the lexical elements belonging to the syntactic category Tense have an active Case feature, in the case of a consistently Nominative systems; or (b) all the lexical elements belonging to the syntactic category Aspect have an active Case feature, in the case of a consistently Ergative system.[13]

Consider now the systems where a split occurs depending on the aspectual specifications of the clause. As described by Dixon (1994), if a grammar shows an Aspect-sensitive split, the Ergative system is found in the perfective paradigm, and the Nominative system is found in the imperfective paradigm. Within the Case Theory laid out in this paper, this type of split can be accounted for given the Case specifications of particular lexical items belonging to the category Aspect. Consider two grammars that display aspectually based splits: Hindi and Georgian.

In Hindi, the perfective paradigm yields and Ergative Case systems, whereas the imperfective paradigm yields a Nominative Case system, as illustrated in (23) (from Mahajan (1990), except for Case notation):

(23) a. *Sitaa   vah ghar   khariddegii*
       sita-FEM-K_T that house-K_A buy-FUT-FEM
       'Sita will buy that house'
   b. *Sitaa ne   vah ghar   kharidaa   thaa*
       sita-FEM-K_T that house-MASC-K_A buy-PERF-MASC be-PAST
       'Sita (has) bought that house'

In (23a), there is no perfective morphology, and a Nominative/Accusative pattern ensues, whereas in (23b), where the perfective aspectual morpheme has been highlighted, an Ergative-Absolutive pattern occurs. Within the current proposal, this variation can be accounted for in the following manner: an imperfective aspect head in Hindi is not specified with an active Case feature, but rather it is specified with a weak Case feature. A perfective aspect head, however, is specified with an active Case feature.

Consider Georgian, where the Aorist series displays an Ergative Case system. As noted by Holisky (1981) and Holloway King (1994), the Aorist series verbs are aspectually perfective. An account along the lines provided for Hindi can thus be provided. Holloway King (1994) argues that the Aorist heads an AspP which is capable of assigning Case. In Holloway King's proposal the Case assigned by the aorist head is Ergative. Here, a modification of Holloway King (1994) will be assumed: the aorist is specified with an active Case feature, and it assigns Absolutive, in the same fashion that the perfective aspect head does in Hindi. This modification yields the same results as far as the Case patterns encountered in the Aorist series, and provides a less language-specific approach to the Georgian split.

In recent literature, a number of proposals have articulated the notion of Aspect as a Case assigner, in various ways (Travis (1991), Borer (1993), van Hout (1994), Yadroff (1994), (to appear)). Some of these works are primarily concerned with the articulation of *aktionsart* in Syntax, whereas others are more concerned with Case alternations induced by various aspectual properties of the predicate. Any attempt to incorporate Aspect into the domain of functional projections faces the difficulty imposed by the multiple ambiguity of the term (Verkuyl (1993), Tenny (1994)). The notion of Aspect intended in this paper is not the one related to the telic properties of the predicate, but rather the more inflectional one related to perfectivity. I will leave for now open the question of how the different relations traditionally included under the label 'aspect' and discussed in the above mentioned works relate to each other and to Syntax.

If Case is a relation involving Tense and Aspect, splits conditioned by particular values of these categories can provide a way to account for their influence in the Case system. Moreover, this approach provides a natural explanation for why the Ergative/Nominative distinction is not a distinction between grammars, and for why both systems can be found in one grammar:[14] it is the specifications of the functional elements implicated in the architecture of the clause that determine what Case system obtains. Therefore, there are no Nominative and Ergative grammars, but rather configurations of Case assigning categories with certain specifications that determine the outcome of the syntactic representations.

7. Conclusion

It has been argued in this paper that Burzio's Generalization derives without stipulation from Case Theory. The Case Theory argued for follows Bobaljik (1992), Chomsky (1992) and Laka (1993b), and it relies crucially on the notion of *active* feature. Case Theory is 'thetablind'; information about particular θ-roles being assigned to particular arguments is not available to Case relations. Case is only sensitive to the number of arguments that require licensing, regardless of their thematic status.

The Case assigners in the clause have been argued to be Tense and Aspect: a Tense active system assigns Nominative whenever a monadic predicate is involved. Burzio's Generalization follows from this fact. An Aspect active system assigns Absolutive whenever a monadic predicate is involved. This results in the absence of Burzio's Generalization (BG) effects in these systems. Moreover, Aspect active systems display 'mirror BG' effects, as predicted by Case Theory. It has also been argued that constructions such as the passive and the antipassive surface only in Nominative and Ergative systems respectively due to the nature of Case assignment. Evidence for Aspect being one of the Case assigning categories in the clause is drawn from split-Case systems, where the specifications of Aspect determine whether an Ergative or a Nominative case pattern results.

Acknowledgments

I would like to thank the organizers and the participants in the *Workshop on Burzio's Generalization* held in Utrecht in June 1994; the organizers and participants of the *1995 International Summer School of Girona*, and the colleagues and students at the University of Vienna where I lectured on Case Theory during the Spring semester of 1994, for the opportunity to discuss some of these ideas, as well as for their extremely valuable criticisms, questions and suggestions. Special thanks to D. Adger, H. Borer, M. den Dikken, M. Haiden, J.C. Odriozola, M. Pinto, M. Prinzhorn, and J. Runner. All errors, misunderstandings and shortcomings are solely mine. The research reported here has been partially funded by the NSF (BNS-9108381) and a research grant from the Department of Education of the Basque Government.

Notes

1. See Levin & Rappaport Hovav (1995) for a proposal and a thorough discussion of the thematic/lexical aspects of unaccusativity and argument demotion. Throughout this paper, it is assumed that the notion of 'thematic role' that is relevant to Syntax is configurationally derived, as argued in Hale & Keyser (1993).

2. It should be noted that the naming of the cases varies in the traditional terminology for each of the systems. The terminology chosen above reflects the configurations responsible for the assigned Case, to avoid terminological confusion. In Bobaljik's proposal, the Case assigned by AgrS is the one labelled Nominative or Ergative, depending on the case system. Similarly, the Case assigned by AgrO is labelled Accusative or Absolutive.

3. The case of Prepositions and Determiners as Case assigners will not be pursued in detail here, where I focus on Nominative/Accusative. See Johnson (1992) and Bittner & Hale (1996a) for proposals related to this issue.

4. Bittner & Hale (1996a) assume that Nominative and Absolutive arguments are not headed by K. They do not assume that Case is assigned by specific Case assigning categories either.

5. This approach is incompatible with the proposal that VSO languages involve VP internal arguments at Spell Out.

6. Andersen shows convincingly that Päri displays verb medial order, thus disproving the generalization that Woodbury attributes to Keenan, while maintaining an OV surface order:

   (i) a. *ùbúr   á-túuk*
           Ubur-ABS ASP-play
           'Ubur played'
       b. *dháagò   á-yàan   ùbúrr-i*
           woman-ABS ASP-insult Ubur-ERG
           'Ubur insulted the woman'

   Examples taken from Andersen (1988).

7. Bittner & Hale (1996b), following Dixon (1972), argue that in Dyirbal and Inuit, the Nominative/Absolutive argument ends up in a higher position than the Ergative argument. Their proposal is illustrated in (i):

   (i) [$_{IP}$ NOM$_i$ [$_{I'}$ [$_{VP}$ ERG$_j$ [$_{VP}$ t$_i$ V]] I]

   where the ERG argument, being the external argument, is adjoined to VP (a position that Bittner & Hale (1996a) assume is the subject site universally). The motivation for (i) is relative clause formation in Dyirbal and Inuit, and Topic chain in Dyirbal. Relative clause formation in Inuit and Dyirbal only licenses gaps in Nominative position, and similarly the gap in Topic chain constructions must be Nominative. Regarding other phenomena, such as control, Dyirbal and Inuit appear to have higher Ergative arguments, however. Bittner & Hale (1996b) assume that control is dealt within the VP positions, regardless of the raising of the Nominative argument. Bittner & Hale argue that Inuit and Dyirbal have Internal Headed Relative Clauses, and account for the restriction in Relativization resorting crucially to (i). For relevant purposes, the representation in (9b) shares all the relevant properties of (i).

8. By 'standard', it is meant versions of Case Theory such as Chomsky (1981), (1986), (1991).

9. This type of approach does not seem able to provide with a straightforward account for Case systems that depart from the one instantiated by English. It remains to be seen how the various types of Ergative systems fit this particular approach to Case.

10. The argument made here does not depend on a particular version of what category is responsible for what Case feature. Thus, this argument can also be made if Nominative/Ergative is argued to be assigned by some other category besides Tense, or if Accusative/Absolutive is argued to be assigned by some other category besides Aspect.

11. Inherent Cases have been argued to be necessarily linked to particular θ-roles. Thus, for instance, Belletti (1988) argues that Verbs assign an inherent Case to their complements,

independently from structural Case assignment. De Hoop (1992) argues extensively that Belletti's inherent Case is 'structural' in the sense that it is not necessarily linked to a particular θ-role.

12. Dixon (1994, page 101) cites a fourth factor, under the heading "Main' versus 'subordinate' clause split', but concludes that this fourth type appears in closer examination to belong to the aspectual split in III.

13. Ezeizabarrena (1996) discusses evidence from language acquisition data, where a correlation between the acquisition of aspectual morphology and Absolutive Case obtains in Basque.

14. Here, it is assumed that what distinguishes a particular grammar from another is a set of morphological specifications on the functional elements available in the Lexicon. The lexical elements (the open class of the lexicon), and the syntactic operations available all form part of Universal Grammar.

References

Abney, S. 1987. The English Noun Phrase in its Sentential Aspect. PhD Dissertation, MIT.
Andersen T. 1988. "Ergativity in Päri, a Nilotic OVS language". *Lingua* 75:289–324.
Anderson, S. 1976. "On the notion of subject in ergative languages". In *Subject and Topic*, C. N. Li (ed.), 3–34. New York: Academic Press.
Burzio, L. 1986. *Italian Syntax: A government-binding approach*. Dordrecht: Reidel.
Baker, M. 1988. *Incorporation: A theory of grammatical function changing*. Chicago: University of Chicago Press.
Belletti, A. 1988. "The case of unaccusatives". *Linguistic Inquiry* 19: 1–34.
Bittner, M. and K. Hale. 1996a. "The structural determination of case and agreement". *Linguistic Inquiry* 27(1):1–68
Bittner, M. and K. Hale. 1996b. "Ergativity: Towards a theory of a heterogeneous class". *Linguistic Inquiry* 27(4).
Bobaljik, J. 1992. "Nominally absolutive is not absolutely nominative". In *Proceedings of WCCFL11*, Los Angeles, CA: UCLA.
Borer, H. 1993. "The projection of arguments". In *Functional Projections*, E. Benedicto and J. Runner (eds) 19–47, Amherst, MA:GLSA.
Burzio, L. 1986. *Italian Syntax: A government and binding approach*. Dordrecht: Reidel.
Chomsky, N. 1981. *Lectures on Government and Binding*. Dordrecht: Foris.
Chomsky, N. 1986. *Knowledge of Language: Its nature, origins and use*. New York: Praeger.
Chomsky, N. 1989. "Some notes on economy of derivation and representation". In I. Laka and A. Mahajan (eds) *Functional Heads and Clause Structure* [MITWPL Vol. 10]. Cambridge, MA: Dept. of Linguistics and Philosophy, MIT. Reprinted in 1991 in *Principles and Parameters in Comparative Grammar*, R. Freidin (ed.), 417–54. Cambridge, MA: MIT Press.
Chomsky, N. 1992. "A minimalist program for linguistic theory". In *MIT Occasional Papers in Linguistics* 1, [MITWPL]. Cambridge, MA: Dept. of Linguistics &

Philosophy, MIT. Reprinted in 1993 in *The View from Building 20: Essays in linguistics in honor of Sylvain Bromberger* [Current Studies in Lingusitic Series 24], K. Hale and S. J. Keyser (eds). Cambridge, MA: MIT Press.

den Dikken, M. 1993. "Auxiliaries and Participles". Ms. Free University Amsterdam/HIL.

de Hoop, H. 1992. Case Configuration and Noun Phrase Interpretation. PhD Dissertation, University of Groningen.

Derbyshire, D. C. 1986. "Comparative survey of morphology and syntax in Brazilian Arawakan". In *Handbook of Amazonian languages* Vol. I, D. C. Derbyshire and G. K. Pullum (eds), 469–566. Berlin: Mouton de Gruyter.

Dixon, R. M. W. 1972. *The Dyirbal Language of North Queensland* [Cambridge Studies in Linguistics 9]. Cambridge:CUP.

Dixon, R. M. W. 1994. *Ergativity* [Cambridge Studies in Linguistics 69]. Cambridge:CUP.

Ezeizabarrena, M. J. 1996. *Adquisición de FLEX en euskera y castellano por niños bilingües*. Bilbao: Servicio de Publicaciones de la UPV-EHU.

Hale, K. and Keyser, S. J. 1993. "On argument structure and the lexical expression of syntactic relations". In *The View from Building 20: Essays in linguistics in honor of Silvain Bromberger*. [Current studies in linguistics series 24], K. Hale and S. J. Keyser (eds), Cambridge, MA: MIT Press.

Holisky, D. 1981. "Aspect theory and Georgian aspect". In *Tense and Aspect* [Syntax and Semantics 14], 127–144. New York: Academic Press.

Holloway King, T. 1994 "SpecAgrP and case: Evidence from Georgian". In *The Morphology Syntax Connection* [Working Papers in Linguistics]. Cambridge, MA: MIT.

Jelinek, E. 1993. "Ergative 'splits' and argument type". In *Papers on Case and Agreement 1* [MIT Working Papers in Linguistics 18], D. Bobaljik and C. Phillips (eds), 15–42. Cambridge, MA: MIT.

Johns, A. 1992. "Deriving ergativity". *Linguistic Inquiry* 23(1): 57–88.

Kayne R. 1984. *Connectedness and Binary Branching*. Dordrecht: Foris.

Kitagawa, Y. 1986. Subjects in Japanese and English, PhD. Dissertation, University of Massachusetts at Amherst.

Koopman, H. and Sportiche D. 1987. "Subjects". M,. UCLA.

Laka, I. 1988. "Configurational heads in inflectional morphology: The structure of the inflected forms in Basque". *Anuario del Seminario de Filología Vasca 'Julio de Urquijo* XXII-2: 343–365.

Laka, I. 1993a. "The structure of inflection: A case study in X^0 syntax". In *Generative Studies in Basque Linguistics* [Current Issues in Linguistic Theory 105], J. I. Hualde and J. Ortiz de Urbina (eds), 21–70. Amsterdam: John Benjamins.

Laka, I. 1993b. "Unergatives that assign ergative, unaccusatives that assign accusative". In *Papers on Case and Agreement 1* [MIT Working Papers in Linguistics 18], J. Bobaljik and C. Phillips (eds), 149–72. Cambridge, MA: MIT.

Lamontagne, G. and Travis, L. 1987. "The syntax of adjacency". In *Proceedings of WCCFL* 6, 173–186.

Larson, R. 1988. "On the double object construction". *Linguistic Inquiry* 19(3): 335–392.

Levin B. 1983. On the Nature of Ergativity. PhD Dissertation, MIT.

Levin, B and Rappaport Hovav, M. 1995. *Unaccusativity: At the syntax-lexical semantics interface*. Cambridge, MA: MIT Press.
Mahajan A. K. 1990. The A/A' Distinction and Movement Theory. PhD Dissertation, MIT.
Mahajan, A. K. 1993. "The ergativity parameter: Have-be alternation, word order and split ergativity". *Proceedings of NELS 1993*.
Marantz, A. 1984. *On the Nature of Grammatical Relations*. Cambridge, MA: MIT Press.
Marantz, A. 1991. "Case and licensing". *Proceedings of ESCOL 1991*, 234–253. [reprinted in this volume].
Ortiz de Urbina, J. 1986 *Parameters in the Grammar of Basque*. Dordrecht: Foris.
Perlmutter, D. 1978. "Impersonal passives and the unaccusative hypothesis". *Berkeley Linguistic Society* 4:157–89.
Phillip, C. 1993. "Conditions on agreement in Yimas". In *Papers on Case and Agreement 1* [MIT Working Papers in Linguistics 18], J. Bobaljik and C. Phillips (eds), 173–212. Cambridge, MA: MIT.
Postal, P. M. 1977. "About a 'nonargument' for raising". *Linguistic Inquiry* 8:141–55.
Stowell, T. 1981. Origins of Phrase Structure. PhDDissertation, MIT.
Tenny, C. 1994. *Aspectual Roles and the Syntax-Semantics Interface*. Dordrecht: Kluwer Academic Publishers.
Travis, L. 1991. "Derived objects, inner aspect, and the structure of VP". *Proceeding of NELS 22*.
van Hout, A. 1994. "Projection based on event structure". In *Lexical specification and lexical insertion*, P. Coopmans, M. Everaert and J. Grimshaw (eds). Hillsdale, NJ: LEA.
Verkuyl, H. 1993. *The Theory of Aspectuality*. Cambridge: CUP.
Williams, E. 1994. *Thematic Stucture in Syntax*.Cambridge, MA: MIT Press.
Woodbury, A. C. 1977. "Greenlandic Eskimo, ergativity, and relational grammar". In *Grammatical Relations* [Syntax and Semantics 8], P. Cole and J. M. Sadock (eds), 307–336. New York: Academic Press.
Yadroff, M. 1995 "Verbal aspect and object licensing". Ms., Indiana University.
Yadroff, M. 1996 "SpecAsP and case assignment". In *Formal Approaches to Slavic Linguistics 3*, J.Toman (ed.), Ann Arbor, MI:Michigan Slavic Publications.

The Aspect–Case Typology Correlation
Perfectivity and Burzio's Generalization

Werner Abraham
University of Groningen

*Der Irrationalismus — als das Gegenbeispiel des Rationalismus —
redet nur schielend von dem, wogegen dieser blind ist.*
Martin Heidegger, Sein und Zeit, 136

Abstract

The present article argues against prevailing assumptions about ergativity and unaccusativity as much as it makes a few new empirical assumptions concerning Perlmutter's and Burzio's positions. In particular, it argues that ergativity, or unaccusativity, at least in certain languages, is not based so much on the canonical set of syntactic distributional criteria (as illustrated in Keyser/Roeper 1984 for English). What counts, rather, is the correlation between past tense/perfective aspect and ergativity, much in the spirit of Comrie (1981). It is this correlation that bridges the two concepts of 'syntax-theoretic' ergativity (in the sense of Burzio and Perlmutter) and typological ergativity (in Dixon's sense). More concretely, the present paper is an attempt to answer and relate to one another two questions: (i) what, if any, is the link between the forms of 'typological ergativity' (in Dixon's sense; cf. Dixon 1994) and the concept at the hands of generative syntax (in the sense of Perlmutter and Burzio)? And (ii) what is the deeper understanding of the syntactic concept of 'unaccusativity' and 'Burzio's generalization'? It will be held that an explanation of ergativity in terms of θ-roles has a good empirical and theoretical motivation and that it derives from a deeper, purely aspectual characteristic, i.e. perfectivity (claimed to hold for Gothic in Abraham (1987)). All of this is exemplified for those Indo-Aryan languages which display split ergativity triggered by past tense and perfective aspect. We consider briefly, and refute, the account by Mahajan (1995) based on an adjacency condition and an incorporation mechanism. By unfolding a perspective on the pronominal character of tense and aspect a set of ergative split characteristics can be covered under the aspectual account that has not received an explanation so far.

I consider Perlmutter's unaccusativity classification to follow immediately from, or lie at the base of, Burzio's (later) generalization. As a consequence, the present attempt at disputing the validity of the claim that there is something like a separate class of 'quasi-passive' (i.e. unaccusative or ergative) predicates will necessarily imply the invalidity of the other generalization. However, this invalidates Burzio's claims only insofar as in languages such as West-Germanic Dutch and German, (still) providing a morphologically as well as syntactically demonstrable sensitivity to perfectivity, ergativity is a sub-phenomenon to perfectivity. Nothing else is claimed. Furthermore, it will be argued that in a language, where perfectivity is no longer identifiable morphologically or syntactically, one is at a risk of identifying 'ergative' properties which are epiphenomena to ergativity at best or, worse, have nothing to do with proper ergativity.

Preliminary survey: typological ergativity and the syntactic 'Unaccusative Hypothesis'

There exists an interesting correlation between aspect realizations and typological ergativity in those languages that exhibit split ergativity: the ergative properties (morphological, sometimes and never totally, also syntactic) are displayed only in the past and the perfect tenses or perfective aspect (among which dominantly the periphrastic perfects), as opposed to the present tense where the nominative-accusative system is adhered to. In typological research, this phenomenon has been known to be restricted to what has been called 'Type-B ergativity', i.e. only in languages with an ergativity split (Trask 1979: 388). Type-A languages of the ergative type do not exhibit this strict correlation. The question why this should be the case (and, in fact, be so overwhelmingly demonstrated by the available empirical evidence) has not received an answer (Trask 1979: 396: "[...] why should the perfective so often be constructed on an ergative basis?"). According to Comrie, there is in fact an obvious and frequently executed pathway from the perfective to the ergative in that the resultant change of state of a two-place predicate is attributed primarily to the role of the object-Patient, rather than the subject-Agent. Given that the perfective generally favors object-Patient orientation, the perfective would be more likely than the non-perfective to correlate highly with passive-like ergative.[1] The present article takes Comrie's position as a point of departure.

If it comes to Dixon (1994: 20 f.), any attempt at a relation between the typological concept of ergativity and that invoked by generative syntacticians is ill-advised. The collapsing terminology just hides the fact that the two concepts are fundamentally distinct. Prior 'ergative' classifications of certain verbal phenomena, such as those by Halliday (1967) and Anderson (1977), appear to suffer from the same misconception. As goes for the latter authors, they infer an 'ergativity relation' between such clausal pairs as *X washed the woollens* and *The woollens washed* well or *Y opens the window* and *The window opens*, respectively. Notice that, in the absence of case assignment in these English examples all we are thrown back to are the syntactic diagnostics — which turn out to be of a dramatically different nature. The following three tests reflect the spirit of exemplification in Dixon (1994: 11 ff.; Dixon's original evidence is on the syntactic relations in Dyirbal, whereas (1)–(3) transfer the radically different diagnostic mechanisms of Dyirbal to English and German).

Diagnostic tests for syntactic ergativity (S: subject of an intransitive clause; A: subject of a transitive clause; O: direct object in a transitive clause): (a)/(b) for NOMINATIVE–ACCUSATIVE LANGUAGES; (c)/(d) for ERGATIVE–ABSOLUTIVE languages; pivot: that pair of clausal relators which exchange functions in the diagnostic distributions below. See, e.g., Dixon (1994: 169 f.) on the 'syntactically deep' ergative Dyirbal (North Queensland), Haspelmath (1991) on the somewhat lesser 'syntactically ergative' Lezgian (Nakho-Daghestanian), Anderson (1976) on Hurrian, or Marantz (1984) on Eskimo. For the ellipsis diagnostics applied to Russian see below (Section 8.3).

Coordination diagnostics: unlike an accusative language, an ergative language gaps the coreferent of the former subject in object position as in (1c, d).

(1) a. Father$_i$(S) returned and e_i(A) saw mother
   S/A pivot; N-A language
 b. Father$_i$(A) saw mother and e_i(S) returned
   S/A pivot; N-A language
 c. *Father$_i$(S) returned and mother saw e_i(O)
   S/O pivot; grammatical for E-A language
 d. *Mother(A) saw father$_i$ and e_i(O) returned
   S/O pivot; grammatical for E-A language

Passivization diagnostics: unlike an accusative language, an ergative language gaps the coreferent of the former subject in instrumental position as in (2c, d).

(2) a. Father$_i$(S) returned and e_i(O) was seen by mother
   S/A pivot; N-A language
 b. Father$_i$(O) was seen by mother and e_i(S) returned
   S/A pivot; N-A language

c. *Father$_i$(S) returned and mother was seen by e_i(A)
    S/O pivot; grammatical for E-A language
d. *Mother(A) saw father$_i$(A) and e_i(S) returned
    S/O pivot; grammatical for E-A language

Relative clause formation: the German version in (3) below reflects the case distribution (subject relative pronominal in the ACCUSATIVE) in ergative Dyirbal (cf. Dixon 1994: 169).

(3)   Den Vater$_i$,   den$_i$ zurückkam, sah Mutter
      the father-TOPIC-OBJ   who-ACC   returned   saw mother-SUBJ-NOM
      S/O pivot as in E-A language (* in accusative German)

The glosses in German and English make obvious that the diagnostics in (1)–(3) have nothing in common with the English examples in Halliday's or Anderson's sense. This holds also for the link between typological ergativity and derived senses applied, for example, to English (see Pullum 1988: 585; Dixon 1994: 20). If *return* as well as *come back* are lexical ergatives, or unaccusatives, as is canonically held in modern syntax, some non-negligeable portion of the standard diagnostics in (1)–(3) should be transferrable to the English 'unaccusative' lexicals also. However, they are not. This raises the question whether the typological meaning of 'ergativity', has anything in common with that in Perlmutter's or Burzio's sense, or else whether 'ergativity' in modern syntax is identifiable by the typological diagnostics. Independently of that, the terminology prevalent in modern syntax (cf. Burzio's term 'ergative' for Perlmutter's 'unaccusative') should have been chosen more carefully and with a eye on the typological import, since, conceptually, it should have been 'absolutive' instead. The precise meaning of the modern syntax-theoretic concept of 'unaccusativity' as well as its diagnostics will be taken up in the subsequent Sections 1 and 2. The ensuing critical discussion is aimed at the stronger assumption that the modern, syntax-theoretic (i.e. Perlmutter's and Burzio's) concept of ergativity should discover deeper distributional properties unifying the syntactic and the typological concepts. However, even if this attempt should turn out not to be successful, the terminological overlap alone would appear to validate the present attempt. Notice, at this point of the discussion, that there is abundant and irrefutable evidence of the fact that representatives of the modern syntax-theoretic concept lay a claim on the homogeneity of their concept of 'ergativity' with the typological concept. See the discussion of Mahajan's point of view below.

In this sense, then, the following paper pursues questions that relate to these observations, which, at first sight, have little, if anything, to do with one another beyond the common terminology. The emphasis will be on empirical issues in this comparison, i.e. on the diagnostics of either concept. If, in the course of this discussion, it should turn out that there is a deeper, contentful conceptual overlap between the two 'ergativities', this is then the most crucial question arising from the data presented (taken from a couple of Indo-Aryan languages as well as West-Germanic, in general, and German, in particular): What do the past and perfect tenses (or: the perfective aspect, and/or: what does the periphrasis on the tense-aspect realization of a predicate) have to do with what has come to be called the 'ergative-absolutive/nominative' morphology and syntax in the languages of the world? And why is this phenomenon restricted to languages of Type B (i.e., to those displaying split ergativity)? The second complex of questions pertinent to the first one is what syntactic ergativity in the sense of modern linguistics (Perlmutter 1976; Keyser/Roeper 1984; Burzio 1986) has to do with typological ergativity and with the aspectual distinction drawn above. Needless to say that this is not a trivial question given the two distant camps of linguistic research; nor is it one that can be addressed on account of the terminological coincidence (cf. for example, Dixon's rash repudiation of the terminological and conceptual mix; Dixon (1995: 20, 232)).[2] In other words, we need to ask: What is the deeper insight to be gained from the claims made in connection with syntactic ergativity (in Perlmutter's and Burzio's understanding of what has come to be called the 'Unaccusative Hypothesis')? These two thematic areas will be pursued in due course. I will relate them to one another in what I hope will be an insightful linguistic scenario. Section 1 discusses syntactic ergativity in the modern linguistic sense showing in which purely empirical way the perfective aktionsart plays a role. This leads to Section 2 in which the generalisations of this concept of syntactic ergativity (Perlmutter, Burzio) are presented. I attempt to provide an understanding as to what these theoretical generalisations may mean within the scenarios displayed by the empirical typological research. Section 3 takes up three languages from Indo-Iranian (Hindi, Urdu, and Balochi) that exhibit split ergativity in a number of morphological categories. The aim is to illustrate that perfect and perfectivity triggers ergativity in these languages. Section 4 extends the morphological categories which have to be accounted for in a systematic description on the basis of Balochi. Sections 5 and 6 present the formal theory set forth by Mahajan (1994): the V-marginal condition and the auxiliary condition for ergativity. However, since Mahajan's assumptions appear not to correlate with a number of empirical data, a competing approach is pursued: the aspect account (Section 7). The last two sections, 8 and 9, wrap up the issues discussed.

I will be claiming that the type of syntactic behavior usually taken to reflect 'ergativity' or 'unaccusativity', as well as Burzio's Hypothesis — which I term collectively the 'Argument-based Hypothesis' — can only properly be understood in terms of what I will call the 'Aspect-based Hypothesis'. The reader of this may find some of the diversions of no direct bearing to this specific goal. Notice, however, that methodically speaking it will be my aim to account for both the theoretical arguments and the typological generalizations made in two rather divergent fields of linguistic reserach. This will in itself require the type of broad approach pursued here. Moreover, it is my aim to ward off possible counter-arguments on different lines which are often levelled only indirectly.

1. 'Unaccusativity': the same phenomenon in Italian and in German?

This chapter discusses the major identifying criteria for 'syntactic ergativity' (Perlmutter 1976; Keyser/Roeper 1984; Burzio 1991). Evidence to the effect that 'unaccusative', or 'ergative' verbs are dependent on perfectivity is derived conclusively from German. Since Italian is usually held to demonstrate that VP-internality of the subject corresponds to ergativity (in Burzio's sense), evidence from West Greenlandic as well as German will be provided to support the claim that VP-internal subjects are due to the specificity, or definiteness, effect and that this phenomenon has nothing to do in a direct way with ergativity. The data drawn from German as well as West-Greenlandic will be used to question Burzio's conclusion that the diagnostics pulled out for Italian is an attestable case of ergativity given the fact that its explanation as VP-internal, since non-specific, subject nominals, on a par with German and West-Greenlandic, would suffice. VP-internal subjecthood as well as nominal non-specificity, as is to be noticed, has nothing to do with ergativity as such since it does not involve lexical properties in the first place.

If it comes to diagnosing syntactic ergativity in Modern German (just as in Modern Italian; see Burzio 1986), it strikes one that each of the crucial tests for such ergative behaviour points at the past participle in attributive function to the designated subject argument of the verb in question (see Keyser/Roeper 1984 for ergatives in English). Since each property of what appears, at the surface, to be independent of the syntax of the past participle can be deduced from the syntactic behaviour characteristic of just this past participle, the observation about the co-occurrence of these factors in split ergative languages becomes more important. I shall first briefly sketch these interdependencies on the basis of Modern German. See the equivalent, for Dutch, in Ackema/Schoorlemmer

(1997). (4)–(5a, b, c) illustrate three main behavioural properties that ergatives are subject to in German (see already Haider 1985; Abraham 1985, 1987; Haider/ Rindler-Schjerve 1987).

(4)   ergative ('unaccusative'; eV) vs. unergative (truly intransitive; iV) verbs (all non-transitive):
eV: German *ankommen, umfallen, aufsteigen, durchlaufen, emporklettern, einschlafen; sterben*
iV: German *kommen, fallen, steigen, laufen, klettern, schlafen.*

Notice that not every verbal prefix classifies in itself for unaccusativity, i.e. for an eV; rather, this appears to depend on the lexical quality of boundedness that is represented, within the derived lexical element, by a prefix (as well as an affixoid; see (29b) and (31) below). Note, furthermore that such 'ergativizing prefixation' extends to constituents with a directional accusative; viz. *in den Garten laufen* 'into the-ACC garden-ACC run' vs. *im Garten laufen* 'in the-DAT garden-DAT run'; the latter is non-ergative in the sense that it does not accommodate any of the diagnostic criteria of unaccusativity/ergativity as shown below).

(5)   a.   adjectival participle test: subject of eV behaves syntactically like a direct object (DO)
der angekommene/umgefallene/aufgestiegene Gast 'the arrived/-fallen/ascended guest'; cf. *geschlagener Hund* 'beaten dog' from *X schlägt den Hund* 'X beats the dog', as opposed to **geschlagener X* 'beaten X'. Furthermore, *das in den Garten gelaufene Kind* 'the-into-the-ACC-garden-ACC-run-child' (as opposed to **das im Garten gelaufene Kind* 'the in the-DAT-garden-DAT-run-child').

Notice that the present participle (presupposing the lexically designated subject, SU, not the DO) does not yield the perfectivizing, and, consequently, the 'ergative' effect: *schlagender X* vs. **schlagender Hund* (cf. the example above). In other words, the present tense and active (underived) (participial) verb does not trigger 'ergative' properties, as opposed to the perfect participle.

(5)   b.   agentivity test: *-er*-nominalizations are generally only possible from AGENTS (note that we consider only productive *-er*-nominalizations from verbs): *Läufer* 'runner', *Kletterer* 'climber', *Steiger* 'riser', *Schläfer* 'sleeper (derived from agentive iV) vs. **Einschläfer*''fall-asleeper', **Zusammenfaller* 'collapser', **Sterber* 'dier' (unless the idea is evoked that the

person doing this does it purposefully). The general conclusion is: the subject of an eV can never be an AGENT.

c. Aux-test: eV select *sein/be,* whereas iV select *haben/have:* the periphrastic perfect forms of eV only go with the Aux *sein*; the equivalent forms of iV never go with *sein: ist-war/*hat(te) angekommen/aufgestiegen/durchgelaufen*; furthermore, the test holds also for projections beyond simple lexicals, e.g. Dutch *in de tuin gelopen hebben* 'in-the-garden-run-HAVE' vs. *de tuin binnen gelopen* ZIJN 'the-garden-into+run-BE'.

d. impersonal passive test: eV cannot undergo impersonal passivization as opposed to iV, which can: iV *laufen* 'run' allows the impersonal passive *es wird (von allen) fest gelaufen* 'it-is-(by all)-hard-run', whereas the eV *ertrinken* 'drown' does not: **es wird dauernd ertrunken* 'it-is-constantly-drowned'.

Notice that (5a) above presupposes the Aux-property diagnosed in (5c): only BE-selecting lexical forms support the distributional participial-attributive diagnostics for 'ergatives'. Since BE-participles have a stative meaning only presupposing an approach phase leading to that participial state (in terms of the grammatical expression of the BECOME+participle, at least where such an option exists such as in German and Dutch), the stative participle always implies completion of an event-part of one single lexical verb. This is what we call a perfective, or terminative, verbal form. If 'ergative' verbs are those that display the distributional properties described in (4) and (5a–c), then the conclusion is forced that this type of syntactic ergative is a perfective. Notice further that (5a–b) suggest that the lexically designated DO can never bear the thematic role of an AGENT, which is in agreement with all available evidence. Notice further that this observation supports the finding in (5b): AGENTS can never have the grammatical status of internal arguments (such as objects). Finally, the ergative property in (5d) is not independent either since impersonal passives can be formed only from agentive predicates. An Agent, on the other hand, can never be the only, and internal, argument of ergatives, since Agents generally do not project inside VP. On the other hand, impersonal passives can only be derived from imperfective predicates — a restriction that relates directly to the aspectual motivation of this test. We shall conclude later that it is exactly the deeper links between (5a–d) that explain, without any extra syntactic stipulation, the fact that 'ergatives' are in fact perfectives.

Italian provides another important diagnostic property, where in certain presentative constructions introduced by the particle *ne* only eV can co-occur, but not iV (Burzio 1986: 20 ff.). Notice that the characteristics displayed in (6a–d) below are of a fundamentally different nature than those in the German examples in (4)–(5c). What appears to be involved is VP-internality of the subjects in question rather than derivational aspects of the verbal lexicals as in German. Nevertheless, the Italian linear conditions correlate distinctly with the distribution of the two Aux-forms, just as do those between the derived and underived lexical verbs in German. For an initial comparison this is what holds: the prefixal forms in German take the BE forms of the auxiliary just as the VP-internal subjects in Italian. Inversely, what are underived simple verbs in German siding with the auxiliary HAVE corresponds to the VP-external subject in Italian. It is not clear at this point what should be common to these correlations.

SVO:
(6) a. *Ne [$_{VP}$ arrivano molti]*
of-them arrive many
... arrivare: eV (selecting *essere*)
b. **Ne telefonano molti*
of-them telephone many
... telefonare: iV (selecting *avere*)
c. **Ne esamineranno il caso molti esperti*
of-them will examine the case many experts
partitive indefinite subject
d. *Esamineranno il caso molti esperti*
will examine the case many experts
non-partitive subject; presentative (Burzio 1986: 20 ff.)

The last observation — which is matched by observations as to the behaviour of Dutch *er* and, in certain respects, also by English *there* and the German expletive pronoun *es* — carries over directly to the following two facts. First, indefinite subjects (among which bare plurals) in German and Dutch can appear only in predicate proximity (i.e. not in a canonical subject position outside the VP); see (7). Such indefinites even appear verb-incorporated in certain incorporating languages as West-Greenlandic (an ergative, incorporating language); and they never allow for a definite (thematic) partitive reading of the subject (van Geenhoven 1995).[3] Compare (7a–c) for West-Greenlandic and (7d–e) for Dutch. The VP-internal (non-specific subject in Dutch is highlighted; the temporal and local adverbs *gisteren* 'yesterday' and *hier* 'here' mark the VP-border to their right).

(7) a. *Niviarsiagga-t cykili-si-pp-u-t*
girl-ABS.PL bicycle-buy-IND-[tr]-3PL
'The girls bought a bicycle/bicycles'

b. *Juuna Kaali-mit marlum-nik   allagar-si-nngi-l-a-q*
J.-ABS K.-ABL.   TWO-INSTR.PL letter-receive-NEG-IND-[tr]-3SG
(i) 'It is not the case that Juuna received two letters from Kaali'
(ii) #'There are two letters from Kaali which Juuna did not receive'
c. *Ilinniartsisu-t   ataatse-mik   allattarfi-si-pp-u-t*
teacher-ABS.PL   a-INSTR.SG board-buy-IND-[tr]-3PL
(i) 'The teachers bought a board'
(ii) #'The teachers bought one of the boards'
d. *Ik zag dat hier gisteren [$_{VP}$ **heel wat kinderen** aan het dansen waren]* ... dansen = iV
'I saw that quite a lot of kids were dancing here yesterday.'
e. *Ik zag dat hier gisteren [$_{VP}$ **heel wat kinderen** aan zijn komen dansen]* ... komen = eV
'I saw that quite a lot of kids had come to dance here yesterday.'

Note that the definite (thematic) partitive reading, (ii), of each of the three sentences, (7a–c), is not available from the sentences whose subjects are predicate incorporated on account of their indefinite epistemology (note the glosses with 'a bicycle/bicycles'). The same phenomenon can be observed, albeit somewhat less systematically, in German incorporated objects.

(8) a. TEPPICH klopfen - *Es   wird hier nicht* TEPPICH *geklopft*
[$_V$ carpet dustout] - it-EXPL is   here not   carpets   dusted
'No dusting of carpets allowed'
b. *Es   wird/kann hier nicht (dreckige) Teppiche*
it-EXPL is/can-SG here not   dirty   [$_{DP}$Ø]-carpets-PL
geklopft werden
dusted   be
c. *Es   können/*kann die   staubigen Teppiche heute nicht*
it-EXPL is/can-SG   the-DEF dusty   carpets today not
geklopft werden
dusted   be
d. *Es   wird heute einmal anständig zähnegeputzt*
it-EXPL is-SG today once   duly   teeth-PL-ACC-brushed

Compare the number agreement on the auxiliary slot, which is not plural as would be suggested by the subject in (8b), as opposed to the non-presentative, subject-outside-VP version in (8c).

The data drawn from German, Dutch and West-Greenlandic demonstrate that Burzio's diagnostics for ergativity in Italian is independently forced on the ground that the distributional phenomena can be accounted for as VP-internal, since non-specific, subject nominals. VP-internal subjecthood as well as nominal non-specificity, as is to be noticed, have nothing to do with ergativity as such. In principle, thus, the behavioral, cross-linguistic evidence weakens the weight of proof of the examples (6a–d), which form the empirical foundation of Burzio's theory. The concrete answer to the question formulated in the title of this section, then, is: it is doubtful that the distributional properties called for in the case of Italian require an explanation in ergative terms. It would be sufficient to subsume, and 'account' for, these properties under VP-internal subjecthood and non-specificity. Both concepts, VP-internal subjecthood as well as non-specific nominality, cannot be subsumed, in any direct and unambiguous sense, under Burzio's Argument account of ergativity or unaccusativity.

As a generalization from the evidence in (4)–(8), one can draw the following preliminary conclusions. See (9a–h).

(9) a. eV have subjects which behave distributionally like a DO; let us call this the 'VP-internal subject property' (VPISP, henceforth); iV do not exhibit the VPISP. Cf. (5a).

b. The VPISP is available only through selection of the past participle, not, however, through the present participle. Cf. the assumption that the passive participle 'absorbs object case' (Baker/Johnson/Roberts 1989). See the attribute test in (5b).

c. There is a deep interconnection between thematic roles and the clausal status of the DO (or ergative subject) such that the syntactic DO-property is matched by thematic non-agentivity. Cf. (5b).

d. There is furthermore a deep interconnection between the event semantics of eV, as opposed to that of iV, such that the syntactic property of eV holds only for perfect participles and their syntactic selection. This is a novel insight as far as modern formal syntax is concerned. Cf. (1).

e. Partitive nominals may, but need not, occur as subjects of eV, nor do definites or indefinites. See (6) and (7). Both nounreferential properties are independent of syntactic ergativity.

f. Indefinite determinations of NPs need to be VP-internal as opposed to definite ones (which allow for either status, VP-external and VP-internal). See (4) and (5).

g. There are languages which express such differences as described in (9e,f) directly in terms of incorporation into the verbal predicate morphology. Such languages are West Green-

landic and German; cf. (7)–(8).
h. There is evidence that the alleged ergative diagnostic of the participial attribute is a constituent property. Think of German directional prepositional phrases governing the telic accusative vs. their non-telic, stative dative counterpart. Think of the aktionsart prefixes on the verb for German. Cf.(5c).
i. There appears to be another deep connection between VP-internal (non-specific and rhematic) argument status and ergativity (think of the *ne*-cases in Italian and their partitive, non-specific reading). Cf. (3)–(4) as well as the linear restrictions on non-specificity of the subject or object.

Notice that we have not answered the question whether or not there is any deeper and explanatory link between the 'ergative' linear characteristic stated for Italian and the derivational verbal property that holds for German. The evidence from another ergative language, West Greenlandic, suggests is that non-specific subject-NPs prefer VP-internal, verb-proximate positions. This at least suggests that VP-internal subjects are not necessarily linked directly, or even indirectly, to ergativity in any interesting sense (as has indeed been argued at length in Abraham (1986; 1995 ch. 9)).[4] I do not wish to decide at this point the question whether this allows for any link to other 'ergative' properties. However, it may just as well be the case that the VP-internality of subjects is an epiphenomenon to ergativity in an interesting sense (for other important ergative diagnostics, mainly in Dutch, see Hoekstra 1984). In what follows I shall focus on those ergative diagnostics which are undisputed across all languages for this type of syntactic ergativity: namely, the two main behavioural criteria illustrated in (4)–(5) above: non-agentivity of the external argument; and that Aux-selection of the eV must be *be* (not *have*). We shall argue also that these two criteria are in concord with perfectivity — a position which will allow us to replace the 'ergative Argument account' with the 'Aspect account'.

2. The 'Unaccusative Hypothesis' and 'Burzio's Generalization'

2.1 *The paradoxality of Burzio's generalization in German*

This section is to show into which types of empirical difficulty Burzio's claims lead us given the evidence of German. Two types of 'ergatives' are presented: lexicals (i.e. X^0-ones; with as well as without verbal particles: cf. German *sterben* 'die'; *absinken* 'down-sink') as well as phrasal (i.e. XP-) ones (i.e. *in den Graben fallen* 'into-the-ditch fall'). It will be argued that the latter, phrasal, evidence alone suffices to cast serious doubt upon Burzio's claim (the 'Burzio/ Perlmutter paradox'). It will furthermore be shown that Dryer's concept of 'intransitive split' (Dryer 1997) does not cover the phenomena which have been held against Burzio's and Perlmutter's conclusions. To the extent that the distributional characteristics demonstrated on German in (4)–(5) above hold for Italian as well, Burzio's syntactic claims follow unambiguously from my Aspect account. Recall that the Italian evidence provided by the *ne*-phenomenon has been recognized as epiphenomenal and may not bear on ergativity in the first place.

It is no doubt striking that the German examples of eV are characterized by verbal prefigation, as opposed to the simple verbal lexicals for iV: German (as well as Dutch and Frisian) eV appear to be classifiable as perfectives. This has led to the early assumption (Abraham 1985) that there is a deep, but yet unexplained connection between the perfective aktionsart and the type of syntactic ergativity described e.g. in Plank (1979) and elsewhere. What precisely is the claim made in connection with 'unaccusativity'?

Part of the conclusions drawn in (9a–i) above have led linguists such as Perlmutter (1976) and Burzio (1986) to make the following two main generalizations. Cf. (10a–b).

(10) a. 'Unaccusative Hypothesis' (Perlmutter 1978, made with the purpose of demonstrating the explanatory force of Relational Grammar): there is a universal class of intransitive verbs whose lexically designated subjects exhibit properties of a direct object. On some covert level of representation, this should turn out as follows:
for Italian SVO:

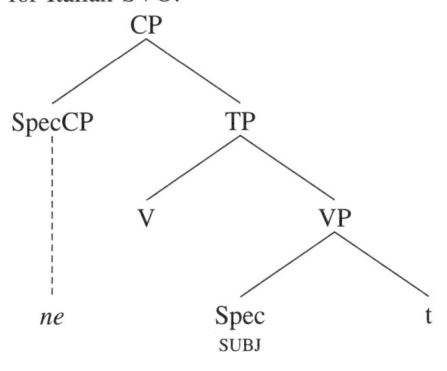

```
              CP
            /    \
         SpecCP   TP
           ¦     /  \
           ¦    V    VP
           ¦         /  \
           ne      Spec   t
                   SUBJ
```

for German SOV:

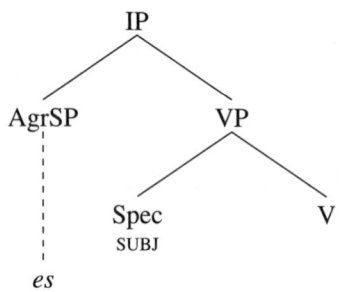

```
        IP
       /  \
    AgrSP  VP
      ¦   /  \
      ¦ Spec  V
      ¦ SUBJ
      es
```

b. 'Burzio's Generalization' (i): "A verb which lacks an external argument fails to assign accusative case." (Burzio 1986: 178 f.; no doubt, to be constrained further, in modern terms; otherwise, i.e. if not so constrained, German subjectless impersonals, with accusative object-EXPERIENCERS, would be straightforward counter-examples invalidating this generalization trivially; for impersonals in German see Seefranz-Montag 1995).

c. 'Burzio's Generalization' (ii): "A verb which fails to assign accusative case fails to θ-mark its external argument." (Burzio 1986: 184; following from case theory, and, no doubt, to be constrained further, in modern terms).

If it will indeed turn out to be the case that the syntactic characterization of unaccusatives in Burzio's (and related) fashion is just too simple and does not do justice to a wide array of empirical linguistic facts which have to be included and accounted for in a general approach — i.e. under examination of semantic and aspectual properties (telicity, change of state, possibility of non- agentive reading). Needless to say that it will be impossible to state the distinction between unergative and unaccusative if:

(i) subjects originate within a (single) VP

and

(ii) vacuous branching is disallowed. See (10c) vs. (10d) below well as Chomsky's analysis (Chomsky 1995) in (10e).

(10)   c.   VP
              / \
            NP   V'
                  |
                  V

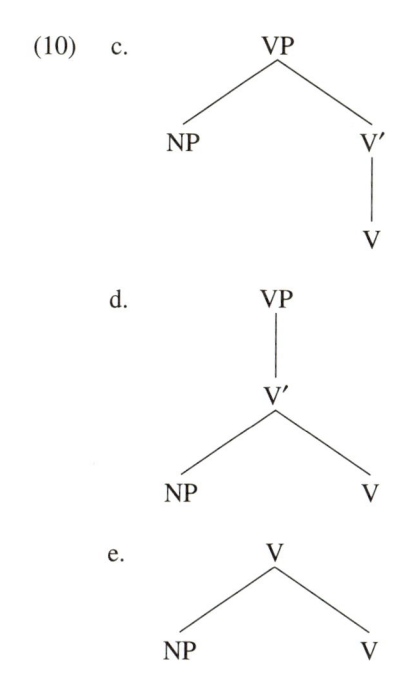

       d.   VP
               |
               V'
              / \
            NP   V

       e.   V
              / \
            NP   V

Beyond such constraints, however, we need an extra format to support our aspectual analysis, e.g. of the lexical-aspectual pair *schlafen* (iV)/*einschlafen* (eV): an analysis in terms of a small clause or embedded VP representing a change of event and the resulting state. This solution is to be expressed more fully in formal terms if eV are indeed perfectives.

It has to be kept in mind that the designation of the lexical subject of eV in terms of objects (such as in the form of (11a) for an SOV-language like German, where the basic (lexically designated) subject position is unoccupied) does not preclude its surface appearance as a subject, due to a universal tendency toward avoidance of subjectless clauses (Extended Projection Principle, or EPP; Chomsky 1981). [θ_i = VP-internal θ-role; θ_e = VP-external θ-role].

(11)   a.   eV: __[θ_i eV] (vs. tV: θ_e[θ_i tV]), where θ_i of eV surfaces eventually as subject due to EPP; cf. eV θ_i-*stirbt* 'θ_i-dies'
       b.   iV: θ_e[iV], where: θ_e for lexically designated subject (external) argument; cf. θ_e-*läuft* 'θ_e-runs'.

Note that if there is a nominative (unmarked case, default case) in contrast to other case morphology, it is the nominative that will identify the subject. Since infinitives never govern subjects or nominatives, one assumes that the nominative is assigned by some clausal function(al category) such as TENSE (or MOOD) of the clausal finite predicate (C/T or C/M), whereas all other case is verbally governed (C/V), either structurally or lexically inherent.

The two generalizations in (11a,b) have a number of principled consequences of a theoretical and a typological nature. The most prominent theoretical question connected with (9a) and the observations in (5a–d) is what aktionsart/ aspect, or, more precisely, the perfect tense, has to do with the syntactic class of eV ('unaccusative' verbs as opposed to iV). Likewise, the important typological question deriving from a comparison of (5) and (9b) is whether it is true that the ergative system has a strong affinity with perfect(ive)s and what the deeper nature of this connection is. Note that a number of other links established in the literature follow immediately from the syntactic property of direct object of the ergative subject, such as its PATIENT or THEME constraint (i.e. NON-AGENTIVITY) as well as, at least in SOV, VP-internality vs. VP-externality, which are linked clearly to noun-referential specificity. Notice, however, that the underlying distinction between unergativity and unaccusativity solely in terms of the structural distribution of θ-roles and (L-related) arguments leads us into a dramatic impasse since we do not know what the perfective equivalent to the PERFECTIVE unaccusative on the two-place, transitive paradigm should be. As is shown in (12a, b), if we accept one-place ergatives, then the aspectual account would force us to speak of 'transitive ergatives' also — which would lead to uninterpretable structures (as in the right column under (12b) below). [Question marks indicate difficulties of categorial identification in the drived structures.]

(12) Burzio/Perlmutter's assumptions lead to an uninterpretable structure:
      [α PERF] Perlmutter/Burzio: demotion of external argument:
   a. −   iV: $\theta_e[\_\_\_]$ tV: $\theta_e[_{VP} \theta_i V_{1+2?}]$
   b. +   eV: $\_\_[\theta_i\_]$ tV: $\_ [_? \theta_e [_? \theta_i V_{1?}] V_{2?}]]$

Notice that perfectivity is not restricted to one-place verbs, but includes transitives ($\theta_e[\theta_i$ tV]; cf. (11a)) as well. Consider the right bottom section in the table in (12b) above. If the external argument, θ_e, is demoted by force of perfectivity, as between iV and eV in German, what would be the status of the perfective tV? To derive the perfective version of tV, the internal argument, θ_i, should be demoted. But it is totally unclear as to what this should yield in structural terms. To be sure, we do know what the 'demotion' (if indeed this is what is going on) should yield empirically: a statal/adjectival passive.[5] But what does the statal passive have to do with the structural θ-role distribution in the perfective tV in (12b)? I will suggest that (12b) for tV is indeed the required structure if the question marks are resolved in terms of a small clause structure for the internal bracketing and distinct components of the prefix verb (V_1 for the 'unaccusativizing', since perfectivizing verbal prefix, V_2 for the simple, non-perfective verbal component). Notice that we would like to arrive at a solution where the fact that the internal argument, θ_i, has subject properties falls out in a natural way. The characteristic responding to this requirement is the logical subject status of θ_i in the embedded small clause predicated of a statal property. If will be seen that this approach is the converse to Burzio's approach.

2.2 *'Intransitive split' as a replacive concept?*

This brief section addresses the concept of 'split intransitivity' introduced by Dryer (1997) and which was intended to replace the syntax-theoretic concept of ergativity in Burzio's sense. In the present paper, Dryer's claim is refuted. In essence, our argument boils down to this: If West-Germanic and in particular German, with their distributional properties, demonstrate lexical as well as phrasal 'ergativity', then Dryer's classification of 'intransitive split' does not cover ergativity in Burzio's and Perlmutter's sense.

In typological work outside the syntax-theoretic schools of thinking, a fundamental distinction is drawn between the ergative patterning as described in Dixon (1994) and what is called 'split intransitive patterning word order' (Dryer 1997). The latter implies that the position of subjects relative to the verb is *pragmatically* (my highlighting; W.A.) governed in such a way that also correlates with their semantics and where it is particularly common for the subjects of certain intransitive verbs to occur in a position normally associated with objects. According to Dryer, this is true for many European languages. The present attempt at a refutation of the 'formal concept' (or 'syntax-theoretic') of ergativity, however, need not be concerned with this distinction on exactly Dryer's terms: first, the explanatory property of perfectivity covers exactly those verbs which are the alleged 'ergative' verbs; and, second, we draw a parallel with those distinctly 'ergative'patterns observed for perfectivity-sensitive phenomena as in the split-ergative languages (see below). Furthermore, a kinship is identified with 'true, typological ergativity' along lines of pronominal and hearer/speaker properties which escapes the 'split intransitive' notion. If 'formal ergativity' (i.e. ergativity in the sense of Perlmutter's and Burzio's 'unaccusativity') covers all that and can be explained in terms of formal grammar, then Dryer's pragmatic 'intransitive split' distinction appears to amount to nothing more than a terminological option.[6]

However, Dryer's classification of split intransitivity is not only just a notational variant. Under the perspective of German it is clearly ill-conceived, since the distributional properties valid for split intransitives ('unaccusatives' or 'ergatives') are shared by transitives as well with respect to one crucial type of behaviour: the distinction between the statal passive and the processual passive. The determining factor is that only ergative transitive verbs admit the statal passive (*SEIN* ('be')+PP; e.g. *ist/*hat herausgezogen "is pulled out"*, which is morphologically distinct from the processual passive (*SEIN*+PP+*worden*; e.g. *ist gezogen *(worden) "has been pulled"*). This distributional property is not shared by unergative transitive verbs, which allow just the processual passive (*gezogen worden sein* 'have been pulled'), but not the statal passive (**gezogen sein*; 'be pulled'). See (1)–(5).

To summarize: From the perspective of Modern German, Dryer's class of intransitives with object distribution of their subjects is inadequate to the extent that the distributional and morphological properties observed for ergatives/ unaccusatives hold for intransitives as well as for transitives. The common property of this larger verbal class, unrestricted with respect to valency, is that of perfectivity, or, perhaps better, telicity/terminativity as an Aktionsart classification (setting the property off from the Slavic notion of perfectivity).[7]

I am not aware of any other European language other than German that shares this 'ergativity split' across verbal valency. See my arguments against Burzio's Italian examples above. Dutch, the language closest to German, has lost the distinction between the perfective ('ergative') and the imperfective distribution in terms of passiveness (*is getogen* (**geworden*); in other words, the *worden*-component has come to be dropped in the course of the history of Dutch). It appears to be the case that, in order to make the comparison between ergativity and telicity work, one needs to look at German and no other European language.[8]

Before we turn to this, however, let us consider a step which is almost self-suggesting: let us look at ergative splits triggered by past tense and perfective aspect.

3. Urdu, Hindi, and Balochi: Specific ergativity splits

Chapters 3 and 4 are to show what typological ergativity is about in languages in which case ergativity is crucially triggered by tense and aspect conditions. Either chapter prepares the ensuing discussion about features and criticism of Burzio's concept of syntactic ergativity.

Let us, inspired by the above, look at split ergativity. We take Balochi (Farrell 1995), Urdu (Butt 1993), and Hindi (Mahajan 1985, 1994, 1997) as

THE ASPECT–CASE TYPOLOGY CORRELATION 149

examples for traits of case morphology that appear to be in partial agreement in these languages. Recall that, in SOV-Hindi, the only Aux is the equivalent of *be*. (9a, b, d) display truly intransitives (unergatives), whereas (9c, e, f) are ergatives (unaccusatives).[9] It should not go unnoticed at this point that, according to Trask (1979), typologically ergative languages appear to be SOV or VSO only and restrict their auxiliary representation to BE. Neither of these characteristics receives any mention in Dixon's book on ergativity. As we shall see, Mahajan (1995) bases his syntactic account on exactly these two correlative properties of typological ergativity.

Now let us see how Hindi splits its clausal case syntax.

(13) Hindi (SOV):
  a. *raam-ne   vah   kitaabē   paṛʰī̃*
     Ram-ERG-MASC those books-FEM-PL read-PERF-FEM-PL
     hē   (Mahajan 1994: 6)
     be-PRES-PL
     'Ram has read those books'
  b. *raam-ne   bhindiiyāā   pakaaī̃   hē*
     Ram-ERG-MASC okra-FEM-PL cook-PERF-FEM-PL be-PRES-PL
     'Ram has cooked okra'   (Mahajan 1994: 7)
  c. *raam   aayaa   hē*
     Ram-MASC come-PERF-MASC-SG be-PRES-SG
     'Ram has arrived'
  d. *raam   bhindiiyāā   pakaataa   hē*
     Ram-MASC okra-FEM-PL cook-IMPERF-MASC be-PRES-SG
     'Ram cooks okra'
  e. *raam   vah   kitabē*
     Ram-NOM-MASC those books-PL-FEM
     paṛʰtaa   (Mahajan 1994: 14)
     read MPER PART-MASC-SG *be*-MASC-SG-PAST
     'Ram used to read those books'
  f. *raam(-*ne) gir geyaa*   verb is inherently ergative
     Ram-(*ERG) fell down
     'Ram fell down'

These examples illustrate the following: case government follows the ergativity distribution, i.e. the absolutive/nominative in two-place predications reoccurs in one-place predications, whereas the ergative case is realized only for the subject of two-place transitives — unless, as in cases such as (9f), Hindi (and, according to Laka 1993, also Basque), the one-place verb is unaccusative. Unaccusatives, in such languages, behave like the absolutive objects in two-place predications to the extent that they cannot appear in the ergative, but must occur in the nominative (term used for the absolutive, in a number of grammatical terminologies). Note, furthermore, that the ergative-absolutive mechanics is active only in the perfect(ive) or past, not, however, in the present or some continuous form; cf. (9a–c) vs. (9d, e). By contrast to unaccusatives ('ergatives), unergative ('truly intransitive) verbs can take either case. Cf. (14).

(14) Hindi (SOV):
a. *kutto-ne bōtkaa*
dogs-ERG bark-PERF-MAS-SG
'The dogs barked'
b. *kutte bōtkee* (Mahajan 1994: 14)
dogs-NOM bark-PERF-MASC-PL
'The dogs barked'

The fact that the ergative case morphology, as in ergative splits, surfaces only in perfective aspect is characteristic of most Indic-European languages (Kachru/ Pandharpande 1979). A similar distribution, carries over to Georgian, some Australian languages and some Tibeto-Burman languages (Mahajan 1994: 14, quoting Marantz 1991 and DeLancey 1980). Two solutions come to mind for a systematic representation and account of this correlation: either, the ergative and absolutive case markings are bound in some way to two structurally different aspectual nodes, one originating outside of VP carrying truly V-independent inflection features; and another one originating from inside VP. Either aspectual node needs to be checked for strong, structural case features: to the extent that the verb is two-place, the perfect(ive) features of the verb trigger the search for the aspectual node for the absolutive (or nominative) case, whereas the outer aspectual node is the landing point for ergative case characteristics. A split with ergative in the imperfective and accusative in the perfective has never been attested (Farrell 1995: 220). Note that the distributive trigger is verb-inherent since it is either the morphological-inflective (perfect(ive) vs. non-perfect(ive)) or the inherent semantic information (unaccusative) of the verbal that decides which of the two structurally different nodes are to be checked for the required overt case morphology. This first scenario can be represented as in (15a, b) representing the two syntactic configurations in (14a, b).[10] [eSubj = ergative subject, aSubj = absolutive subject].

(15) a. for *bark₁*: __[V]

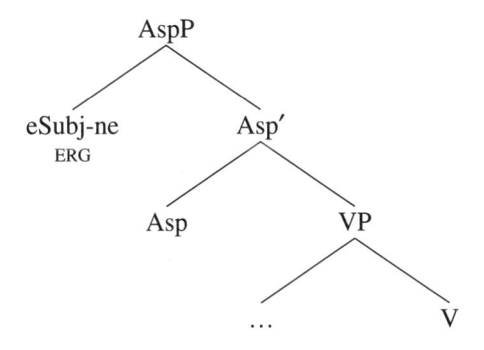

```
           AspP
          /    \
     eSubj-ne   Asp'
       ERG     /    \
             Asp     VP
                    /  \
                  ...   V
```

b. for *bark₂*: [_V]; cf. *fall* as eV

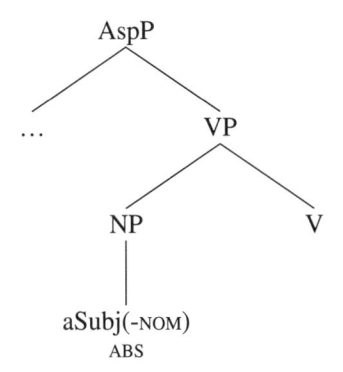

```
          AspP
         /    \
       ...     VP
              /  \
            NP    V
            |
         aSubj(-NOM)
            ABS
```

The second scenario starts out from the observation that ergative languages generally appear to have no auxiliary for *have*, but only one for *be*, as opposed to NOM-ACC-languages. Hindi would be a good example; see (9a–e) above, where *be* appears as the only Aux of the periphrastic perfect. This scenario is somewhat complicated and will be discussed in the following section. Following up on this issue, the bipartition of the structural representation of the clause in a (split) ergative language is not basic as in (15) above, but derived, i.e. the result of the principled distribution of the Aux *have* vs. *be* and the principled link between the two Aux's (see Marantz 1991; Guéron 1995; Hoekstra/Rooryck 1995; Bittner & Hale 1996).

In what follows I shall be brief on Urdu, since it is closely related to Hindi. What is highlighted, however, is what appears to be a dependency on the specificity of the VP-internal argument.

(16) Urdu (SOV):
  a. *naadyaa-ne xat likh-aa*
     N.-FEM-ERG letter-MASC-NOM wrote-PERF-MASC-SG
     basic word-order in perfective constructions: SOV
     'Nadya wrote a letter'
  b. *naadya-ne hassan-ko xat*
     N.-FEM-ERG Hassan-MASC-DAT letter-MASC-NOM
     di-yaa
     give-PERF-MASC-SG
     'Nadya gave Hassan a (particular) letter'
  c. *naadya-ne hassan-ko xat*
     N.-FEM-ERG Hassan-MASC-DAT letter-MASC-NOM
     jaldii-se di-yaa
     quickness-INSTR give-PERF-MASC-SG
     'Nadya gave Hassan a (particular) letter quickly'
                                   (Butt & King 1995: 3)
  d. *anil g^{h}ore bec-taa hai*
     Anil-MASC-NOM horse-MASC-PL sell-IMPERF-MASC-SG be
     'Anil does horse-selling'
  e. *naadyaa subah-se shaam-tak xat*
     Nadya-FEM-NOM morning-INSTR evening-until letter-MASC-NOM
     likh-tii hai
     write-IMPERF-FEM-SG be-PRES-SG
     'Nadya writes letters from morning until evening'
                                   (Butt & King 1995: 7)

As is illustrated in (16c), the specific reading of the direct object is available also if the object is outside of VP. As soon as an indefinite object is instantiated, incorporation into the predicate takes place. A position outside the VP is no longer available then. See (16d), with the direct object, *g^{h}ore*, without case marking. (16e), finally, testifies to the observation above that it is only under the perfective that the ergative mechanism (and not the nominative/accusative mechanism) is activated.

Hindi presents a rather homogeneous case of aspect-triggered ergativity. Let us have a look at Balochi where other conditions appear to be responsible for case ergativity — evidence which may help us finding out about deeper features linked with ergativity explicable also in syntactic terms.

4. Balochi: Ergative split according to heterogeneous criteria

The following examples on the Northwestern Iranian language of Balochi are taken from Farrell (1995). Balochi is interesting insofar as two variants can be distinguished: Southern/Eastern Balochi and Western Balochi, of which only the first exhibits the ergative split, whereas the latter displays a pure nominative/accusative pattern except in discourse where ergativity occurs occasionally. Furthermore, the areal ergative/accusative distribution in Balochi allows for the conclusion that ergativity in the Southern/Eastern part follows the track the Western district with the nominative/accusative pattern has taken, i.e. follows the former on its way out of the ergative system. Furthermore, Balochi displays a number of interdependencies that are telling in the evaluation of ergativity conditions. Next to the aspectual condition for the split, Balochi is specific to the extent that the ergative/absolutive case marking in the perfective is confined to third person nouns and pronouns (in line with all findings so far on ergativity split; see Silverstein 1976; Rumsey 1987: 27). First and second person pronouns are marked in the nominative/accusative pattern.

(17) Balochi (SOV):
    a. *jinik sho*   (Farrell 1995: 221)
        girl-DIR go-PAST-3SG
        'The girl went'
    b. *jinik-a becik ja*
        girl-OBL boy-DIR hit-PAST-3SG ergative pattern
        'The girl hit the boy'
    c. *men te-ra gir-ã*
        I-DIR you-SG-OBL catch-PRES-1SG accusative pattern
        'I will catch you'

Note that DIR, in the traditional grammatical terminology of Balochi, stands for 'direct' (case)' without case marking, therefore absolutive/nominative; OBL oblique case; (Farrell 1995: 219).

The reason for this person split is obviously that first and second persons are the prototypical AGENTS, as opposed to third persons. AGENTS, we generalized above, can never enter into the lexically designated VP-internal argument position. Consequently, they are out as carriers of the absolutive/nominative/direct case, particularly in a system that displays a tendency toward another pattern in the first place. Note that the AGENT cannot surface in a lexically designated object position in any of the Indoeuropean nominative/accusative languages (Abraham 1978).

According to Farrell's (1995) analysis of Balochi, one can factor out the following triggering criteria for ergativity: the aspectual (perfectivity) factor, the definiteness factor, and the person factor. To this, Mahajan (1994: 14 ff.) adds the following criteria: the unaccusativity factor; the auxiliary factor; and the reflexive factor. According to Mahajan (1994), all of the factors are epiphenomena of one basic factor, namely whether or not the language in question has the clausal predicate, V, in marginal position (thus, SOV or VSO). Since the line of argument pursued in the present paper questions this basic assumption and its consequences, each of these five criteria for ergativity will have to be discussed separately.

In order to arrive at a full set of conditioning factors for the emergence of ergativity let us survey Farrell's findings with respect to the person and the definiteness factors. (18) and (19) display nicely the complementary distributions of case characteristics as dependent from such factors (none of which were considered by Mahajan 1994).

(18) Person-definiteness factor for ergativity in Balochi (Farrell 1995: 223): third person patient marking in the perfective and the non-perfective

Abbreviations: DIR = direct (absolutive, nominative) case; OBL = oblique case; S = subject; A = agent; P = patient; IND = indefinite; DEF = definite; EMPH = emphatic; 1,2,3 = 1st, 2nd, 3rd person.

	non-perfective	perfective
indefinite patient	direct case	direct case
definite patient	oblique case	direct case
definite emphatic patient	oblique case	direct case

(19) Case and verb agreement factor for ergativity in Balochi (Farrell 1995: 225)

	S	A (1&2)	A(3)	P(Ind)	P Def (1&2)	P Def (3)	P (Emphasis)	Verb Argument
non-perf.	DIR							with S
non-perf.		DIR	DIR	DIR	OBL	OBL	OBL/DAT	with A
perf.	DIR							with A
perf.		DIR	OBL	DIR	OBL	DIR		with P
perf.		DIR	OBL				DAT	with 0

The Balochian examples above as well as the generalisations in (18) and (19) permit the following conclusions which appear to be relevant for our present purposes. Let us first generalize, from properties exhibited by German as an SOV-language, to ergative SOV-languages (such as Balochi, Hindi, and Urdu). Clearly, we are not in a position to exploit these data to yield final directions of further research. It is for this reason that just a number of questions are jotted down. While no clear answers can be seen as yet it appears intriguing enough to formulate these questions.

(20) a. [–definite] verbal arguments/actants, rather than [+definite] ones, appear in the ABS. The reason is that [–def] occurs closer to the verb (inside VP, as a case governed by the verbal predicate, C/V⁰), whereas [+def] occurs distant from the finite predicate (outside of VP; as C/T, i.e. under the tense category of the whole clause).
It is to be asked whether this indicates that ergativity in these (SOV) languages has a deep link with the THEMA-RHEMA split of the clause. If this should indeed turn out to be the case an explanation in clause-grammatical terms could not be found unless THEMA-RHEMA were to be anchored firmly in clause-structural terms. For such an approach (vs. the approach in terms of an independent module, e.g. after spell-out) see Abraham for German (Abraham 1992; 1995: Chapter 11).
b. ABS, rather than ERG, occurs as PAT, and consequently as [–animate]. This, is presumably linked to the fact that VP-internal θ-roles such as for the ABS cannot be AGENTS.
c. ABS is closer to the clausal focus position, which makes ABS rhematic in nature, if in its basic position. Again, this has to do with the fact that an SOV-language splits the structural field for its arguments/actants (subject and objects) into VP-internal and VP-external portions. Departing from Heim (1982), Enç (1991) and following Abraham (1992), VP is taken to be the locus of rhematic material, whereas the structural area above VP (IP or AgrPs, TP, CP) is the locus of thematic material.[11]

What (20a–c) point to, however, is a categorical distinction between V-marginal languages (SOV, VSO) and V-medial languages (SVO), since only the former open a structural space for NP-scrambling and, consequently, for the distinction of thematic vs. rhematic status of scrambled nominals (in terms of Heim (1982): the 'restrictive', VP-external space vs. the clause 'kernel', VP-internal, space). This is the basic typological split that Mahajan (1994, 1997) takes as a point of departure for his account of ergativity and the non-occurrence of the auxiliary

HAVE in ergative languages. Mahajan's position will be sketched in the following section. Before we do that, however, let us generalize further on Balochi.

(21) a. The ABS is morphologically and paradigmatically the unmarked case — some sort of 'copular' case; unless the features [–def] and [–human] are supported by perfectivity, the NP-(object) case morphology appears marked.
   b. ABS (≠ ERG) only surfaces under perfective or past tense conditions.
   c. The ABS in split ergativity patterns co-occurs with the default focus or non-focus of the clause in total agreement with the accusative in the nominative-accusative pattern.
   d. According to some optimality mechanics, the ergative split can find expression on different levels of representation: in terms of case (Erg-Abs vs. Nom-Acc), [α Animate] or [α Reference], i.e. [± def]. One may ask whether there is reason to assume that the latter features surface in a language whose ergativity is fading (such as in Western-Southern Balochi vs. Eastern Balochi). Compare the assumptions made by Farrell (1995: 239).
   e. In terms of a strong tendency, first and second persons are prototypical AGENTS, since they are invariably [+human], even in the least ergative dimension in an ergative language (cf. (18) above, following Farrell 1995: 223). The question is, however, how agentivity relates to the perfective. If ergativity is to be accounted for on the basis of the striking link with perfectivity, all the generalizing observations in (21) and (18) should follow naturally from this basis, in particular the conditioning factors such as agreement, focus, θ-role of 1st and 2nd persons vs. 3rd persons, and, possibly, also the auxiliary split between ergative and non-ergative languages.

In what follows two approaches to ergativity will be evaluated against these criteria and facts: Mahajan's (1994; 1997) typological split and the aspectual syntax approach (Abraham 1992, 1994a).

5. The V-marginal vs. V-medial split and the Aux-correlation: ERGATIVE *BE* vs. NOM-ACC *HAVE*

In Chapters 3 and 4 we noted that the ergative-split languages employ only *be* as an auxiliary verb in their pasts and perfects, which co-occur with case ergativity. This may or may not be pure chance. The discussion in this section will depart from Mahajan's repeated claim (Mahajan 1994; 1997) with respect to the occurrence of HAVE/BE and their distribution across ergative languages. The key to Mahajan's conclusions is his typological split into V-marginal vs. V-medial languages as well as the observation (Trask (1979: 399 f.),[12] Kayne (1993) next to quite a number of others, notably Benvéniste 1952), that ergative languages do not appear to select the auxiliary HAVE for periphrastic constructions. This was an early observation in typological research and has led linguists such as Klimov (1973) — reported by Comrie (1976: 254) and Trask (1979: 399) — to suggest that there may be a correlation between ergativity and oblique subject constructions (in the DATIVE, GENITIVE, OR LOCATIVE) to give form to a possession predicate (see the similar discussion in Dixon 1994: 191). The latter generalization (if indeed correct; see, however, Basque, which is ergative and nevertheless possesses the auxiliary distinction) and explanation hinges crucially on the claim that HAVE is BE + an empty adposition, i.e. something like *be with* or LOC/DATIVE + *be* (reminiscent of Latin; see (23)). Note the case affix for the ergative in Hindi (Mahajan 1994: 6) in (24) below. Thus, if BE is a category representing tense and agreement, then HAVE incorporates the properties of BE and configurates simultaneously both a grammatical case (as in the case of some ergative languages) and the semantics of some locality. See (22) and (23) below (following Kayne 1993).

(22) Possession in Latin:
mihi est SUBJECT$_i$
I-DAT cop-3SG nom(-SG)
'I have OBJECT$_i$'

(23) Lexical decomposition of possessive *have*:

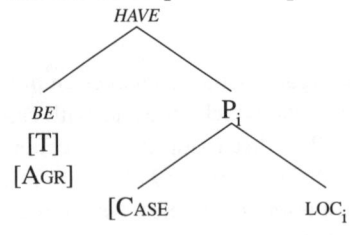

```
         HAVE
        /    \
      BE      P_i
      [T]    /   \
     [AGR] [CASE]  LOC_i
```

(from Guéron 1995; see also Guéron 1998)

Latin *mihi* "(to) me" in (22) is taken up in (23) by both [Case] and LOC, daughters of P, no doubt a constituent highly marked with respect to case morphology and syntactic mobility. Consider the following Hindi example, where the person-GOAL dative of Latin in (22) corresponds to what is the subject in the (equally marked) ergative case in Hindi, *raam-ne*. Notice that ergative case is inflection marked with *-ne* deriving from a former postposition, while the case of the object, *kitaabẽ*, is the pure nominal stem (unmarked; in many of the terminologies also called 'nominative' or 'direct case').

(24) *raam-ne   vah   kitaabẽ   paṛʰiĩ   hɛ*
Ram-ERG-MASC those books-FEM-PL-Ø read-PERF-FEM-PL be-PRES-PL
'those-books-have-been-read ('are-read)-to/for/by-Ram'
'Ram has read those books'   (Mahajan 1994: 6)

According to Mashajan, in V-medial languages (SVO, like all European Romance languages as well as the Germanic ones with the exception of German, Dutch, and Frisian), due to the direct vicinity of finite V in second position, this adposition appears V-incorporated and therefore does not surface as a separate adposition morpheme or as a case marker. In V-marginal languages, however, this adposition surfaces either as a separate morpheme or as case morphology, thereby making superfluous the separate HAVE/BE distinction.

Mahajan's idea is perhaps best illustrated by the change of agreement in French. As is well-known, agreement for gender and number on the participle is expressed with preverbal pronominal clitic objects, not, however, with postverbal full NPs.

(25) a. *Jean les_i a repeint[-es_i]*
proclitic object — object agreement on the predicative participle
b. *Jean a repeint[-Ø_i] les maisons_i*
postverbal object-NP — no (object) agreement on the participle

c. *Jean les$_i$ a cuit[-s$_i$]*
d. *Jean a cuit[-Ø$_i$] les pommes de terre$_i$*

What Mahajan claims is this: the subject in French, like *Jean* as in (25), originates as a PP, the head of which is incorporated into Aux in the course of derivation from the underlying structure to the surface. This pertains to those positions of the finite predicate (Aux or full verb) immediately adjacent to the subject, *Jean*. Where such adjacency is interrupted as by a preverbal clitic object, such incorporation is blocked and object-agreement applies, as in Hindi. The clitic constructions in French (25b, d), in a way, can be regarded as ergative-like orders.

It is to be noted that in Dixon's most recent survey of typological ergativity, no mention is made of an Aux-ergative correlation. In any case, what is indicative of a systematic correlation between typological ergativity and tense/aspect is his remark to the effect that, if an ergative split is conditioned by tense or aspect, then the ergative is always found either in past tense or in perfective aspect (Dixon 1995: 99). Recall that the present article does not base its account on such a strict correlation between the choice of Aux in a language and ergativity. What counts, as we have claimed from the beginning, is the correlation between past tense/perfective aspect and ergativity. We have claimed also that it is this correlation that bridges the two concepts of 'syntactic ergativity' (in the sense of Burzio and Perlmutter) and typological ergativity in the explanative scenario of the "aspect account".

6. Mahajan's thesis contested on empirical grounds

The present chapter intends to provide evidence that Mahajan's Aux-criterion is not consistent with the evidence from German and West Greenlandic. Furthermore, Mahajan's V-marginality generalization is compared with more general conclusions drawn in the typological literature. The conclusion will be that Burzio/Perlmutter's argument-based position on ergativity advocated by Mahajan cannot solve the problems encountered. Rather, as the ensuing chapter will argue, it is the aspect-based position that can take care of all the open questions.

6.1 The Aux-criterion

Departing from Kayne (1993), Hoekstra/Rooryck (1995), and Guéron (1995) developed the idea that HAVE results from the incorporation of a locative element into BE.[13] Mahajan (1994) also bases his account of split ergativity in Hindi on this idea. It is not without reservations, however, that one can accept Mahajan's (1994) typological account.

Note, first, that the Latin possessive construction displaying the HAVE-less type so typically, should be ergative; however, this is not so. Latin is as nominative/accusative as can be. Second, what is more, the correspondence with Latin (Kayne 1993; Guéron 1995) is ill-drawn since the Latin example does not exhibit the lexeme in Aux-status at all; rather, it is a full verb in the possessive construction. It remains unclear why Mahajan (1994) emphasizes the typological criterion in terms of the auxiliary status rather than the full verb status. Third, French, as other Romance languages, provides dubious evidence for Mahajan's assumption that the proverbal clitic blocks P-incorporation to yield HAVE; there is no P on the subject in the first place. Fourth, and perhaps foremost, there appear to exist crucial differences between the HAVE morphemes that depend on an important criterion which may be at the bottom of the distinction that Mahajan is after. Let us look into that. Note that under the approach chosen by Mahajan (1994), in order to align the fact that German (along with Dutch and Frisian) is SOV and clearly has HAVE as an Aux next to BE, one would be forced to assume an independent criterion enforcing the incorporation of the ergative P into BE. Note that this criterion cannot be the one employed for SVO-languages such as French and English. It appears, thus, that nothing is gained in terms of simplifying the typological account.

Furthermore, it is interesting to see, to say the least in the face of Mahajan's assumption, that an unquestionably ergative (as well as incorporating) language such as West Greenlandic does exhibit HAVE. See, first, examples from German which mimick the occurrences in West Greenlandic. Note that this HABEN is fundamentally different from the possessive HABEN. It is appropriate to call it 'ergative HABEN'. Accordingly, there is what one can call German 'ergative HABEN' side by side with possessive HABEN. See (26). [# for a clause which is out of the pregiven context, although not ungrammatical as an individual clause.][14]

ergative HABEN:
(26) a. *Es hat heute keine Milch bei uns*
it has today no milk with us
= Es gibt heute keine Milch bei uns
it gives today no milk with us
b. *Es hat hier jede Menge Schnee*
it has here every number of snow
= Es gibt hier jede Menge Schnee
it gives here every number of snow

THE ASPECT–CASE TYPOLOGY CORRELATION   161

    c. *Es hat heute alle/jede Milch bei uns
    = *Es gibt heute alle Milch bei uns

ergative HABEN – ambiguity with clause negation (based on (26a):

(26) d. (i) 'Es ist nicht so, daβ es bei uns Milch gibt'
       = It is not the case that we got milk
      (ii) 'Es ist da Milch, die es bei uns nicht gibt'
       = There is milk which is not to be had at our place

possessive, non-ergative HABEN:

(27) a. *Ich habe einen Schlüssel*
      I have a key
    ≠ Es gibt bei mir einen Schlüssel
      it gives with me a key
   b. *Ich habe jeden Schlüssel*
      I have each key
    ≠ Es gibt bei mir jeden Schlüssel
      it gives with me each key

cf. (26c) with (27b)

POSSESSIVE HABEN – non-ambiguity with clause negation ([#]means: contextually inadequate): cf. with (26d)

(28)   *Hans hat keinen Hund*
     Hans has no dog
    (i)   'Es ist nicht so, daβ Hans einen Hund hat'
    =   It is not the case that H. has a dog
    (ii) [#] 'Es gibt einen Hund, den Hans nicht hat'
    =   There is a dog which H. does not have

We conclude from this that there would be some 'ergative' HAVE to be distinguished from an unergative, 'possessive' HAVE — see the object status of the HAVE-subject in those cases where a paraphrase with an oblique object is possible as in (26a–d), as opposed to (27a, b)–(28). According to the typological survey on (split) ergativity provided by Trask (1979) we expect that only this ergative HAVE occurs in the ergative languages, not, however, the possessive HAVE pointing at the nominative/accusative typology. Exactly this, however, is exhibited by the following examples (van Geenhoven 1995) from West Greenlandic (Inuit). Recall, from the German examples above, that for incorporated object+negation the existential reading, as in (ii) above and below, is not available.

(29) a. *Nuka   qimmi-qa-nngi-l-a-q*
Nuka-ABS dog-have-NEG-INDIC-[−tr]-3SG
(HAVE+incorporated indefinite object *dog*: no existential reading under predicate negation)
   i. It is not the case that Nuka has a dog/dogs
   ii. # There is/are a dog/dogs that Nuka doesn't have
b. *Festi-mi   qallunaar-passua-qar-p-u-q*
party-LOC Danes-many-HAVE-INDIC-[−tr]-3SG
(HAVE+existential reading only in unnegated clauses)
'There were many Danes at the party'
(van Geenhoven 1995: 6)

See again (30a, b) where English exhibits exactly the same restriction, grammatically even stronger so than in Inuit. The English examples relate to the Inuit ones above.

(30) a. *John doesn't have a dog*
   i. It is not the case that John has a dog
       no existential reading under predicate negation
   ii. # There is a dog that John doesn't have
b. **John doesn't have every dog*
c. **There was every Dane at the party*
(van Geenhoven 1995: 6)

Incorporated indefinites lack non-narrow and partitive readings; non-incorporated indefinites get a specific and partitive reading. This is in line with findings by Enç (1991) and Abraham (1992, 1994) that specific readings are assigned to clausal constituents outside of VP, whereas non-specific ones are confined to VP.

All this means in the present context is that, first, the form of the article alone is not relevant for the syntactic restrictions (VP-insideness vs. VP-outsideness) exhibited across languages. Rather, there is an intricate, but systematic, interplay between (non-)specific reference and the linear position of elements; and, second and more prominently here, the Aux HAVE need not be inexistent in principle for ergative languages (as proposed by Trask 1979 as well as brought into an explanatory perspective by Mahajan 1994, who bases himself on Trask's typological survey). Rather, according to what the examples from both Inuit and German exhibit, there is what one can call an ERGATIVE HAVE, which is not to be accommodated in the framework unfolded by Mahajan since, quite obviously, Mahajan would have to posit two different mechanisms: one for unergative HAVE incorporating into BE, and another one which defies incorporation and thus surfaces as HAVE despite the ergativity features of the language in question.

Recall that the 'ergative' HAVE does not have the possessive denotation, which alone allows for the DATIVE+BE correspondence, which in turn is necessary for the P-incorporation mechanism. Quite aside from other arguments raised above, this alone appears to be reason enough to look for a different syntactic account and explanatory scenario.

6.2 *The criterion of V-marginality*

According to Trask (1979: 398 f.) it is still an unanswered question why the ergative/absolutive system should co-occur only with languages of the linear types VSO/SOV/VOS. This is where Mahajan takes up the thread. See (31) vs. (32) (from Mahajan 1994: 9 f., somewhat abbreviated: P stands for what can be a local preposition or an oblique case marker designating a similar locality; i.e. NP-P in the subject category below stands for either nominal postposition or for nominal case marking). This is what Mahajan's account in (31) tries to represent: P-incorporation takes place, in the sense of (22)–(23) and (25) above, only if the subject (*Jean*) and Aux (*a* 'has') are directly adjacent. The mechanics of P-incorporation to be yielding HAVE from BE takes place only under strict locality conditions (in somewhat non-structural terms: if 'S(-PoP)BE-O' holds, (-PoP)BE yields HAVE). No such PoP-incorporation takes place, however, if this locality condition (direct adjacency) is suspended by a pro-clitic, as in French ('S(-PoP)CL-V-O'). Here and elsewhere, the basic, underived position of the subject is taken to be VP-internal. The angled brackets, $\langle\rangle$, denote alternative surfacing: either *les$_i$ a cuites* or *a cuit les tomates$_i$*.

(31) for S(O)VO (V-medial):

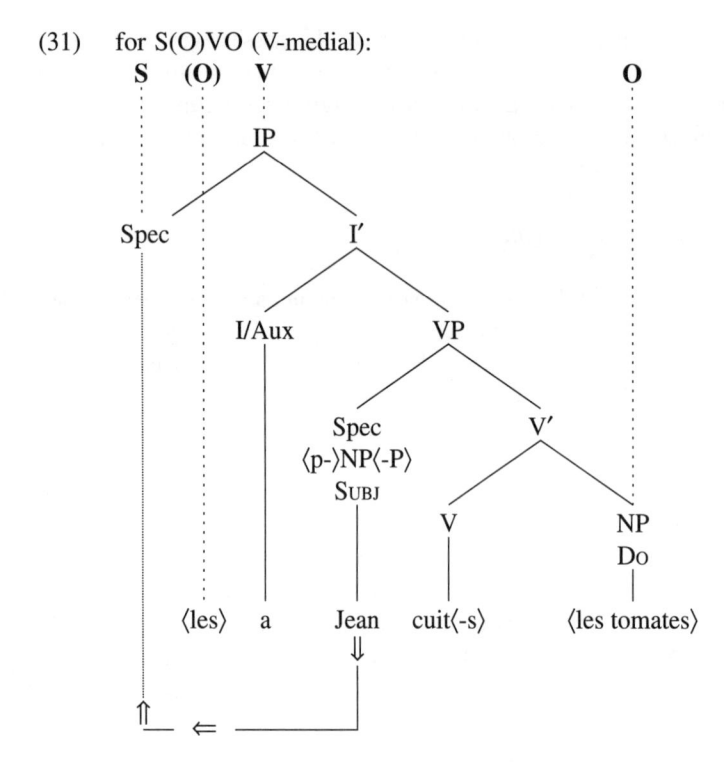

```
  S        (O)       V                                    O
                      IP
                    /    \
               Spec       I'
                         /  \
                      I/Aux  VP
                            /   \
                         Spec    V'
                      ⟨p-⟩NP⟨-P⟩ /  \
                         S_UBJ  V    NP
                                     Do
                         ⟨les⟩  a  Jean  cuit⟨-s⟩  ⟨les tomates⟩
                                     ⇓
       ⇑    ⇐
```

Now note that in Hindi, (32), Aux can govern the subject but will not be adjacent to it, since it is clause-final. If adjacency between Aux (not just any full finite predicate) and the subject case marker is a crucial condition for incorporation, then incorporation of Po(stposition /case marker) of the subject-NP into Aux is bound to fail (Mahajan 1994: 10). The Aux will then always surface as the copula BE, and the subject will surface with an oblique case, i.e. the ergative case in Hindi:

(32) for ⟨V⟩SO⟨V⟩ (generally V-marginal, here V-final):

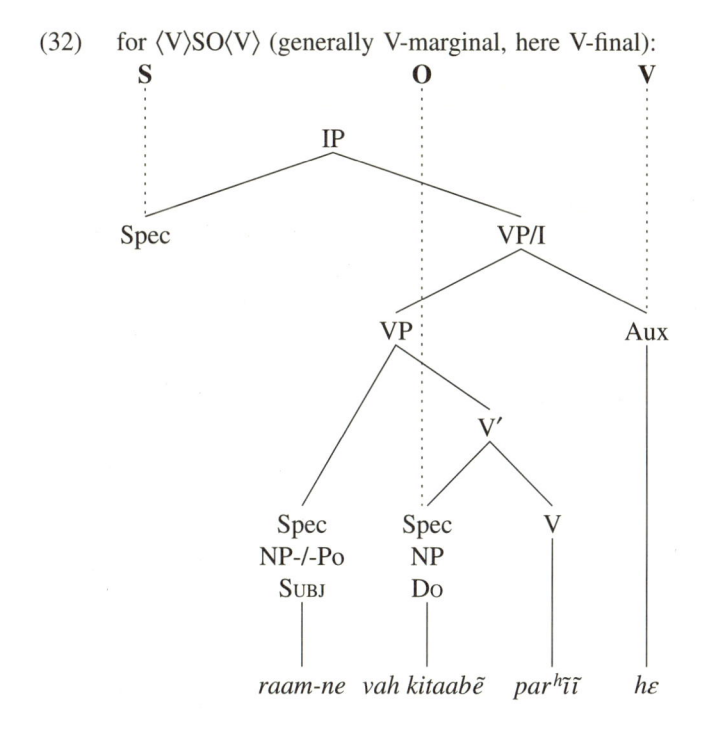

```
         S                    O                    V
         ┊                    ┊                    ┊
              IP              ┊                    ┊
          ╱      ╲            ┊                    ┊
       Spec      VP/I                              ┊
               ╱    ╲
              VP     Aux
            ╱   ╲
           ╱    V'
          ╱    ╱  ╲
        Spec  Spec  V
       NP-/-Po  NP
        SUBJ    DO
         │      │
         │      │
      raam-ne  vah kitaabẽ  parʰĩĩ   hɛ
```

(31) vs. (32) shows that, according to Mahajan, the difference between French and Hindi is to be derived from the underlying word order (SVO vs. SOV) and the adjacency criterion between Aux$_{fin}$ triggering P-incorporation into the Aux. This yields the auxiliary lexeme HAVE, as opposed to SOV languages where, in the absence of this trigger, this Aux surfaces as BE. This is the whole theory-based story, no doubt attractive in its simplicity, but too strong in the face of the empirical facts.

For whatever the descriptive merits of Mahajan's account, it is to be noted that there are in fact ergative languages which are not V-marginal (see Dixon (1995: 50–52), who counts at least five soundly ergative languages from all parts of the world not coinciding with the V-marginal requirement, Basque being one of them). This should be taken as a serious obstacle to Mahajan's account, just like the Aux-condition. See Section 6.1. above. Furthermore, it is of a highly speculative nature, at best, to derive support from the data in French, since no case incorporation — the crucial requirement to explain the occurrence and the derivation of *avoir* from *être*, despite the 'ergative-like' phenomenon of object agreement with V-preposed pronominal object clitics — is visible in any instance of French. Furthermore, it is the common opinion in typological work that there is a vast majority of BE-languages in the world. This being so, any strict correlation, and, consequently, any causal link between *be* and ergativity is on shaky ground.

There is one further problematic case. Mahajan's analysis does not relate to the empirical fact that HAVE appears to be missing in languages which display split ergativity only (Type B; Trask 1979: 398 f.). Since it is Type B, but not Type A (full ergativity, i.e. without a split between the ERG/ABS and NOM/ACC case paradigms), that correlates strongly with the aspectual (perfect(ive)) condition, Mahajan's theory would predict that both ergative types, A as well as B, were to surface with the Aux BE. However, this is counter to fact: type A ergativity does provide HAVE occasionally (Trask 1979: 398). Consequently, any explanatory scenario should build in, as an essential component of the triggering mechanism, the aspectual property such that Type A, which does not share the aspectual condition for ergativity, is excluded as a natural consequence. This is achieved under the 'aspect account' in the next section. Notice what the chain of argument would be: if, as we have claimed, there is a deep link between the resultative/statal passive and ergativity, to the extent that the perfect participle in periphrasis gives expression to this ergative marking, it may be concluded that this ergative arose in the following way. The synthetic, inflectional perfect was lost and replaced by the periphrastic construction based on the passive participle. The crucial point in this suppletion is this: while in the imperfect the intransitive subject and the transitive subject were marked in the same way with the direct object being different, in the periphrastic perfect the DO was marked in the same way as the intransitive subject, with the transitive subject marked by the instrumental inflection, in line with its marking function for the demoted subject in the passive. Notice that this is exactly the function the direct object (DO) obtains in the Small Clause construction: it takes the subject function of an intransitive (adjectival) predication. We shall come back to this in the following section.

7. The aspect-based account contesting the argument-based account

Chapters 1 and 2 have demonstrated that perfectivity, or telicity, plays a major role in explaining the alleged ergative character of phenomena, lexical as well as phrasal, in languages such as Continental West Germanic (German, Dutch, West Frisian, and Yiddish) as well as West Greenlandic. In the present chapter, other languages will be adduced to support the aspect-based approach to lexical 'ergativity'.

It is important to see that the linearity argument raised by Burzio (1986) and others (cf. den Besten 1985; Grewendorf 1989) is not directly related to the diagnostic status of the past participle as well as the auxiliary diagnostic of syntactic ergativity. Recall Burzio's observation in Italian: *ne* allows for ergative verbs in its syntactic domain, not, however, for truly intransitive ('unergative') verbs; see (6a,b) above. However, recall also that the diagnostics on transitive verbs showed that a second property is at play in such collocations, namely the quantifier-like behaviour of *ne*: it normally triggers a partitive reading on an indefinite NP in its scope — see (6c, d); however, the position of the object-NP, *il caso*, within VP (in close vicinity to the finite clausal predicate) excludes such readings. The sentence, (6c), is ungrammatical. This makes the illustrations inconclusive with respect to the decision whether argumental ergativity or a definiteness factor is at play. In SOV-languages, on the other hand, definite partitive readings, as a subset of specific readings, are possible only for NP-positions outside of VP (definites, or themas, go outside of VP, indefinites, or rhemas, are base-generated inside; cf. Abraham 1997). Since the subject-NPs of ergative verbs display the same type of sensitivity as direct objects with respect to a partitive reading, ergative subjects should be VP-internal subjects irrespective of the definiteness factor.

What then is the link between the VP-relative position and aspect displayed so unquestionably important in a wide number of ergative languages and, in particular, in split ergativity? Recall that what is ergative in the continental West Germanic languages, appears to be restricted to the perfective domain (perfect participle with the copula BE). Recall furthermore that the subject of the perfect participle predicate has the property of a direct object (TH or PAT). All sensitivity to specificity appears to be secondary to the property of perfectivity. However, none of this explains, in an obvious way, why and how aspect (perfectivity) comes into the play.

In what follows only the most crucial steps toward this systematic link are unfolded (for more detailed arguments see Abraham 1992; 1994). Consider what perfectivity amounts to in terms of event structure, as opposed to non-perfectivity, or durativity. The languages which demonstrate this most clearly are the continental West Germanic ones, German, Dutch, and Frisian, which are all languages with a rich derivative verbal paradigm (prefixed verbs changing not only the valency of the predicate verb, but also verbal gender and aspect). This is highly reminiscent of how Samoan, a Polynesian split ergative language language, classifies its verbs. According to Milner (1973: 552; see Trask 1979: 395), only those verbs are used with the accusative that go without a suffix; suffixed verbs, on the other hand, always go with the ergative. Moreover, it is the class of suffixed, ergative verbs that express the totality, or consequence, of the action rather than the action itself. Quite similarly, Catford (1976: 298), on referring to North Caucasian languages, relates ergativity to a "tight, penetrating, effective relation between the verbally expressed activity and its object." (Trask 1979: 396).[15] Milner also draws the comparison with the perfective in Slavic. This type of lexical ergativity, then, relates perfectly to perfectivity, just as German does. The following generalisations appear to be in place. (SMALL CAPS for main word accent)

(33) a. There is a class of verbal prefixes, and verbal particles, in the continental West Germanic languages which change the non-perfective meaning of a verbal simplex to a perfective one. This class is open and actively productive to the extent that it is enriched by adjectivals and those adverbials that designate states to be reached through some prior (approach) process. Among such adverbials are adverbial constituents (PPs) designating direction (without exception P+accusative in German, as well as in Latin and Ancient Greek). See the following groups of examples, where the first one is the one-place durative, whereas the second one represents the perfective (with the typical, obligatory EMPHASIS on the verbal prefix).

b. *schlafen* "sleep" — *EIN*+schlafen (VERBAL PREFIX) "fall asleep", *welken* "wilt" *WEG*+ *welken* (ADVERBIAL) "away-wilt", *laufen* "run" — *sich MÜDElaufen* (ADJECTIVAL PREFIX VERBAL AFFIXiod) "to run oneself tired", *(im Garten) laufen* "in-the-garden-run" — *in den GARTEN laufen* (DIRECTIONAL ADVERBIAL PP) "into-the-garden- -run".

For such perfectivization by means of lexical prefixation, see the productive prefixal paradigms in Modern Russian, among which *po-* or *na-* (Gawronska 1993 as well as Smith 1995):

(33) c. *Ona pro-stoja-l-a   na uglu   celyi   čas*
she PRO-stand-PAST-agr on corner-P entire-ACC hour-ACC
'She stood-PERF on the corner for an entire hour'
(Smith 1995)

(34) a. Any of these derived predicative perfectives are covered without exception by the participial and auxiliary diagnostics of ergatives (see Burzio 1986 for Italian; Haider 1985; Abraham 1985 for German; Haider/Rindler-Schjerve 1987 for the contrast

between Italian and German). Note that this is an empirical finding, which is in need of a structural account just as much as Burzio's generalisation. But the claim, according to these exceptionless observations, is that ergatives in the languages under inspection (languages with an actively productive derivative system producing perfective verbs) are perfectives. Note, further, that this is in line, in a fashion yet to be explained, with the equally general observation that in split ergative vernaculars, the ergative is bound to the perfect(ive) forms. See the following example from Hindi (Mahajan 1994: 6; the example repeats (9) above):

    b.   *raam-ne   vah   kitaabē   paṛʰīĩ*
       Ram-ERG-MASC those books-FEM-PL read-PREF-FEM-PL
       hɛ
       be-PRES-PL
       'Ram has read those books'   (Mahajan 1994: 6)

(35) a. Any of these perfectivized constructions can most adequately (i.e. rendering the semantic interpretation of an accomplishment or achievement semantics in the most direct fashion) be represented as predicatives (i.e. copular predicates + prefix/adjectival/adverbial) for the object in transitive two-place constructions or the subject in one-place constructions. See the small clause representations in (b)–(c) below. Note that such perfectivizing small clause constructions derived from transitives can be paraphrased systematically in accordance with the following pattern: subject-verbal event-SUCH THAT-[$_{sc}$ direct object = SC-subject COPULA+TENSE+AGREEMENT XP], where XP = {adjective, verbal prefix, verbal affixoid, NP, perfect participle (= adjective)}. Note, at the same time, that one-place ergatives such as *sterben/die*, representing the approach as well as the resultative phases in (36) below, do not take a statal predicate in the small clause. It has to remain open for the time being whether there are other one-place perfectives/ergatives that do in fact take such a small clause predicate. [t/riV = transitive or reflexive intransitive verb as in (35b) below; eV = ergative verb as in (35c)].

    b. θ$_1$ t/riV [θ$_2$ AgrP ADJ]
       [sie$_{θ_1}$ [$_{iV}$ tanzte [$_{sc}$ sich$_{θ_2}$ [$_{ADJ}$ müde]]]]
       she   danced   herself   worn out

c. θ_2 eV [t$_2$ AgrP]
   [sie$_{\theta_2}$ [$_{iV}$ starb ([$_{SC}$ t$_2$/*(sich$_{\theta_2}$) [$_{ADJ}$ zu Tode])]]]]
   she   died   herself   to death
   where θ necessarily = TH, and AgrP is restricted to states; θ_2 with iV = reflexive pronouns with subject coreference.
d. for eV: NP$_j$ [$_{VP}$ [$_{SC}$ t$_j$ AgrP] V]
e. for t/riV: NP$_i$ [$_{VP}$ [$_{SC}$ NP$_j$ AgrP X(P)] V]
   where NP$_j$ necessarily = TH; AgrP is restricted to states; NP$_j$ with iV = reflexive pronouns with subject coreference.[16]
f. Now note the bracketing below, which is fully in line with the predicative representation in (a, c, d) above (from Mahajan 1994: 6; my bracketing, W.A.):
   [$_{CP/IP}$ raam-ne   [$_{SC}$ vah kitaabẽ   pa$\mathrm{\underline{t}}^h$ĩĩ
   Ram-ERG-MASC   those books-FEM-PL read-PERF-FEM-PL
   hε]]
   be-PRES-PL

These are the corresponding features between (35a, d, e) and (35f) above: copular reading in the small clause (whether hidden or not) — see hε in Hindi; agreement not with the matrix subject, but with the object (= subject in the small clause) as well as the participial adjective and the BE-copula. Cf. the bracketing for French with identical structural identifications:

(35)   g.   [$_{CP/IP}$ Jean [$_{SC/AGRO}$ les$_i$ [$_{TP}$ a$_j$ [$_{VP}$ t$_i$ t$_j$ repeintes$_i$]]]][17]

Where no proclitic is present as in (35h) below, no such agreement features are exhibited:

(35)   h.   Jean a repeint-Ø les bouteilles

Note that the formal representation of the perfective predication in terms of a small clause (predicative, or secondary predication) has all the properties that the typological research has ascribed to ergatives: the copula as Aux; the adjectival participle; agreement with the small clause subject, which is not the surface subject; furthermore, what cannot be shown in detail here, a directional prepositional constituent + ACCUSATIVE incorporated in the matrix predicate appears decomposed in the small clause predication to yield a local-statal prepositional phrase + HIDDEN COPULA PREDICATION (cf. explicitly Abraham (1994) for German). The latter feature relates in a conspicuous way to the distinction between 'approach phase' and 'resultative state' explicitly referred to in the event denotation in (38a) below.

The following list of examples is to illustrate the wide-spread nature of small clause constructions in the diachrony of German (see in more detail Abraham 1996).

(36) a. *(Habet filia) arbores transplantatos*   Late Latin
has-3SG daughter trees-ACC-PL transplanted-ACC-PL
b. (Tho quad her thesa ratissa:)   Old High German
dicebat autem hanc similitudinem:
then   spoke he   this simile
phígboum habeta sum giflanzotan
                       (Tatian Γ 102,2, CII 23; Sievers 1960: 146)
arborem fici   habebat quidam plantatum
figtree-4SG-MASC had a   certain planted-4SG-MASC
in sinemo uuingarten
in vinea   sua
have-3PL tree-ACC planted-ACC in vineyard
c. *(habda them heriscipie   herta   gisterkid,) that sia habdon*
(had   they retainership heart-ACC reinforced) that they had
bithuungana   thiedo   ghuilica,...
superceded-4PL   peoples-2PL every-4PL,...
'they had reinforced the hearts of their retainers such that they superceded all peoples'
                      Old Saxon (Tatian 2,1–2,55–56) B/M 195866
d. *Sume sâr verlorane Uurdun sum erkorane*
some-1PL became forelorn-1PL become-3PL some selected-1PL
'some will be forelorn, some will be selected'
                                  Schumacher 1963: 57
OHG Ludwigslied XXXVI,13): B/E 1966 perfective (eV) verb
e. *... uuit   hebbiat unk   giduan mahtigna   god,*
we two have   us-two-3SG done   mighty-4SG-MASC god
uualdand uureðan. ...
master-4SG-MASC enraged-4SG-MASC with the direct object
Old Saxon (XLIV. Annex: B., from the Genesis, 24) B/E 1966
active past participle agreeing
f. *thes   ni   habda he êniga   geuuuruhte te thi,*
thereof not had   he anything done   to you
sundea gisuohta, thoh   thu ina nu   aslagan hebbias,
sin   sought, although you him now slain   have
dôdan giduanan.
dead made
                         Old Saxon, Genesis 46 ff.; from Doane)

g. *Thô geng im   thanan mid grimmo hugi,*
then went him-ETHIC thence with grim   mind
habda ina god selbo suîdo farsakanan.
had   him god self given up
                              Old Saxon (Genesis 80 f.; from Doane)

Returning to (35b–f), (37)–(38) spell out what is behind an aspectual reading of small clauses.

(37) The subject of the predicative construction (small clause, SC) is transferred to the subject position of the whole construction according to the EXTENDED PROJECTION PRINCIPLE (strong universal tendency to fill the subject position of any predication). See (35c, d).

Perfectives have the following event structure (see Abraham 1990, 1994).

(38) a. biphasic event structure for *einschlafen* 'fall asleep' (ergative verb and terminative): the event structure consists of two lexically inherent components, E_1 and Zu_2, carrying together the Aktionsart reading and, consequently, the lexical meaning. [t_1, t_m, t_n = temporal points on the event-constituting axis; E_1 = approach event component, Zu_2 (*Zustand* "state") = state phase resultating from E_1]. Read: *einschlafen* 'fall asleep' is characterized by the telic approach phase (>>>), whereas *eingeschlafen sein* 'fallen asleep' is the result of the aforegoing event component.

schlafen =
einschlafen   eingeschlafen (sein)
|>>>>>>>>|----------------------|
t_1 E_1 t_m Zu_2 t_n

b. monophasic event structure for *schlafen* 'sleep' (intransitive verb and interminative): the event structure is restricted to one single homogeneous, durative component, inherently not complex (≈≈≈≈≈). The graph below represents the temporal points of reference, t_1 and t_m, as well as the relative point of the speech act, t_s (relation of anteriority), thus a temporal relation, that for *schlafen* 'sleep' and that for *geschlafen haben* 'have slept'. Note that one does not have to distinguish two inherent event components as in (a), i.e. E_1 and Zu_2.

                    geschlafen
    schlafen   *(haben)*
    |≈≈≈≈≈≈≈≈≈|≈≈≈≈≈≈≈≈≈|
    t_1 t_m t_s

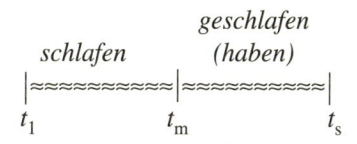

This concludes the general discussion about the continental West Germanic languages. Note that the generalisation to cover also non-derivative languages such as Hindi, Urdu, and Balochi etc. is based on the structural similarity displayed in (35e, f) above. The overall conclusion is drawn that derivative ergativity such as in German and non-derivative ergativity such as in the Indo-Iranian languages exemplified here permits an identical account based on the aspectual condition of perfectivity.

It is to be noted that German appears to provide a linear argument in support of Mahajan's assumption that only V-marginal languages (VSO, VOS, SOV) can be ergative. Notice the two readings of the periphrastic perfect in German, which gets disambiguated, in the sense of the perfective adjectival, only in co-occurrence with a strict V-last in the V-complex. The order is optional otherwise.

(39) a. *daß die Mutter Juden hatte versteckt*
          that mother   jews   had   hidden
          (i) 'that mother had hidden jews'
               event reading only
          (ii) *'that mother had jews hidden'
               no object predicate reading
      b. *daß die Mutter Juden versteckt hatte*
          that mother   jews hidden   had
          (i) 'that mother had hidden jews'
               event reading
          (ii) 'that mother had jews hidden'
               also object predicate reading

From among the linear options it is only the one with the perfect participle next to the object -NP, (396), that permits the small clause, object-predicative reading.

Recall, however, that we have abstained from concluding, in the face of Dixon (1995), that there is a forceful, general systematicity behind that. In fact, our perfective account does not require such a V-margin requirement for an overall account such as Mahajan's which rests crucially on the adjacency condition for the finite predicate (Aux) and the object (= small clause subject). Recall the discussion about the derivation of HAVE from BE (allegedly already in the spirit of Benveniste).

8. Conclusions

8.1 Perlmutter's and Burzio's Generalisations revisited

It has been demonstrated that the relation between the type of θ-role ergativity, or unaccusativity (in Perlmutter's and Burzio's sense)[18] and perfectivity (Abraham 1996a, b, c), hinges crucially on the following criteria.

(40) Ergative/unaccusative verbs, categorially X^0, are a subclass of phenomena displaying identical ergative properties both below the zero projection, X^{-1}, and above, XP. Whatever the common solution to a description, the multilevel character of this phenomenon has to be involved.

(41) Due to ergative phenomena on the level of XP as well as to the apparent and unexplained asymmetry with 'ergative' transitives, the thematic solution proposed by Burzio cannot be correct. Rather, as we suggested, the perfective properties are accounted for by the small clause syntax (object predication) both for one-place (ergatives) and two-place perfectives.

(42) Both the θ-role restriction and the condition that the subject of ergative verbs displays distributional properties of a structural, internal argument are epiphenomena in relation to the aspectual account, both semantically and syntactically.

(43) There are two seemingly contradictory properties to be accounted for under one single explanation:
(i) the pivot, or focal, status of the object as opposed to the non-pivotal status of the subject in ergative languages; this has lead to the conclusion that ergativity is a phenomenon closely akin to the passive.
(ii) Both the order and c-command relation between subject and object and binding relations for the assignment of reflexive pronominals are identical in either accusative and ergative languages.

No doubt, the small clause solution takes care of all these criteria: the perfectivity semantics is plausibly reflected; likewise, the focal, pivotal status of the internal argument as well as the subject criterion safeguarding the binding requirements are singularly motivated by the small clause syntax; the focal phenomenon is further supported by the fact that the small clause predicate is always the stress-focussed component of the derived predicate. Beyond doubt also, the event semantics is best reflected by the resultative syntax of the small clause description. Notice, furthermore, that the typical small clause order is naturally reflected by the distribution in (39) above.

Now, recall Perlmutter's 'Unaccusative Hypothesis', which says this: there is a universal class of intransitive verbs whose lexically designated subjects exhibit properties of a direct object (Perlmutter 1978). However, following Kayne (1995) and Chomsky (1995), there are no non-branching nodes any more. See what comes of the assumptions made in Comsky (1981) concerning the distinction of iVs and eVs in (44a, b) and in the new templates in (45)–(46).

(44) a. one-place iV: NP [V]
subject = external argument

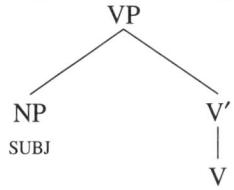

```
      VP
     /  \
   NP    V'
  SUBJ   |
         V
```

b. one-place eV: _ [V NP]
subject = internal argument
(raised following EPP)

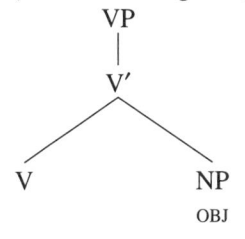

```
   VP
   |
   V'
  /  \
 V    NP
      OBJ
```

If, according to Chomsky (1994: 11), one is to avoid non-branching projections, this excludes either representation in (44). While Perlmutter's observation is not affected empirically, it is not clear how it should be accounted for in a simple constituent structure. Chomsky's own solution to this problem is to assume that unergative (un-unaccusative) verbs are in fact transitive; in other words, the V' in the structure tree for iV in (46) is branching, despite the absence of an overt internal argument (see already Hale/Keyser 1994, who argue for DO-incorporation into the verb). See (45).

(45) iV with DO-incorporation:

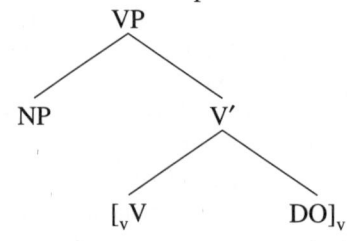

```
        VP
       /  \
      NP   V'
          /  \
        [vV   DO]v
```

It remains unclear, under this proposal, what the underlying structure of eV should be. If we accept Vanden Wyngaerd's account for perfective past participles and perfectivizing verbal prefixes, such an ergative structure should have the form in (46) (according to Vanden Wyngaerd 1996).

(46) eV (underlying):

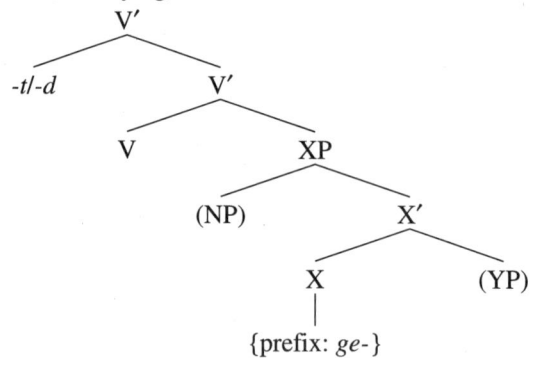

```
           V'
          /  \
        -t/-d  V'
              /  \
             V    XP
                 /  \
              (NP)   X'
                    /  \
                   X    (YP)
                   |
              {prefix: ge-}
```

{pref} stands for *ge-*, characteristic of the past participle in German, Dutch, and West Frisian as well as of perfectivizing (ergativizing) verbal prefixes (both separable and inseparable in German). The prefix will be raised to adjunction positions to the left of, and higher than, V, in two cycles: one to prejoin to V, and a second one to prejoin to the participial suffix, *-t/-d* (German and Dutch/West Frisian, respectively). Notice that, under this assumption, the items classified under {pref} are inflectional, not derivational. This is made plausible by the traditional linguistic wisdom that the modern participle is verbal rather than adjectival.

There is, to be sure, ample evidence, from diverse languages, that, indeed, there is such a phenomenon as a single internal argument surfacing as a subject. The question to be asked here is whether it is true that, for all languages with a syntactic characteristic as in (44b), this scenario carries over to our conclusion, i.e. that 'ergative' constructions in this sense are to be considered as (i) perfectives (of both X^0- and XP-status; think of the directional XP-constituents in the three Continental West Germanic languages such as sketched in (4)–(5c) above) and (ii), consequently, are to be seen as small clause constructions.[19] In other words, to the extent that the Perlmutter-'ergativity' ('unaccusativity') is displayed by virtue of the distributional properties in (4)–(5a–c), Perlmutter's claim needs to be revised in the following way.

(47) Perlmutter's 'Unaccusativity Hypothesis' revisited: Syntactic unaccusatives are perfectives; consequently, their syntactic form is that of a small clause (in the sense of (35a–g)).

Note that Perlmutter's term 'external argument' with distributional properties of a direct (internal) object needs to be translated, according to the revisited formulation, as 'subject of the small clause'. Note, further, that, ECM applies for the small clause subject in more-than-one-place cases and that the SC-subject raises to the position of the matrix subject in the case of a one-place predicate, in accordance with the EPP. See (35b, c) above.

To the extent that the small clause structure replaces the internal object component in Burzio's generalization, the latter is in need of reformulation, too. Let us repeat Burzio's claims.

(48) a. "A verb which lacks an external argument fails to assign accusative case." (Burzio 1986: 178 f.).
      b. "A verb which fails to assign accusative case fails to θ-mark an external argument." (Burzio 1986: 184).

Note, first, that the generalization in (48a) is not confirmed by languages such as Latin and German. Both languages display accusatives without any external arguments. In German, such verbs are frequently used, although not frequent in type (Seefranz 1995). Furthermore, beyond any doubt, (48b) is, prima facie, very problematic, too. There are intransitive verbs with a θ-marked external argument, but no accusative. Recall, however, the option to treat them as transitives.

Discounting all this for the time being, it is not immediately clear that, indeed, Burzio's generalization, as represented in (48a, b), is identical to Perlmutter's hypothesis. In fact, it has nothing to do with it unless one of the following components is added to identify the two generalizations. Witness (49a, b).[20]

(49) a. revised: A verb which lacks an external argument fails to assign structural accusative case.

b. revised: A verb which fails to assign structural accusative case fails to θ-mark its external argument.

(49a) appears to be able to account for the range of subjectless accusative-governors in German (see Seefranz 1995), none of which can be passivized and which, therefore, should be said not to govern a structural accusative. On the other hand, (49b) cannot be made any better by the revision in order to accommodate truly intransitive, one-place predicates with a θ-marked external argument — unless we consider, much in the sense of Hale/Keyser (1993) and Chomsky (1994), admitting only intransitives with a cryptic accusative object which is incorporated in the course of lexicalization. It is quite possible that Burzio thought of the revised forms when formulating (48a, b). Recall that lexical incorporation of a surfacing one-place verb (with a θ-marked external argument) should be considered as a predicate that is saturated, on the basis of some pre-lexical mechanism, in the sense of the 'absolute' verb as opposed to its two-place homonym (think of verbs such as *cook, drink, eat, see, hear, feel* etc., all of which can be used as two-place verbs and as 'absolute' one-placers). The component that changes in the absolute version is that the θ-property of the DO is implied in an existentially quantified sense. Thereby, total defocussing of this DO ensues. I will not go into this any further at this place.[21]

Another revision of Burzio's assumptions is contained in (50).

(50) revision of (49a): A verb which lacks an external AGENT argument fails to assign *structural* accusative case.

The reason for assuming (50) is the fact, among others, that in German the accusative of the internal argument is structural (passivizable) only if the external argument bears the θ-relation of AGENT (and is not structural on the basis of distributional criteria, for example, if the external argument is EXPERIENCER). Notice that agentivity, and nothing else, is the triggering feature for passivization in German (Abraham 1995: Chpts. 1 and 12). We shall come back to this diagnostic property presently.

It has been argued in this paper that syntactic unaccusativity or 'ergativity' is of the type that was called 'perfective ergativity'. Only unless Burzio's two generalizations pertain to this type of 'perfective ergativity' as they no doubt do only under extension in the sense of either (46) or (47), then, clearly, (50) has a meaningful overlap with this concept of ergativity. Recall that Burzio's claim in (48) cannot accommodate anything crucial about full typological ergativity (Dixon 1995), nor does my account of split ergativity in the present paper, for that matter. How do the revised assumptions fare under the perfectivity account?

It would seem that the replication of (50) does indeed bear on this question. AGENT can never be internal argument in a single clause structure. Thus, a structural internal argument (object) can never be an AGENT. This is directly derivable from the status of small clause subjects: since they are predicated of statal (resultative) predicates (adjectivals, nominals) their θ-status has to be that of a THEME. The fact, thus, that internal arguments cannot have the thematic properties of external arguments is directly derivable from the perfectivity account of unaccusatives presented here as well as the fact that small clause predicates are never 'durative' statals. Rather, what they have in common as adjectivals as well as nominals is their resultativity as a statal. Recall the pattern in (35b, c).

Finally, for whatever fate Vanden Wyngaerd's (1996) account will eventually have, his story carries over easily to the perfectivity account presented here. Notice that the XP dominated by V' and sister to V may stand for the small clause, with the {*ge*-prefix} as head of the constituent. This is in line with our resultative small clause account as sketched in (35b, c).

8.2 *The V-marginal account defended and refuted: scrambling in _SO_ and the* THEMA-RHEMA *distinction*

The present systematizing proposal with respect to ergativity and a theory-based account of Burzio's generalization departs from the same assumptions as those held by Mahajan (1994), i.e. the claim that only V-marginal languages (SOV, VSO) can exhibit ergativity. But it differs from Mahajan to the extent that the criterial property of ergativity is claimed to lie in the fact that the matrix predicate is subcategorized for small clauses, which themselves map the perfective properties of the participle and its subject (either the surface object in [SpecAgrO] or the only subject of the construction, which later raises from the small clause to the [SpecAgrS] of the higher categorial node). This mechanism, it is claimed, is possible only as long as there is linear and structural variance between the finite predicate component of the entire clause and the subject. In short, the aspectual solution hinges on the suggestion that there has to be a structural 'middle field' (a term introduced by the German grammatical tradition; see Abraham 1995: Ch.3) between VP (with the subject and the objects inside VP) and subject/objects outside of VP. Unless this type of structural middle field is present, scrambling between verbal arguments cannot shift an element outside of VP. Unless an NP-argument can change position across the VP-border (i.e. between what Heim 1982 has distinguished as the 'nuclear scope'and the 'restrictive clause', or what has been identified to distinguish thematic from rhematic material; see Abraham 1992, 1995) yielding distinct object and subject readings depending upon VP-internality or VP-externality, one will not get syntactic ergatives and, by the same token, small clause predicates. Only small clause predicates yield a resultative semantics expressed in terms of copular readings, agreement, and adjectival participles. This is not feasable in SVO-structures. Note, however, that this line of argument, though based upon V-marginality (Mahajan's term), is not forced to consider the question of which Aux is assigned, which would be undesirable on empirical grounds (ergative HAVE in ergative languages) anyway. Consider also that in order to make Mahajan's account work for fully ergative languages as well, one would have to derive that the Aux HAVE is missing. This is an assumption, however, which appears to be empirically unfounded, to the best of our knowledge about the data. On the other hand, the aspect account fully covers the distinction between split and undivided ergativity to the extent that only in the first type, but not in the latter, perfect and perfectivity play the structurally distinguishing role.

Needless to say this article has nothing to say about languages with full ergativity (in the typological sense). Vice versa, all this paper dealt with was the type of language displaying split ergatvity conditioned by tense/aspect. We have drawn the conclusion that, if a language has lexical expression means for perfectivity (or terminativity or boundedness), then it may display the type of 'syntactic ergativity' that Perlmutter and Burzio deal with in purely syntactic and distributional terms. This article also argues that it does indeed make sense to merge, and treat alike, the two concepts of ergativity under the following two conditions: if the language under inspection has a means to distinguish verbal perfectivity paradigmatically and productively, and if it keeps perfectivity and non-perfectivity lexically (as through the Aux-distinction between HAVE and BE) or syntactically distinct. German and Dutch are such languages, whereas English is not.

8.3 *Passives and ergatives*

Unaccusatives have traditionally held to be very similar to passives. What is the difference between the ergative and the passive? What are the characteristics that are alike? If we want to go along with a description of the two types of ergativity and an equivalence between ergativity and perfectivity, the Perlmutter-Burzio type and the typological one (including split ergativity and its triggering conditions), we are bound to elucidate the true relation. What, for example, does the restriction tell us about Russian where the ellipsis of the direct object is possible only under the control of the imperfect, but never of the perfect aspect? See (51a, b) below (Kotin 1993: 88; see (51d, e)) where the perfective marker is the prefix *pro-*. The grammatical distribution is not dependent upon any temporal marking.

Modern Russian
(51) a. *čital (knigu)*
        read-PAST-IMPERF a/the book
     b. *čitayet   (knigu)*
        reads-PRES-IMPERF a/the book
     c. *pročital   *(knigu)*
        has read-PAST-PERF a/the book (completely)
     d. *On spokojno   spal   (vsju noč)*
        he slept-IMPERF deeply through the whole night
     e. *On spokojno   prospal *(vsju noč)*
        he slept-IMPERF deeply   throughout the whole night

German would render (51e) differently from (51d). Notice that the verbal particle *durch-* "through" perfectivizes the imperfective verbum simplex, *schlafen* "sleep". Recall that we pointed out this strongly productive and paradigmatically well-established characteristic of German; see (51d). [PREF =verbal prefix]

German
(51) d. *Er ist (die ganze Nacht) gegangen*
        he AUX   the whole night   gone
        'He walked (the whole night)'
     e. *Er ist *(die ganze Akte) durchgegangen*
        he AUX   the whole file   through-gone
        'He went through the whole file'
     f. *Er mordet (Hilflose)*
        he murders helpless
        'He murders helpless ones'
     g. *Er ermordet   *(Hilflose)*
        he PREF-murders helpless

Lezgian (Haspelmath 1991)
(52) a. *Zamira-di get'e   xa-na*
        Zamira-ERG pot-ABS break-AOR
        'Zamira broke the pot'
     b. *Get'e   xa-na*
        pot-ABS break-AOR
        'The pot broke'

Quite clearly, (51a–c) are not identical structurally with the subsequent (51d–g), to the extent that the latter provide an adverbial accusative (of duration) rather than true direct objects. Yet, there is a common property, namely the duration-delimiting, or telic, accusative. This delimiting accusative is dispensible in Russian only with the imperfective, not the perfective predicate regardless of tense.

Consider again our original tenet with respect to the fundamental syntactic nature of perfectives (cf. above (35)–(38)). We have established beyond doubt that perfectives are to be taken syntactically as embedded small clauses (object predications, or secondary predicatives). In this configuration, the Russian perfective prefix *pro-* will be the secondary (small clause) predicate. Its argument needs to be the object, unless the verb is a one-place perfective (in which case the only subject argument will serve as a small clause argument, too, and will be subject to subsequent raising to serve as derived subject, due to the EPP). Perfectives as in (51c, e) therefore need an object to provide the internal external subject. Imperfectives, on the other hand, do not take small clause objects. Their object is dispensible for syntactic reasons, other than that of perfectives where the prefix-predicate (small clause predicate) is in need of an external subject. This is behind the distribution in (51), and as such it provides a nice support for the perfective syntax hypothesis introduced above.

The Lezgian examples in (52a,b) are somewhat different, of course. But they show that, while the non-pivot DO is elliptically dispensable in the typologically accusative Russian and German, the (ergative-derived) DO-ABS in Lezgian is not, since it is the syntactic pivot. Thus, quite expectedly, the non-pivot ERG-subject can be eliminated without violating the grammaticality and interpretability of the Lezgian clause (Haspelmath 1991: 8).

It is interesting to note that accusative and ergative languages present a certain symmetry with respect to the verbal derivative morphology and the pivoting clausal part. While accusative/non-perfective languages such as English merge intransitive and transitive forms in one single verbal morpheme (*cut, move, break, render*, also called 'labile' verbs in the literature; cf. Haspelmath 1991: 13 ff.), the ergative Lezgian does so with deleting the ergative subject (in a way 'antitransitivizing') where, clearly English would have to use a passive form on the verbal predicate. We can thus consider a typological criterion by which languages are distinguished on the distribution of dispensability under ellipsis (see, for a typological attempt, Abraham 1996c,d).

8.4 *Tense/aspect and binding*

What remains as an open question are the conditions of split ergativity which are outside of perfectivity (person split). Recall Section 4 above. Is there any link to the type of explanation on the split under perfectivity conditions? Or do we deal, in this instance, with completely unrelated phenomena? Notice that Dixon (1994) does not relate these phenomena in any way.

One of the ways to think of tense is in terms of pronominality (though metaphorical and relating to binding theory, this comparison dates back, as far as I can see, to Partee 1973; see also Hornstein 1990 and Guéron 1993). Now, if this is to make sense one should assume two points of time, the reference point and the speaker's time point. Any Past tense, then, would refer to some anaphoric time relation, i.e. looking back to some antecedent. Future tense, in this perspective, would be a cataphoric time relation, i.e. looking forward to some reference point to come in relation to the speaker's reference time. And the present would be non-pronominal since no pronominal relation would be established between the reference time and the speaker's time. The relation between the two reference points on the time scale are can be seen to mimick binding, subject to Principle B of the Binding theory, i.e. like true pronouns (relation to some occurrence in the previous text, thus as highly thematic, but without any syntactic local binding, or coreference, property as holds for reflexives). See the following graph sketching these relations.

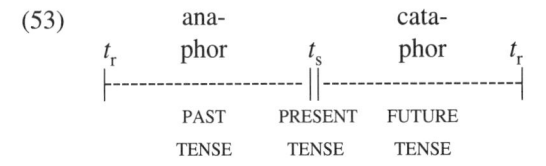

(53)   ana-   cata-
   t_r phor t_s phor t_r
   |--------------------||--------------------|
        PAST   PRESENT   FUTURE
        TENSE   TENSE   TENSE

Now, assume that *past*, as opposed to *present* and *future*, establishes true anaphoric relations on the basis of Principle B ('unbound within the syntactic local domain, i.e. unbound by the subject within the minimal clausal domain created by this subject'). Then, what would be the tense relation correlative to the reflexive, for which Principle A holds ('coreference with the subject in the minimal syntactic domain'). Think of the relation established in (38a). The best candidate, beyond all tense differences mentioned above, is the bi-phasic relation holding for perfectives. This is so because the relation of coreference holds within the minimal domain of the lexical meaning of the verb, or the verbal stem plus the affixoid, or the prepositional constituent in the accusative of direction plus the movement verb. Recall the examples about lexical as well as syntactic unaccusatives in German in (4)–(5a–c) above. This truly close, or reflexive, relation is established in terms of the bi-implication between the two phases holding for perfectives, or resultatives: the approach phase always implies the result to be achieved, and, vice versa, the result state presupposes the aforegoing phase leading to it. There is some intuitive plausibility to holding that a perfective, then, is subject to local binding in terms of Principle A. But what is the subject to which we need to make the local clausal binding domain applicable, needed for the relation of coreference under Principle A? Notice that invoking a coreference relation with some object would not do, since for intransitives we cannot refer to an object. To invoke a binding-A relation for one-place unaccusatives, or perfectives, we need the local domain of a subject, unless there is reason to go beyond the domain of the subject-predicate domain. But there is no such reason. Now, the only way to determine a subject domain for the predicate is by appealing to a small clause construction embedded under the stem of the main verb and with the prefix, the affixoidal adjective, or the prepositional constituent of directional movement predicates as secondary predicates. The embedded small clause, then, is the local domain for binding under A-conditions, i.e. between the embedded secondary predicate and the small clause subject.[22]

Notice that this pronominal-reflexive link in syntactic terms is supported by two old observations. First, as regards the pronominal nature" of the past tense category, both the 'past pronoun' and the 'perfective reflexive' are highly thematic (in the discourse-functional sense of the Prague School; thus, as much as 'given'). This is borne out by the syntactic constraints for the only landing sites of weak pronominals and their clitic correspondents: outside of the '(existential) nuclear sentence' (or 'nuclear scope', to use Heim's 1982 term) on the right edge of CP, or the section restricted to anaphoric material (the restrictive portion of the clause, in Heim's terms). Weak pronouns and their clitic forms can never occur within VP, whatever the underlying word order (SVO or SOV). This clarifies the truly discourse-thematic nature of weak pronouns. Second, the observed discourse thematicity is in line with the equally old observation that perfectivity is enhanced, or created, by definite object-NPs. They are presupposed, or given, on the basis of their categorially inherent thematicity as going with definite articles, and they are perfective in that they invoke the whole of the event as a completed result. Results, thus, are always more thematic; and past events, by their very past nature, are closer to such completed events. In other words: if pronominals are discourse themata, then past and perfect can be seen as being thematic, too. If, on the other hand, the perfective is thematic, then results and resultatives are thematic also.

What we have done so far is relating pronominal and reflexive binding to discourse-functional relations, on the one hand, and to tense and aspect relations, on the other hand. At this point, a caveat is in place, however. Pasts and perfect(ive)s need not denote completed events (cf. Dixon 1994: 97, Figure 4.6., where he addresses exactly this phenomenon). All that appears to depend on is whether you look at the event as a semantic unit or in its relation to the time scale. If the latter, temporal rather than aspectual, view is expounded pasts will not correlate with, or trigger, perfectives or unaccusatives, or absolutives. This may be the typological situation of unsplit ergative languages.

What all this yields is the following. Aspectual perfectives and, likewise, aktionsart terminatives, can be seen as discourse-thematically associated. This may be achieved in several ways, which display no direct correlation at first sight:

(50) (i) in terms of their aspectual property, i.e. the biphasic event relation;
 (ii) the category-inherent specificity of the definite article; and
 (iii) the even higher specificity, and discourse thematicity, of the first and second persons vs. the third person.

See our (18)–(20) above, where we were still speculating about the true nature of an underlying, common denominator for the split triggered by person deixis and specificity of the nominals involved.

Now note what all this permits one to conclude with respect to the concept of unaccusativity, or "ergativity" (in the sense of Perlmutter, Anderson, Halliday, Burzio, Pesetsky, Grewendorf, Belletti and others in the generative syntactic tradition). If indeed, this syntactically explained concept of unaccusativity can be reduced to the all-and-more encompassing concept of perfectivity then this is: (i) a syntactic concept only to the extent that perfectivity is. I have argued that indeed all perfectivity is to be accounted for in terms of secondary predication, or the predicative, or small clause embedding as displayed in detail in (35a, b). Note that the simpler generalization and explanation on the basis of case theory as under (5b, c) not only is a subconcept under the account in (35). What is more, it is wrong given the impossibility to relate, and make symmetrical, the representation of unaccusatives/ergatives as one-place perfectives (with the lexical grid '_[internal θ-role V]' (_[θ$_i$ _]) and true unergatives as one-place non-perfectives (with the lexical grid 'external θ-role[_V]' (θ$_e$[_]), on the one hand, and non-perfective transitives/two place predicates (with a corresponding external argument), on the other hand. Consider what we called the 'Burzio-Perlmutter paradox' in connection with (12) above. After all, this would require to bring on a par the clause type "external θ-role [internal θ-role V]" ('θ$_e$[θ$_i$_]) and the perfective correspondent (which would have to "demote" its internal argument to some lower case position, parallel to the object-like subject of unaccusatives). This is not imaginable, however. Recall (9) above. Thus, what remains is to conceptualize perfectives in terms of biphasics, with the result that its semantics is mapped onto an embedded small clause. The latter yields the subjecthood of its only argument required by the resultative, or stative-adjectival, predicate type.

This leaves us with little, if anything, to be added for Perlmutter's Unaccusative Hypothesis and Burzio's Generalization. The German unaccusative facts have to be subsumed totally under the perfective account anyway. What might remain are the observations with respect to *ne* in Italian (cf. (6a–d) above). But we have extended these observations to include facts from West Greenlandic as well as from German to show that, while they appear to concern VP-internal subjects and non-specific, predicate-incorporated objects in rhematic discourse function, nothing convincing carries over to ergative properties of the case or syntactic ergativity facts observed in truly ergative languages. The *ne*-phenomena, to all appearances, are cases which are to be kept separate from the distributive ergative scenario and which probably have to do with grammatical generalizations of a totally different denomination (non-specificity; VP-internality; discourse-functional rhematicity). It appears, then, that, on the one hand, what is called unaccusativity or ergativity in Perlmutter's and Burzio's sense is but an epiphenomenon within a much more pervasive perfective scenario. While perfectivity covers the grammatical nucleus of this phenomenon, together with its small clause construction, other triggers such as discourse thematicity and pronominality are less central, but, eventually, must also be accounted for in syntactic terms. As for the distribution of *ne*, we speculated and made amenable on the basis of parallels in West-Greenlandic and German, that discourse functional accounts play a role.

It has been pointed out repeatedly (among others by Anderson 1976) that languages can develop in either direction: from ergativity to accusativity and conversely. In either case perfectivity plays a crucial role: either as a property taking on a stronger triggering role for grammatical properties, or losing this conditioning force. If ergativity follows it cannot be predicted which of the observed conditions (discourse thematicity by way of pronominal person, by VP-internality, or by aspectual definiteness) it will propagate. But the accompanying distributional facts, notwithstanding that they resemble ergative properties, are to be subsumed under the larger denominator of aspectual perfectivity.

Notice that it would be attractive to infer from the observed data in German that the modern stage is a weak reflex of an Indoeuropean ergative stage (as has often been claimed, though without much convincing evidence). Now, if perfectivity is the fundamental property from which the epiphenomenon of ergativity follows, then it would appear that to conclude from the observed distributional data that such an Indoeuropean ergative stage existed (cf. Rumsey 1987) has become a little more than pure speculation. Our observations about German and other modern Indo-European languages allow one also to study from close and on-line the mechanisms that have always been claimed for non-

European languages: namely the links between the perfect/perfectivity and ergativity as well as the diachronic changes between nominative-accusative languages to ergative ones and perhaps even backwards.

Acknowledgments

This paper has been presented to various audiences in Leiden, Vienna, Klagenfurt, Vancouver, Madison, Berkeley, Dublin, and Oslo. It has gained from personal communications with Jan Witok (Vienna), Martin Prinzhorn (Vienna), Carlota Smith (Austin), Rolf Mehlig (Kiel), Vladimir Klimonow (Berlin), Theodora Bynon (London), Elly van Gelderen (Arizona State University), Harry Bracken (Arizona State University), Mickey Noonan (Milwaukee), Alice Davison (Iowa City) and respective academic audiences in general. I would like to thank all persons involved, notably also the editor of the present issue, Eric Reuland, for valuable constructive criticism and his insistence to make the paper more readable.

Notes

1. Given the relationships between perfect, past perfective, and past, one would also expect to find correlations between past perfective and passive-ergative, between past and passive-ergative. Notice that this generalization can be true only for predicates effecting the object referent (i.e. with resultative object predications, not with non-resultative transitives), which is exactly the case for perfective aspect or terminative aktionsart.

2. Dixon appears to endorse Pullum (1988: 585) who has called this "a truly crackbrained piece of terminological revisionism".

3. Van Geenhoven's observations are reminiscent of Egede's conclusions some 230 years ago (Egede 1760 on Eskimo) echoed many times later, although they do not fully cover the facts (Kalmár 1979: 122 f.). Egede sees the definite direct object realized in the unmarked nominative, whereas the indefinite direct object is in the marked *mik*-case and can only appear in the antipassive. Kalmár (1979: 123) emphasizes that Egede's identification does not cover all empirical facts to the extent that definiteness subsumes two contextual categories: specificity and givenness. Note that van Geenhoven carefully distinguishes properties of specificity to the extent that she observes data with quantifiers and not only article lexemes.

4. VP-internal subjects can be accounted for on discourse-functional grounds. They are invariably indefinite and, thus, rhematic. See Heim 1981 for supporting arguments and evidence.

5. It should be noticed, in this context, that according to ergative typologists, there is a deep link between passive and ergative (Dixon 1994: 189 f.) to the extent that both passives, perfect(ive)s and ergatives share one semantic property: namely that they both tend to focus on the state which the referent of the underlying object NP is in, as a result of some action. See also Anderson (1977: 366); Comrie (1976: 85 f.); Hopper/Thompson (1980: 271); Shibatani 1984.

6. The term 'formal' account of ergativity, as contrasted here with 'pragmatic' account, is purely nomenclature. However, as I have been made aware, it may be an issue of confusion. I do not claim that a good pragmatic approach to any linguistic description can do without formal representation — quite on the contrary (albeit in contrast to many a pragmatic description and

the intention of its author). All that is meant in the present paper by 'formal' is a syntax-theoretic account of ergativity, much in Burzio's, Marantz', and Mahajan's sense, among others.

7. Although, as I have argued elsewhere (Abraham 1995), this is not crucial in that the Aktionsart property of telicity fully carries over, in event-logical terms, to the notion prevalent in the Slavic tradition of grammar writing, including, as it were, telicitation by means of adverbials, i.e. means other than verbal prefixation.

8. In case there are readers who feel that it necessary to fill in a position modestatis auctoris at this point, here is one: German appears to be a very dull language with respect to the temporal paradigm to the extent that it has no aorist-imperfect distinction, nor has it a clear distinction between the preterite and the perfect, let alone a distinctive future tense. See Dahl 1995 and Thieroff 1996.

9. Recall the distribution of cases in ergative systems, ABS(OLUTIVE) is often formally equivalent with NOM(INATIVE)):

    in ergative case systems:
    two-place verbs: ERG-ABS
    one-place verbs: ABS
    in non-ergative case systems:
    two-place verbs: NOM-ACC
    one-place verbs: NOM

10. For a more detailed discussion as to what aspectual conditions can mean in syntactic representation terms see Abraham 1996.

11. This is made plausible also by the fact that clitic pronominals, by contrast to their full nominal counterparts, cannot occur in situ within VP. Note that pronominal clitics are highly thematic, often to the extent that they can be dropped completely (pro drop).

12. Trask (1979: 399 f.): "Finally, the correlation with SOV word order is again the most difficult problem, and here I have no satisfactory explanation."

13. Hoekstra/Rooryck (1995), in particular, identify the BE-element as an element which imposes an anaphoric condition on the complement of HAVE referred to as SE (reminiscent of the reflexive in Romance). This is to make BE a detransitivized derivate of HAVE and to refer to the relation between the ergative and the passive, or medium (SE), as opposed to the unergative/active.

14. The GIVE-paraphrase is not a reliable diagnostic test fo ergativity; see (i), which, for obvious reasons, has a non-possessive meaning.

    (i) a. Er hat es kalt   'Ihm ist kalt' (*...hat...)
            he has it cold   him is cold (*... has ...)
        b. Er hat es schwer damit   'Es ist ihm dabei schwer' (*...hat...)
            he has it difficult therewith   it is him on this difficult (*... has ...)

15. Note, incidentally, that this is not compatible with, albeit not in outright contradiction, either what Hopper/Thompson (1980) have suggested for the gradient property of the transitive accusative, as long as they remain silent on the interconnection between transitive accusativity, ergativity, or such connected properties as specificity and VP-internality.

16. I am aware of the unaccomplished precise description of directional perfectivizing constituents such as *der in den Garten (hinein) gelaufene [Gärtner]* "the-into-the-garden-run-gardener", which should yield the paraphrase "der Gärtner lief, bis/so daβ er in dem Garten war" ('the gardener ran until he was in the garden'). Since the small clause predication is always statal the directional *accusative* in German has to give way to the statal *dative*. Notice that this case shift

is always accompanied by a shift in the deictic verbal prefix. Thus, *in den Garten (hinein-)* will eventually become *im Garten (drinnen)* in the statal small clause predication — something which cannot be accounted for by a simple morphological shift.

17. This is reminiscent of Sportiche (1995: 302 ff.). The rationale behind the distinction with (35g) above is that the past partciple with object-agreement needs to be under government both by *avoir* and the pronominal in pro-clitic position.

18. Cf. Perlmutter 1976; Burzio 1981/1986; Belletti 1988; den Besten 1986; Marantz 1984, 1991; Pesetsky 1982 among others.

19. Under the present concept, there holds a bi-implicative relation between perfectivity and small clause syntax — one that is supported by the semantic event-related account of perfectivity; cf. (38a, b). This is not the view customarily expounded in modern syntax, notably among 'ergativists'. In my view, it is not only a methodological virtue, but a methodological necessity that syntactic solutions are coupled with unambiguous semantic representations.

20. The extensions discussed below may have been assumed all along. This is not the issue, though. Under these assumptions, German and Spanish have often been quoted as problematic (see, e.g., Reuland 1985). The position developed here is that German, at least, does not behave exceptional under the aspect account to cover the ergativity phenomena. It would not be surprising if Spanish, a notable aspect language, were to provide an identical solution. Notice that this position embraces the one-way implication that the aspect account embodies the wider solution and that Burzio's Generalization is a sub-phenomenon of this aspectual account. See also the inceptive abstract to this paper.

21. It is only a short step from the above to investigate the question whether there are (possibly more-than-one-place) 'ergative verbs' with an incorporated internal argument such that this structural argument does not surface at all, and what would, if indeed it does, exclude such verbs on universal grounds.

22. E. Reuland warns me, at this point, that the comparison of temporal reference and binding relations may be a lot more complex than alluded to in this section. No doubt, the discussion at this point suffers from a touch of superficiality and metaphoricity. What I meant to have to point out, though, was the ease with which the aspectual scenario can be captured, no doubt in purely metaphorical terms, by binding relational concepts. Notice that the discussion above is in the spirit of others (among which Partee 1971) and has been conducted in order to relate ergative triggers in the typological spirit other than tense and aspect (see Chapters 3 and 4 above) to the present discussion

References

Abraham, W. 1978. "Epilogue: Valence and case. Remarks on their contribution to the identification of grammatical relations". In *Valence, semantic case, and grammatical relations*, W. Abraham (ed.), 695–729. Amsterdam: John Benjamins.

Abraham, W. 1985. "Transitivitätskorrelate und ihre formale Einbindung in die Grammatik". *Groninger Arbeiten zur germanistischen Linguistik (GAGL)* 28: 1–72.

Abraham, W. 1987. "Burzio meets Wulfila. Zu den distributionellen Eigenschaften von *wairðan*, 'werden' und *wisan* 'sein' im gotischen Passiv". *Groningen Papers in Theoretical and Applied Linguistics — TTT* 9.

Abraham, W. 1990. "A note on the aspect-syntax interface". In *Progress in Linguistics,* M. Mascarò and M. Nespor (eds) 1–12. Dordrecht: Reidel.
Abraham, W. 1992a. "The emergence of the periphrastic passive in Gothic". *Leuvense Bijdragen* 81: 1–15.
Abraham, W. 1992. "Clausal focus vs. discourse rhema in German: A programmatic view". In *Language and Cognition 2,* D. Gilbers and S. Looyenga (eds), 1–18. (Yearbook of the Research Group for Linguistic Theory and Knowledge Representation of the University of Groningen).
Abraham, W. 1994. "Ergativa sind Terminativa". *Zeitschrift für Sprachwissenschaft* 12(2): 157–184.
Abraham, W. 1995. *Deutsche Syntax im Sprachenvergleich. Grundlegung einer typologischen Syntax des Deutschen.* Tübingen: Narr.
Abraham, W. 1996. "The interaction between aspect, case, and definiteness in the history of German". In *Parameters of morphosyntactic change,* A. van Kemenade and N.Vincent (eds), 29–61. Cambridge: CUP.
Abraham, W. 1997. "The base structure of the German clause under discourse functional weight: Contentful functional categories versus derivative ones". In *German: Syntactic problems — problematic syntax* [Linguistische Arbeiten 374], W. Abraham and E. van Gelderen (eds), 11–42. Tübingen: Niemeyer.
Abraham, W. 1999. "Die angebliche Passivbedeutung des Perfektpartizips im Deutschen: Argument-Hypothese und Aspekt-Hypothese". *Groninger Arbeiten zur germanistischen Linguistik* 42.
Abraham, W. and Klimonov, V. 1999. "Typologisch-kontrastive Miszellen: Perfektivität ubiquiter Ergativität nusquam." In *Deutsch kontrastiv-typologisch,* H. Wegener (ed.), 1–32. Tübingen: Stauffenburg.
Ackema, P. and Schoorlemmer, M. 1994. "The middle construction and the syntax-semantics interface" . *Lingua* 93, 59–90.
Anderson, John M. 1968. "Ergative and nominative in English". *Journal of Linguistics* 4: 1–32.
Anderson, Stephen R. 1976. "On the notion of subject in ergative languages". In *Subject and topic,* C. Li (ed.). New York: Academic Press.
Anderson, S. 1977. "On mechanisms by which languages become ergative". In *Mechanisms of Syntactic Change,* Charles Li (ed.), 317–363. Austin: University of Texas Press.
Baker, M.C., Johnson, K. and Roberts, I. 1989. "Passive arguments raised". *Linguistic Inquiry* 20(1): 219–251.
Belletti, A. 1988. "The case of unaccusatives". *Linguistic Inquiry* 19(1): 1–34.
Besten, H. den. 1986. "Some remarks on the ergative hypothesis". In *Erklärende Syntax des Deutschen,* W. Abraham (ed.) 53–74. Tübingen: Narr.
Bittner, M. and Hale, K. 1996a. "The structural determination of case agreement". *Linguistic Inquiry* 27(1): 1–68.
Bittner, M. and Hale, K. 1996b. "Ergativity: Towards a theory of a heterogeneous class". *Linguistic Inquiry* 27(4): 531–604.

Burzio, L. 1986. *Italian Syntax. A government-binding approach*. Dordrecht: Kluwer.
Butt, M. 1993. The Structure of Complex Predicates in Urdu. PhD Dissertation, Stanford University.
Butt, M. and Holloway King, T. 1995. Optionality in 'free' word order languages. Ms., Univ. Tübingen. (Paper GGS-meeting in Jena, 26th May, 1995).
Catford, J.C. 1976. "Ergativity in Caucasian languages". *NELS* 6: 37–48.
Chomsky, N. 1981. *Lectures on Government and Binding*. Dordrecht: Reidel.
Chomsky, N. 1994. "Bare phrase structure". *MIT Occasional Papers in Linguistics 5:* 1–48.
Chomsky, N. 1995. *The Minimalist Program*. Cambridge, MA: MIT Press.
Comrie, B. 1976. Review of Klimov (1973). *Lingua* 39: 252–260.
Comrie, B. 1981. "Aspect and voice: Some reflections on perfect and passive". In *Tense and aspect*, P.J. Tedeschi and A. Zaenen (eds), 65–78. New York: Academic Press.
Dahl, Ö. 1996. 'Das Tempussystem des Deutschen im typologischen Vergleich". In *Deutsch — typologisch*, E. Lang and G. Zifonun (eds), 359–368. Berlin: De Gruyter. (Institut für deutsche Sprache. Jahrbuch 1995).
DeLancey, S. 1980. An interpretation of split ergativity and related patterns. IULC Publication, Indiana University.
Dixon, R.M.W. 1995. *Ergativity* [Cambridge Studies in Linguistics 69]. Cambridge: CUP.
Dryer, M. 1997. "On the six-way word order typology". *Studies in Language* 21(1): 69–104.
Egede, P. 1760. *Grammatica Groenlandica Danica-Latina*. Copenhagen: Gottmann.
Enç, M. 1991. "The semantics of specificity". *Linguistic Inquiry* 22: 1–25.
Farrell, P. 1995. "The structure of Balochi". In *Ergativity*, Th. Bynon et al. (eds). In *Subject, voice, and ergativity. Selected essays*, D.C. Bennett, Th. Bynon, and B.G. Hewitt (eds), 218–243. London: SOAS.
Gawronska, B. 1993. *An MT-oriented Model of Aspect and Article Semantics* [Traveaux de l'institut de linguistique de Lund, 28]. Lund: University Press.
Geenhoven, V. van. 1995. "Semantic incorporation: A uniform semantics for West Greenlandic noun incorporation and West Germanic bare plural configurations". *Proceedings of the 31st Meeting of the Chicago Linguistics Society*. University of Chicago.
Grewendorf, G. 1989. *Ergativity in German*. Dordrecht: Foris.
Guéron, J. 1993. "Sur la syntaxe du temps". *Langue Française* 100: 102–124.
Guéron, J. 1995. "On *have* and *be*". Paper Univ. of Paris, Nanterre (read at Groningen, April 26, 1995; hand-out).
Haider, H. 1985. "Über *sein* oder nicht *sein*: Zur Grammatik des Pronomens *sich*". In *Erklärende Syntax des Deutschen*, W. Abraham (ed.) 223–254. Tübingen: Narr.
Haider, H. and Rindler-Schjerve, R. 1987. "The parameter of auxiliary selection: Italian-German contrasts". *Linguistics* 25: 1029–1055.
Hale, K. and Keyser, S.J. 1993. "On argument structure and the lexical expression of syntactic relations". In *The view from Building 20*, Hale, K. and S.J. Keyser (eds), 53–109. Cambridge, MA: MIT Press.

Halliday, M. A. K. 1967. "Notes on transitivity and theme in English, part 1". *Journal of Linguistics* 3: 37–81.
Haspelmath, M. 1991. "On the question of deep ergativity: The evidence from Lezgian". *Papiere zur Linguistik* 44/45, Heft 1/2: 5–26.
Heim, I. 1982. The Semantics of Definite and Indefinite Noun Phrases. PhD Dissertation, University of Massachusetts, Amherst.
Hoekstra, T. and Rooryck, J. 1995. "Dynamic and stative *HAVE*". Paper Leiden (read at the 10th Comparative Germanic Workshop at the University of Brussels, 17–19 January, 1995).
Hopper, P. and Thompson, S. 1980. "Transitivity in grammar and discourse". *Language* 56: 251–299.
Hornstein, N. 1990. *As time goes by*. Cambridge, MA: MIT Press.
Kachru, Y. and Pandharpande, R. 1979. "On ergativity in selected South Asian languages". *South Asian Language Analysis* 1: 193–209.
Kalmár, I. 1979. "The antipassive and grammatical relations in Eskimo". In F. Plank (ed.) 1979, 117–143.
Kayne, R. 1993. "Toward a modular theory of auxiliary selection". *Studia Linguistica* 47: 3–31.
Keyser, J. and Roeper, T. 1984. On the middle and ergative constructions in English". *Linguistic Inquiry* 15:381–416
Klimov, G. A. 1973. *Očerk obščej teorii ergativnosti*. Moscow: Nauka.
Kotin, M. 1993. "Zum Ursprung der deutschen Passivperiphrasen". *Wort* 1993: 80–91.
Laka, I. 1993. "Unergatives that assign ergative, unaccusatives that assign accusative". In *MIT Working Papers in Linguistics* 18, J. Bobaljik and C. Phillips (eds), 149–162.
Mahajan, A. 1990. The A/A-bar Distinction and Movement Theory. PhD Dissertation, MIT.
Mahajan, A. 1994. "Universal Grammar and the typology of ergative languages". Paper UCLA (read at the FAS-meeting Berlin, November 1994).
Mahajan, A. 1997. "Universal Grammar and the typology of ergative languages". In *Studies on Universal Grammar and Typological Variation* [Linguistik Aktuell/ Linguistics Today 13], A. Alexiadou and T. A. Hall (eds), 35–57. Amsterdam: John Benjamins.
Marantz, Alec 1984. *On the Nature of Grammatical Relations* [Linguistic Inquiry Monographs 10]. Cambridge, MA: MIT Press.
Marantz, A. 1991. "Case and licensing". *Proceedings of ESCOL* 91. [reprinted in this volume].
Milner, G. B. 1973. "It is aspect (not voice), which is marked in Samoan". *Oceanic Linguistics* 12: 621–639.
Partee, B. 1971. "Some structural analogies between tenses and pronouns in English". *Journal of Philosophy* 70: 601–609.
Perlmutter, P. 1976. "Impersonal passives and the unaccusative hypothesis". *Publications of the Berkeley Linguistic Society* IV: 157–189.
Pesetsky, D. 1982. Paths and categories. PhD Dissertation, MIT.

Plank, F. (ed.). 1979. *Ergativity. Towards a theory of grammatical relations.* New York: Academic Press.
Pullum, G. K. 1988. "Topic ... comment: Citation etiquette beyond thunderdom." *Natural Language and Linguistic Theory* 6: 579–588.
Reuland, E. 1985. "Representation at the level of logical form and the definiteness effect". In *Grammatical Representation,* J. Guéron, H. G. Obenauer and J. Y. Pollock (eds), 327–362. Dordrecht: Foris.
Rumsey, M. 1987. "Was Proto-Indoeuropean an ergative language?" *Journal of Indo-European Studies* 15: 19–37.
Seefranz-Montag, A. 1995. "Impersonalien". In *Syntax. Ein internationales Handbuch zeitgenössischer Forschung* Volume 2., J. Jacobs, A. von Stechow, W. Sternefeld and Th. Vennemann (eds), 1277–1287. Berlin: W. de Gruyter.
Shibatani, Masayoshi 1985. "Passives and related constructions: a prototype analysis.' *Language* 61: 821–848.
Silverstein, Mark 1976. "Hierarchy of features and ergativity." In *Grammatical categories in Australian languages,* R. M. W. Dixon (ed.), 112–117. Canberra: Australian Institute of Aboriginal Studies.
Smith, Carlota S. 1995. Aspectual viewpoint and situation type: the two-component theory. Paper LSA Leiden, January 1995 (handout).
Spencer, Andrew 1995. "The ergative parameter." In *Subject, voice, and ergativity. Selected essays,* D. C. Bennett, Th. Bynon, and B. G. Hewitt (eds), 244–262. School of Oriental and African Studies, University of London.
Sportiche, Dominique 1995. "French predicate clitics and clause structure." In *Small Clauses* [Syntax and Semantics 28], A. Cardinaletti and M. T. Guasti (eds), 287–315. San Diego etc.: Academic Press.
Tieroff, Rolf 1996. "Das Tempus-Aspekt-Modus-system des Deutschen aus typologischer Sicht." Rolig-paper 58, 23.
Trask, Robert L. 1979. "On the origins of ergativity." In *Ergativity: toward a theory of grammatical relations,* F. Planck (ed.), 385–404. London: Academic Press.
Vanden Wyngaerd, Guido 1996. "Participles and bare argument structure." In *Minimal ideas. Syntactic studies in the minimalist framework* [Linguistik Aktuell/Linguistics Today 12], W. Abraham et al. (eds), 283–304. Amsterdam: John Benjamins.

Anatomy of a Generalization

Luigi Burzio
Johns Hopkins University

Abstract

'Burzio's Generalization' (BG) is argued to result from the fact that, in unaccusative-type structures, the 'Extended' Projection Principle imposes one more grammatical relation, and hence one more Case, than there are θ-roles. This will violate the requirement that θ-roles and Cases be associated one-to-one, unless one Case is suppressed — object Case being the one suppressed in Nominative-Accusative languages. With the object Case suppressed, the subject Case will then link with the object directly, assuming Case assignment falls under Relativized Minimality. Movement and expletive constructions are on the proposed analysis similarly local because they are both constrained to the domain of a single Case under Relativized Minimality. The syntactic mechanisms that give rise to BG are argued to be the same as those that exclude 'Quirky' subjects, hence accounting for the fact that Icelandic, that has quirky subjects, indeed violates BG. The overall analysis relies crucially on violable constraints, giving indirect evidence for the 'optimality theoretic' character of syntactic organization.

1. Introduction

Work of the LGB (Chomsky 1981) era drew the conclusion that A-movement, such as that of passive, raising, and unaccusative structures, was driven by Case requirements, the dictum 'Movement is to get Case' gaining universal acceptance. Much of Chomsky's (1993, 1995) 'Minimalist Program for Linguistic Theory,' (MPLT) rests on the correctness of that conclusion. If movement is 'to get Case' -the implicit reasoning goes- then at least some Cases are gotten by movement, and conceptual parsimony may then suggest that all of them are, whence the MPLT hypothesis that all Cases, at least the 'structural' ones, are assigned by an inflectional head 'Agr' to its Spec, to which the relevant argument has moved in the course of the syntactic derivation.

In this article, I argue there was never any basis to the assumption that A-movement was 'to get Case'. The reason is that, in order to understand movement as the need for Case, one must first understand why that need exists, specifically why in passive, raising, unaccusative structures, the argument affected by movement does not just get the object Case that it would get in the corresponding active, ECM, and transitive structures, respectively. What one finds in that connection is a statement that it does not, commonly referred to as 'Burzio's generalization' (BG), which says that if a verb does not assign θ-role to the subject, then it does not assign Accusative Case to the object, as in (1).

(1) **BG**: No subject θ-role ⇒ no Accusative Case

The reason why the account of movement to subject as the need for Case fails is that it presupposes BG (1), which, however, is not a principle of grammar. Rather, (1) is essentially a restatement of movement in so far as it refers to the two positions: subject, object, that movement implicates. Since lack of subject θ-role (absence of a subject argument) is obviously what makes it possible for an object to move to subject, BG (1) is restatable as in (2a), while the Move-to-get-Case hypothesis is restatable as in (2b).

(2) a. **BG**: If an object can move to subject, then there is no object Case.
b. **Move-to-get-Case hypothesis**: If there is no object Case, then the object must move to subject.

The conjunction of the two conditionals in (2) is purely tautological. It has the form 'if the object can move to subject, then the object must move to subject'. Now, the 'must' in the second conjunct is actually incorrect, since the movable object does not always move, as in Italian *Arrivo io* 'arrive I', English *There arrived a man*, etc. The 'must' thus needs to be revised to 'can', and then (2a, b) become, indeed, fully tautological. In sum, the Move-to-get-Case hypothesis presupposes BG, but the latter is uninterpretable except as a recapitulation of movement, which will reduce the latter hypothesis to the unenlightening statement that if movement is possible, then it is.

In what follows I will argue that BG, along with a corresponding generalization for Ergative languages noted in Marantz (1991, this volume) is in a sense a reflex (rather than the cause) of movement possibilities, which is why it is statable as in (1)/(2a). Specifically, I argue that when movement connects two different grammatical relations (GRs) — specifically, subject and object, then one of the corresponding Cases needs to be suppressed to avoid assigning two Cases to a single θ-role (violating the 'Visibility' hypothesis on Case). In turn, I will take movement to be essentially driven by the need to fill the subject position, a result of the Extended Projection Principle (EPP). From this perspective, there will be no reason to suppose that objects of transitive verbs also move (to Spec of AgrO), since there appears to be no object counterpart to the EPP. There will also not be adequate reason for postulating that subjects of non-unaccusative verbs come from a VP internal position.

Taking thus a rather different approach than in MPLT, I will claim that Cases basically reflect GRs, the relations that verbs or other heads hold to their arguments. While there are instances in which such fixed mapping does not hold, such as the Nominative objects of various constructions and the Accusative subjects of ECM constructions, I will argue that those are to be dealt with in terms of further principles or constraints of higher rank, in the framework of Prince and Smolensky's (1993) 'Optimality Theory', and the relevantly similar one of Burzio (1994).

The theory of Case I propose is in some respects less parsimonious than the one of MPLT, in that it does not reduce all (structural) Case assignment to Spec–Head relations, but it achieves alternative reductions, in subsuming the locality of A-movement under natural principles of Case assignment, as I will show. In addition, it will also makes sense of the structural/inherent Case distinction, formerly stipulated.

The discussion will proceed as follows. In Section 2 next, I review the basic empirical problems posed by the distribution of Case, along with some recent attempts to deal with them. In Section 3, I outline the proposed approach and give some of the arguments for it, while in Section 4 I show that it successfully deals with expletive constructions, without the problematic LF movement of Chomsky (1993). In Section 5 I give an analysis of ECM and other clausal arguments from the proposed perspective, and in Section 6 I show how, with all the pieces now in place, BG reduces to effects of the EPP. Section 7 addresses the phenomenon of 'Quirky' subjects in Icelandic, and argues that it is consistent with and supports the proposed conception, via one single peculiarity of that language. Section 8 concludes.

2. Cases versus Grammatical Relations

A naive conception of Case would claim that Cases are simply a reflection of Grammatical Relations (GRs), Nominative being the Case of the subject,

Accusative that of the direct object, other Cases representing indirect objects of various sorts. The notion of GR raises no particular problem in this connection, since it is independently needed to map those aspects of lexical meaning usually referred to as θ-roles into syntactic representation. The standard wisdom here is that agents map into subject, patients into direct objects, goals into (some type of) indirect objects, etc., that basic view having many different refinements (see, in particular, Levin and Rappaport 1995). However, if GRs are defined for purposes of the lexicon-syntax interface, then, that definition will presumably be available for Case purposes as well. In fact, given the θ-role-to-GR mapping just mentioned, one might consider a stronger version of the naive view, holding that Cases directly reflect θ-roles. The latter may well seem incorrect, for reasons I come to next, but it is correct at least to some extent, as it corresponds essentially to the definition of 'inherent' Case, i.e. the type of Case that is indeed supposedly linked to θ-roles. It seems incorrect for cases like (3b), however, compared with (3a).

(3) a. She fired **me**
    b. **I** was fired

In (3b), Nominative *I* bears the same θ-role as Accusative *me* of (3a), breaking the Case to θ-role correspondence. The standard response to this has been to suppose that, alongside of 'inherent' Case, which is θ-role based, there exists 'structural' Case, which is based solely on structural position, (3a, b) instantiating the latter. While we may thus want to abandon the stronger version of the naive view in the light of (3), the weaker version still seems tenable, so long as one takes the surface rather than the underlying GRs to be what counts for Case in (3). Other structures, however, make trouble even for the weaker version, such as those in (4).

(4) a. *Sarò   licenziato **io***   (Italian)
        will be fired   I
    b. *There comes **a man***
    c. *Henni   voru sýndir **bílarnir***   (Icelandic)
        her-DAT were shown the cars-NOM

The NPs in boldface in (4) are Nominative. For the one in (4b), the Nominative Case is inferred from the fact that it triggers verb agreement, like the ones in (4a) and (4c). Yet those NPs are plainly not in subject position. As has been argued in the literature, they in fact appear to be in direct object position, despite the subject Case. The dative of (4c), arguably in subject position as we see below, also represents a 'misalignment' between Cases and GRs. Further misalignments are also systematically found in Ergative languages, where subjects can receive the same Case as direct objects, as in (5), from Marantz (1991, glosses adapted).

(5) a. *raam-ne roṭii khaayii thii* (Hindi)
Ram-ERG bread-ABS eat be
'Ram has eaten bread'
b. *siita aayii*
Sita-ABS arrived/came

Such facts have led linguists to suppose that, while there is an algorithm for mapping Cases into GRs, the algorithm is not the one-to-one mapping of the naive view, but a more complex one. One notable attempt in this connection is the 'Case in Tiers' (CT) approach of Yip et al. (1987), who proposed that Cases and GRs are organized as in (6).

(6) a. **Case tier**: Nominative Accusative ...
b. **GR tier**: Subject Direct Object ...

The relevant algorithm here would be one that simply drew association lines between the tiers, normally linking Nominative with subject, Accusative with direct object, and so forth. The cases of (4) above would be dealt with in terms of the subject not being available for such association, hence letting the Nominative automatically link with the direct object — the next available GR, as desired. Yip et al. argue that the non-availability of the subject in (4c) is due to the presence of 'lexical' Case, a notion similar to that of 'inherent' Case, and presumed to be assigned independently of the tier system. As for the subjects of (4a, b), while they are not discussed in that work, one can easily imagine attributing their non-availability to their non-argumental status. The facts of Ergative languages illustrated in (5) would be accounted for as well, in that system, by supposing that in those languages associations proceed from the right rather than the left, so that 'Absolutive', just another name for Accusative in this and other analyses, would connect with a direct object if there is one, as in (5a), but with a subject otherwise, as in (5b).

The general approach to Case proposed in Chomsky's (1993) MPLT bears considerable similarity to the CT approach, and can be illustrated as in (7), intentionally reminiscent of (6).

(7)   Nominative... Accusative... [$_{VP}$ Subject... Object...]

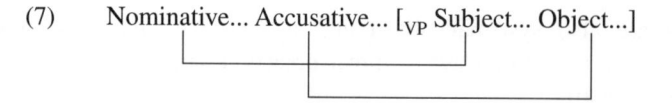

In (7), linear order stands for C-command in a syntactic tree, Nominative/ Accusative stand for MPLT's SpecAgrS/SpecAgrO, positions in which these Cases are respectively taken to be assigned, and Subject/Object stand for the respective initial positions of these two arguments, both within the VP. The main difference from CT is that the association lines in (7) are not drawn by principles of tier association, but rather by an especially crafted theory of A-movement, which enables the subject to reach the farther position and the object the nearer one, excluding other choices. In this system, the Nominative objects of (4) above, aside from the one of Icelandic (4c) which is not discussed, are handled by supposing that they move to SpecAgrS (the 'Nominative' of (7)) at LF, where they adjoin to the expletive element (null in Italian), and where their Case is 'checked', so that there is never any need to use the SpecAgrO in these structures. Ergative languages would in this system be those that utilize object rather than subject Case first, hence consistently using object Case (AgrO) with single-argument verbs, much as in the CT system.

In contrast to this general type of approach, I will propose that the naive conception, which associates Cases directly with GRs one-to-one is substantially correct, and that the instances in which that basic association falters, like those in (4) and (5b), are due to the operation of another associational mechanism which is able to override the first, as we see in the next section.

3. Where Grammatical Relations meet the θ-roles

I will propose in fact that, in a sense, both versions of the naive view are correct, that is that Cases are constrained to reflect both θ-roles and GRs. In certain structures, such as those of (3b), (4) and (5b) above, the existence of the 'Extended Projection Principle' (EPP), stated in (8) below, will induce a misalignment between θ-roles and GRs, with Case thus having to choose which association, with a θ-role or a GR, to maintain, and which one to forego.

(8)   *The Extended Projection Principle* (EPP): A clause must have a subject GR.

Concerning the association of Cases with θ-roles, it appears that an 'Equal Opportunity' version of it is at work, one that imposes that each and every Case must be associated with one single θ-role, though not necessarily a specific one. This is the 'Visibility hypothesis' of Aoun (1979), Chomsky (1981, 1986) and other work, which I will adopt here. A more discriminating constraint imposing specific associations is also at work, however, and this will yield the so called 'inherent' Cases (Goal= Dative; Possessor = Genitive; etc.), but I put that aside for the time being. I thus postulate the two constraints in (9), ranked in that order, Case-uniqueness of θ-role (9a) being the present term for the 'Visibility hypothesis'.

(9) a. *Case uniqueness of θ-role* (UNI C-θ): There is exactly one Case for each θ-role and exactly one θ-role for each Case.
 b. *GR consistency of Case* (CONS GR-C): There is one specific Case for each specific GR and vice-versa.

The general intuition behind this approach is that the grammar is fundamentally constrained by invariance of surface patterns (as I argue for morpho-phonology in Burzio 1996, 1998, 1999, to appear). Thus, the EPP (8) is consistent presence of the subject GR, while the constraints in (9) express consistency of certain associations. Variation arises from competition between different patterns of invariance. Abstracting away here from certain apparent or potential difficulties for (9b), such as double-object constructions and various Case syncretisms one finds across languages, we consider that the two constraints in (9) are in conflict in exactly the class of cases in which there is no subject θ-role. In those cases, because of the undominated EPP (8) that imposes a subject GR, there will be one more GR than there are θ-roles, with (9a) and (9b) thus demanding different outcomes, as in the typical unaccusative structure in (10).

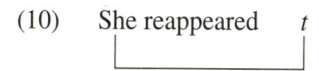

(10) She reappeared *t*
 |_____|

In (10), GR-consistency (9b) would impose object Case on the trace and subject Case on the moved NP. Those two positions, however, share a single θ-role and are thus prevented by the higher ranked (9a) from bearing two cases, so that one Case will need to be suppressed. The choice of which Case is suppressed appears to make the distinction between Nominative-Accusative (N-A) and Ergative languages. I express this by supposing that GR-consistency (9b) stands for a family of constraints, with each GR yielding one member. The difference between the two groups of languages will then come from the different rankings in (11).

(11) a. *Nominative-Accusative languages*:
 CONS GR-C$_{SUBJECT}$ >> CONS GR-C$_{OBJECT}$

b. *Ergative languages*:
   CONS GR-C$_{OBJECT}$ >> CONS GR-C$_{SUBJECT}$

The analysis of (10) for N-A languages will then be as in (12).

(12)

appeared pron.	EPP	UNI C-θ	CONS GR-C$_{SUBJ}$	CONS GR-C$_{OBJ}$
a. appeared her$_{ACC}$	*			
b. she-NOM appeared t$_{ACC}$		*		
c. her$_{ACC}$ appeared t$_{ACC}$			*	
d. ☞ she$_{NOM}$ appeared t$_{NOM}$				*

In (12), the combined effects of the EPP and Case-uniqueness (Visibility) force a violation of GR-consistency as in (c, d). By the language-specific ranking (11a), the lesser violation will be to change the object Case, yielding a Nominative trace as in (d), a point that I pick up in the next section. Candidates in which the object is not moved will be considered in 4.2 below. It is clear that under the alternative ranking (11b), (12c) rather than (d) would be optimal. Once we trade in the label 'Accusative' for 'Absolutive', the one used for the Case of objects in Ergative languages, indeed this is what we find, as in the Hindi example (5b), where the subject of the unaccusative verb is Absolutive.

The proposed system is partially similar to the others discussed, in ranking or ordering subject and object Cases relative to one-another, but is crucially different in confining the relevance of such ranking to A-chains (passive/unaccusative structures). Unless an A-chain is involved, there could be no Case interaction between different GRs. One consequence of this is a direct account of the Accusative objects in boldface in (13).

(13) a. Bill expected [him to hire **me**]
     b. [His hiring **me**] surprised Bill

These structures show that Accusative is not in general dependent on the presence of a Nominative as one might expect from the other systems discussed. From the present point of view, there is no such expectation, since the Accusatives in question are just those predicted by GR-consistency (9b), which is here not in conflict with Case-uniqueness. Unlike the objects, the subjects *him*, *his* in (13a, b) will require further comment, however. For the genitive in (13b) I take the standard view that the bracketed structure is partially NP-like, genitive being the canonical subject Case for NPs. This means that GR-consistency (9b) is at least partially category-specific, or depends on the nature of the Case assigner. As for the Accusative subject of (13a), I return to it in Section 5.

Another important empirical difference in the present approach is that it draws a needed distinction among single argument verbs: unaccusatives, which give rise to A-chains as in (10), and other intransitives that do not. In this connection, it is relevant to consider Ergative languages. It is a common belief that Ergative languages instantiate the Case generalizations in (14).

(14)   Subject Case (Erg)   Object Case (Abs)
      a.   Subject of transitive   ✓
      b.   Object of transitive   ✓
      c.   Subject of intransitive   ✓

As is clear from Marantz (1991), Legendre et al. (1993), and other work, however, the generalization in (14b) is not the correct one. What is general about Ergative languages is only that the subject of unaccusatives bears object Case, while the subject of other intransitives varies language specifically, as in (15).

(15)   Subject Case (Erg)   Object Case (Abs)
      a.   Subject of unaccusative   *   ✓
      b.   Subject of unergative   ✓   ✓

That is, as Marantz (1991) notes, parallel to BG (1) above for N-A languages, Ergative languages instantiate the generalization in (16).

(16)   No subject θ-role ⇒ no Ergative Case

The difference between (15a) and (15b) reflected in (16) follows immediately from the present proposal. With unaccusatives, the object Case follows from the presence of the A-chain and the effects of Case-uniqueness discussed. With unergatives, there is no A-chain, which accounts for the contrast between (5b) above (*Sita*-ABS *arrived*) and (17).

(17)   *kuttoŋ ne bhoŋkaa*   (Hindi)
        dogs-ERG barked

As for the cross-linguistic variation within (15b), that is also consistent with the present approach. Given the absence of an A-chain, subjects of unergatives will be bound only by GR-consistency (9b), which means that these subjects should just have the Case of other subjects. Other subjects, however, come in two flavors in these languages: necessarily Ergative with transitive verbs (since Absolutive, already used by the object, would violate Case-uniqueness); and necessarily Absolutive with unaccusatives as argued. Hence, if the subjects of the third category, the unergatives, were Ergative, they would satisfy GR-consistency of Case relative to the transitive class. But if they were Absolutive, they would satisfy it relative to the unaccusative class — a toss up. This seems correct, as languages vary apparently idiosyncratically here — some, like Hindi, allowing in fact both choices. Hence *kutte* 'dogs-ABS' is also possible alongside of *kuttoṇ ne* 'dogs-ERG' in (17), while **siita ne* 'Sita-ERG' is not possible for (5b) (Marantz 1991, this volume). In terms of concrete constraint ranking, the two types of Ergative languages can be characterized by the opposite rankings in (18a, b).

(18) a. SUBJECT-ERG >> SUBJECT-ABS
      b. SUBJECT-ABS >> SUBJECT-ERG

Both constraints in (18) will be subcases of GR-consistency for subjects. As such, they will be dominated by Case-uniqueness, which will compel their respective violations, imposing Ergative subjects in transitive structures, and Absolutive ones in unaccusative structures, thus limiting the effects of (18a) or (b) to unergative verbs.

Approaches that do not recognize the GR-consistency of Case, and rather link GRs to Cases in a more free-wheeling fashion, will fail to draw such important distinctions among single-argument verbs. Specifically, in the CT system of (6) above, the Absolutive Case, which needs to be associated first, should associate equally well to an object-of-transitive, or to a subject-of-intransitive, whichever is found — that ability being the essence of the system. Analogously, in the MPLT system in (7), any single argument of a verb should look like any other once it moves out of the VP in search of Case.[1]

A problem similar to the one just described arises in N-A languages as well. This is illustrated in (19).

(19) *Questo$_i$ è successo t$_i$ *me/a me*   (Italian)
      this   is happened   me/to me
      'This has happened to me'

Cases like (19) are indicative of the general fact that unaccusative verbs fail to assign Accusative not only to a first object, but altogether. This abstracts away again from double object constructions, in which a second Accusative appears to be available through some language-specific mechanism. Thus, in English, which permits *I gave him the book*, the structure *This befell him* has an Accusative object, despite the fact that the verb is likely unaccusative in the same thematic sense as the one in (19). Aside from this, (19) expresses a true generalization so far as I know — a subcase of BG. This generalization follows directly from the present system. Under GR-consistency, the Case of a second object will never be Accusative, because that is the Case of the first object (again, double object constructions aside). The Accusative of the first object is indeed missing in violation of GR-consistency, but that is because of the A-chain invoking the higher ranked Case-uniqueness as discussed. This will have no effect on the second object, which therefore bears Dative — just the canonical Case for that GR. Matters are different for the alternatives in question. Just as they failed to make the distinction among single-argument verbs, they will fail to make the distinction among double-argument verbs, and hence treat the structure in (19) as they would a transitive one. Indeed, the CT system would first assign Nominative to the subject in (19), making then Accusative available for whatever the next argument may be. Similarly, in the MPLT approach, the two arguments of (19) should be able to move out of the VP like any other argument pair, and then find whatever Cases (Nominative, Accusative) other argument pairs find.

In sum, the naive view that Cases simply reflect GRs proves correct once it is seen as subordinate to another rather simple and familiar idea that sees Cases associating one-to-one with θ-roles. In contrast, more complex algorithms for associating Cases and GRs yield various unwanted classes of misassociations.

4. Case Uniformity

4.1 Why traces have Case

The common assumption that traces of A-movement do not have Case stems from two premises: (i) that movement is 'to get Case', and (ii) that an argument and its trace cannot both have Case, since they have a single θ-role. As I argued in 1. above, there is no basis to the first premise. We know that Case can be attained without movement, as shown in (20a) compared with (20b).

(20) a. *Sarò licenziato io*   (Italian)
will be fired   I
b. *Io$_i$ sarò licenziato t$_i$*
I will be fired

We also know that movement still occurs even when there is clearly no need for Case, as in (21a), where the dative Case is obviously due to the D-structure position of that argument, the one it has in (21b).

(21) a. **Henni** *voru sýndir bílarnir*   (Icelandic)
her-DAT were shown the cars-NOM

b. *Bílarnir$_i$ voru sýndir t$_i$ henni*
   the cars-NOM were shown her-DAT

Furthermore, whatever 'need' there may be for the object to move in (21a), it does not seem to reside, at least not entirely, within the object itself (contra MPLT's 'Greed'), since the other object can move instead just as well, as in (21b). As for the second premise above that there cannot be two Cases with a single θ-role, it is accepted under Case-uniqueness (9a)/'Visibility', but only in the sense that antecedent and trace could not have separate or independent Cases, leaving open the possibility that the trace may share the same Case as the antecedent. In this regard, two ways come to mind to test for the presence of Case on the trace. One is to consider minimally different structures in which some lexical NP rather than the trace occupies the same position; the other is to consider structures in which some lexical material is required to agree in Case with the position occupied by the trace. Both tests are available and reveal that the trace indeed has Case. The first is provided by (20a) and (21a) above. In each example, the object position is evidently able to receive Nominative Case, and it then seems plausible to suppose that, when the trace occupies that same position, (as in (20b), (21b)), it may also receive that Case. The second test is provided by the following type of example.

(22) a. *Ég tel   [hana vitlausa]*   (Icelandic)
        I believe her-ACC crazy-ACC
    b. *Hún   er talin   [t vitlaus]*
        she-NOM is believed crazy-NOM

In Icelandic, adjectival predicates of small clauses agree in Case with their subjects, as shown in (22a). In (22b), then, the subject — a trace, must evidently be Nominative, the same Case as its antecedent. This evidence leads to the conclusion that A-movement chains are Case uniform, in the sense that both the moved NP and its trace have the same Case. I will take such uniformity to reflect a specific syntactic condition given in (23).

(23) *Case Uniformity*: In an A-chain, all positions must receive the same Case by the same assigner.

A condition like (23) seems natural, and in fact comes at no cost. The reason is that it is merely a specific interpretation of the Case-uniqueness (Visibility) hypothesis of (9a) above, which imposes that an A-chain be associated with a single Case. Within the latter hypothesis, one cannot determine a-priori whether the single Case of an A-chain needs to be associated with one position in that chain or with all positions, and the decision becomes an empirical matter. Taking the latter alternative to be correct in the form of (23) will account for facts like (22b) directly, and it will have the further important consequences that we see below.

In the above discussion, I took Cases simply to reflect GRs, without specifying the structural conditions involved. However, it turns out that the Case exhibited by each GR depends on that GR's association with some Case assigner. This is why some Cases are not GR-invariant across lexical categories, e.g. *I(Nom) lost* vs. *My(Gen) loss*. Turning then to the conditions controlling the association between a Case assigner and a GR, I take Nominative to be assigned to the subject by an inflectional element I, under the same relation that provides for subject verb agreement, presumably an instance of the more general Spec–Head agreement. I further assume that Case is generally assignable under C-command, so that in an unaccusative type structure the inflection will in effect assign Nominative to both subject and object, as in (24) (See also Sigurðsson 1989, 1991 for similar ideas).

(24)   The window I broke *t*
       └─N─────┴─N─┘

On this analysis, movement in (24) will satisfy Case-uniformity (23). If Case assignment is thus not constrained to Spec–Head relations, it obviously needs to be constrained to some other local domain. The simplest hypothesis is that Relativized Minimality (Rizzi 1990) applies, as in (25).

(25)   *Minimality of Case*:
       a. A Case must be assigned by the closest assigner.
       b. A Case assigner α for Σ is the closest, if there is no category X that contains both Σ and an alternative Case assigner β, but not α.

In cases like (24), there is no closer assigner than the inflection, since the verb must not be an assigner given Case-uniqueness/uniformity, in contrast to transitive cases like (26).

(26)   They I [$_{VP}$ broke the window]
       └─N──┴─*N─ └─A─┘

In (26), assignment of Nominative by the inflection is blocked by the presence of the verb which is here both a Case assigner for the direct object and closer, by virtue of being contained in a VP which does not contain the inflection. The non-assignment of Nominative to the object in (26) would thus follow from Case minimality. Note, however, that it may also follow from Case-uniqueness, barring multiple associations between Cases and θ-roles. Suppose it is the case that Accusative can only go to the object for structural reasons, and not to the subject. Then the only possibility given Case-uniqueness will be for Nominative to go to the subject. The assumption that Accusative can only go to the object seems challenged by the fact that, in Ergative languages, the object Case, Absolutive, can in fact go to the subject. But it is well-known from 'split Ergative' languages, that mix the N-A and Ergative patterns, that Absolutive does not correspond to the Accusative, but rather to the Nominative. We may then assume that Nominative/Absolutive is the only bi-directional Case, universally. In transitive structures, in which that Case cannot be used bi-directionally, languages would then differ. N-A languages would utilize a special Case for the object: the Accusative, while Ergative languages would utilize a special Case for the subject: the Ergative. The case in (26) is then consistent with Case-uniformity, but the more general Case-uniqueness may be sufficient for it. Consider in this connection also the contrast in (27).

(27) a. She I seems [t happy]

b. *She I seems [t I is happy]

This contrast would also follow from Case-uniformity (23). In (27a), the matrix I succeeds in linking with both the moved NP and its trace, just as in (24) above. In (27b), however, it cannot link with the trace, because there is a closer Case assigner for the lower subject: the lower I, the crucial difference between small clauses and full clauses. Compliance with minimality of Case would thus force a violation of Case-uniformity. Again, however, the more general Case-uniqueness may be sufficient in this case as well, since a single θ-role would receive one Nominative from each inflection. The more specific interpretation of Case-uniqueness as Case-uniformity becomes finally necessary, however, with 'super-raising' structures, like (28).

(28) John I is likely [it I seems [t happy]]

In (28), the lower inflection is again the closer Case assigner for the trace of the matrix subject. But in contrast to (27b), the initial position would not have Case here, so that only Case-uniformity, and not Case-uniqueness, is violated. This account of super-raising is substantially parallel to the one of MPLT based on 'shortest move', i.e. minimality of movement, except that the 'shortest move' effect is here derived from minimality of Case via Case-uniformity. This interpretation is supported by the fact that it also applies to (27b) as we just saw, in contrast to the 'shortest move' account of MPLT which does not. The reason is that the movement of (27b) is structurally just as 'short' as the one in (27a), showing that Case, rather than distance, is what makes the difference here. MPLT indeed gives a Cased-based account of (27a, b), in terms of movement being only allowed for the self-serving purpose of 'getting Case' (the principle of 'Greed' to which I will return). The present proposal is that Case is *always* what controls the possibility of movement, hence not only in (27), but also in (28).

If Case-uniformity is what makes A-movement possible, the remaining question is what compels it. I take that to be a combination of semantic and syntactic conditions. In non null-subject languages, the subject position has to be filled with lexical material. In structures in which no subject θ-role is assigned, there will be two possibilities: to insert a lexical element that bears no θ-role — an expletive, or to move an object to subject. The two options appear to have different semantic consequences noted in the literature: the first yields the definiteness effect, and an interpretation of the post verbal NP as 'new information'. Specific expletive elements may also carry specific syntactic or semantic restrictions, hence indirectly forcing movement when such restrictions are not met. Null-subject languages, on the other hand, are those in which the subject position need not be filled. Hence they do not face the specific requirements that come from overt expletives, thus resulting in 'freer' inversion, but still yielding a 'new information' versus 'old information' reading of the relevant NP based on its position. Aside from the Quirky subject phenomenon of Icelandic (e.g. (21a) above), in N-A languages the choice of which argument to move is limited to those arguments whose Case can be suppressed, non-suppression being barred by Case-uniqueness. Apparently, the only Case that can be suppressed is Accusative, resulting in the generalization that only would-be Accusatives can move to subject. This restriction is not accounted for by the above discussion and is provisionally stipulated. I will return to it and a similar restriction for Ergative languages below. In sum, then, movement is made possible by the EPP and is made necessary by semantic conditions, movement structures and their non-moved counterparts (with null or expletive subjects) having different interpretations. In non null-subject languages, restrictions associated with overt expletives make the movement imperative somewhat more general.

4.2 Expletive Constructions

A crucial advantage of the Case-uniformity proposal is that it generalizes across movement and expletive constructions, as we can see by considering the pair in (29).

(29) a. There I appeared a man
 └─N──┴──N──┘

b. A man I appeared t
 └─N──┴──N──┘

In both (29a, b), the inflection will connect with the subject, driven by GR-consistency. In either case, this will not be sufficient, however. In (29a), the subject position does not contain an argument, and hence fails to provide a θ-role. The inflection will thus need to connect with the object position as well where a θ-role is found, to satisfy Case-uniqueness. In (29b), the inflection also needs to connect to the object, to satisfy Case-uniformity, the specific interpretation of Case-uniqueness proposed here. Both cases in (29) violate GR-consistency for direct objects, by creating Nominative ones, but that will be compelled by the higher ranked Case-uniqueness/uniformity. Calculation of (29a) will be as in (30), assuming satisfaction of both the EPP and the ban on null subjects in English tensed clauses.

(30) appeared a man	Uni C-θ	Cons GR-C$_{SUBJ}$	Cons GR-C$_{OBJ}$
a. there appeared a man-ACC		*	
b. there-NOM appeared a man-ACC	*		
c. ☞ there-NOM appeared a man-NOM			*

In (30), the first candidate, in which *there* is a subject with no Case, violates GR-consistency for subjects. On the other hand, Nominative Case confined to the expletive as in the second candidate violates Case-uniqueness. Hence the optimal candidate is the third, since it only violates the bottom-ranked GR-consistency for objects.

The account of (29a) carries over to the other type of expletive construction in (31).

(31)   It   I is obvious [that she is happy]
       └─N──┴────N────┘

Here, the matrix inflection connects again not only with the subject, which has no θ-role, but with the object as well, here a clause. It cannot connect with material internal to the clause for the reasons discussed for (27b), i.e. Case minimality.

This analysis of expletive constructions accounts in obvious ways for all of their properties, specifically the presence of a Nominative object and the fact that the latter participates in verb agreement, though either property or both may not be directly detectable in all instances. Both properties follow from the link between inflection and the object. This analysis will also account for the fact that the locality conditions on expletive-argument relations mirror strictly those on NP-trace relations. This follows from the fact that locality conditions on Case assignment, namely Case minimality, are at work in both cases. Such parallelism is further evidenced by the examples in (32).[2]

(32)   a. *There are [many people] in the room*
       a'. *[Many people]$_i$ are t_i in the room*
       b. **There are a picture of [many people] in the room*
       b'. **[Many people]$_i$ are a picture of t_i in the room*
       c. *It was believed [that John was here]*
       c'. *[That John was here]$_i$ was (widely) believed t_i*
       d. **It was believed a claim [that John was here]*
       d'. **[That John was here]$_i$ was believed a claim t_i*

The grammatical examples in (32), given for comparison, are straightforward, and like others already discussed. The ungrammatical pairs (b, b'), (d, d') involve parallel violations of Case minimality in both members. Thus, in (b), *many people* is an object of the noun *picture*, hence minimally assigned Case by it, excluding a connection with the more remote verb inflection. The trace in (b') is then similarly prevented from connecting with inflection, resulting in a violation of Case-uniformity. The same holds for the pair in (d, d') where the closer Case assigner is the noun *claim* and the argument which is prevented from being connected with inflection is its object, a clause.

On this approach, there is therefore no need to postulate 'LF movement' of the argument with adjunction to the expletive as in MPLT. The latter hypothesis would seek to account for the various parallelisms noted by reducing expletive constructions to movement structures, but seems sharply inconsistent with known 'LF' facts. For instance, in *There weren't many people in the room*, the relative scope of negation and quantifier is different than in *Many people weren't in the room*.

Note that there is, however, one divergence between movement and expletive constructions, illustrated in (33).

(33) a. *Some data had suddenly appeared [t$_i$ (to be) out of order]*
 b. **There had suddenly appeared [some data (to be) out of order]*
 c. *There had suddenly appeared some data on the screen*

The asymmetry of (33a, b) obtains with both infinitival and small-clause complements, as indicated by the parenthesized portion. It also obtains with all types of small clauses (adjectival, participial, prepositional) as can be easily shown. The case in (33c) shows that the problem of (33b) strictly depends on the configuration being 'raising' rather than unaccusative. In (33c), the PP is not the predicate of a small clause, but presumably just a locative complement of *appear*, which is thus simply unaccusative. I will leave this contrast unaccounted for (but see note). So far as I can see, there is no account of it in the MPLT analysis either, since in (33b) LF movement should be allowed, just like the overt one in (33a).[3]

Note that the above discussion has only considered expletive constructions with unaccusative-type verbs, but is potentially extendable to other cases, such as the transitive expletive constructions of Icelandic discussed in Bobaljik and Jonas (1993) and other work. What limits expletive constructions to unaccusative structures in English and other languages is the presence of a vacant D-structure subject position only with those verbs, the expletive being inserted in that position (Burzio 1986). In languages in which (overt) expletives are not limited to unaccusative verbs, it must be the case that there is an additional position available for insertion. The above proposal makes no commitment to what positions may be structurally available, and only entails that in all cases both the expletive and an argument must be within reach of a single Case assigner, which seems consistent with known facts.[4]

In sum, and aside from the residual problem of (33b), if we re-state Case-uniqueness (Visibility) as the more specific Case-uniformity condition, imposing that all GRs sharing a single θ-role must receive the same Case, then locality of A-movement falls out of minimality of Case assignment. In addition, by generalizing to expletive constructions directly, Case-uniformity will account for the movement-like locality of those constructions, without requiring LF movement. We will see below that this apparatus then enables us to reduce BG to effects of the EPP. First, however, I will consider how the present approach deals with other familiar structures.

5. ECM, Raising and PRO

As noted above, small clauses differ from full clauses in lacking a Case-assigning inflection. As a result of this, their subjects will receive Case from an external assigner, as in each of (34).

(34) a. We believed [her happy]
         └──A──┘

   b. She I seemed [*t* happy]
      └N─┘└──N──┘

The structure in (34a) provides one more instance of non-canonical Case: Accusative subjects. As in the case of Nominative objects, I take this phenomenon not to falsify the hypothesis that Cases are GR-based, but rather to represent a principled deviation from that general correlation, due to overriding constraints. The constraint at work here is again Case-uniqueness. The lower subject in (34a), which has a θ-role, needs a Case, and the nearest Case assigner is the main verb. The Case that the verb assigns canonically to its object, the clause, is thus allowed to 'percolate' to that clause's subject. Hence, in effect, Accusative in (34a) goes apparently to both the clause and its subject. I leave open the question of whether this would still constitute a violation of Case-uniqueness (perhaps unavoidable). The Case of the lower subject in (34b) can also be regarded as non-canonical for the manner in which it is assigned, although it is Nominative. It is in fact the type of relation with the Case assigner that is relevant, rather than the nature of the Case itself.

We have thus uncovered two main conspiracies behind the misalignment of Cases and GRs: (i) the Case 'surplus' that one finds with verbs not assigning a subject θ-role; and (ii) the Case shortage that one finds with predicates of small clauses. Turning now to infinitival complements, we find that some behave like small clauses, as in (35), parallel to (34).

(35) a. We believed [her to have left]
         └──A──┘

   b. She I seemed [*t* to have left]
      └N─┘└──N──┘

Others, however, do not, as in (36).

(36) a. *John decided [her to leave]
   b. *Mary$_i$ was decided [t$_i$ to leave]

While the infinitival complements of verbs like *seem* and *believe* (raising and ECM, respectively) are thus to be assimilated to small clauses, the natural move regarding the complements of the verbs in (36) is to assimilate them to tensed clauses, whose inflection will block both raising and ECM by Case minimality (See (27b)). Specifically, I am proposing that the inflection in (36a, b), which we can identify with the particle *to*, is a Case assigner, hence assigning Case to 'PRO' in the grammatical variants of (36a, b) given in (37).

(37) a. John decided [PRO to leave]

   b. It was decided [PRO to leave]

As a closer assigner, *to* will then block either the Accusative that would be assigned by *decide* in (36a), or the Nominative that would be assigned by the main inflection under Case-uniformity in (36b), as desired. As for the Case of PRO in (37) and in general, it appears to be no different from the Case of subjects of tensed clauses, as is clear from relevant tests, especially as discussed in Sigurðsson (1991). I thus take the PRO of (37a, b) to be Nominative, hence satisfying GR-consistency. On this view, the fact that such subjects cannot show up overtly can thus no longer be related to Case, as in Chomsky (1981, 1986). Rather, omitting details that would take us too far afield, I will relate it to the fact that infinitival 'inflection' is actually uninflected, hence inherently unable to serve as an agreement element. This leaves open the only other option that inflection appears to have — that of functioning as an element bearing a θ-role linked with an empty category, as in null subject languages, where the empty category is labeled 'pro'. This explains the null character of PRO, by reducing it to that of 'pro'. The interpretive differences between the two will come from the fact that the 'feature rich' inflection of null subject languages yields the properties of a pronoun (pro), while the featureless character of infinitival inflection yields the property of an anaphor (PRO), as argued in Burzio (1991, 1992).[5]

The hypothesis that 'PRO' is a reflex of infinitival inflection now predicts correctly that it should not occur in small clauses, whence (38).

(38) a. *Mary decided/hoped/wanted [PRO to be happy]*
   b. **Mary decided/hoped/wanted [PRO happy]*

It also predicts correctly, as shown in (39), that PRO should not occur in complements of verbs like *believe, seem* if those complements are to be reduced to small clauses as I suggest next.

(39) a. *We believed [PRO to have won]
 b. *It seemed [PRO to have won]

Considering then that the availability of such ECM and raising complements as those in (35) above is clearly a matter of selection by the main verb, and supposing that the inflection is the head of a clause, I take verbs like *believe* and *seem* to select for complements with an 'inactive' inflection, whence their small clause-like behavior. The fact that such ability to be 'inactive' is limited to infinitival inflection presumably follows from the fact that only the latter is independently 'weak'. Given an inactive inflection in (35a, b) above, then, both the Accusative by the main verb, and the Nominative by the main inflection will be able to reach the embedded subject thanks to the absence of a closer assigner. The proposed common account of both ECM and raising in terms of selection by the main verb will of course account for the fact that ECM verbs regularly serve as raising verbs in the passive, as in *She was believed to have left* compared with (35a), while non ECM verbs do not, as shown in (36) above. Furthermore, the hypothesis that both phenomena are a matter of selection also accounts for the fact that neither raising nor ECM are possible in the presence of intervening structure, in contrast to PRO, as shown in (40), where (a, b) hold for any X.

(40) a. *John X-ed [what [her to have done]]
 b. *John$_i$ X-ed [what [t_i to do]]
 c. John decided [what [PRO to do]]

This follows from supposing that selection is local and only from head to head, hence correctly blocked by the intervening C in (40a, b), while PRO of (40c) (active inflection) requires no selection.

Recall now that in passive/unaccusative structures I am taking both subject and object to be within the Case domain of the inflection, as in (24), (29b) above. When such structures are embedded under ECM or raising verbs, then, we will expect both positions to be turned over to the external Case assigner, as schematically indicated in (41).

(41) a.
 John believed [her to have disappeared *t*]

b. Mary was believed [t to have disappeared t]

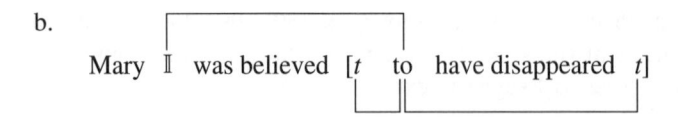

That is, I presume that, due to the demise of the closer Case assigner *to*, both the trace and its antecedent will be Accusative in (41a), while both traces are Nominative in (41b), Case-uniformity being satisfied throughout. Similar considerations will hold for embedded expletive constructions, as in (42).

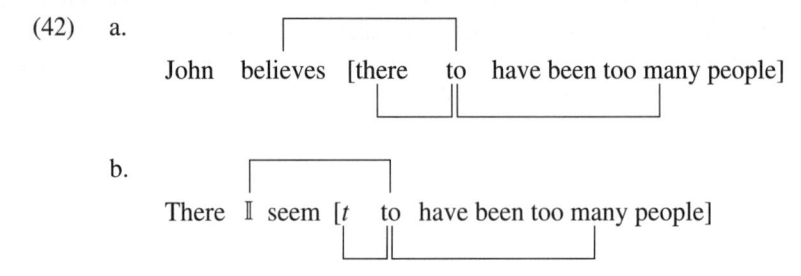

(42) a. John believes [there to have been too many people]

b. There seem [t to have been too many people]

I take both the expletive and the argument to receive Accusative in (42a), while both the trace of *there* and the argument receive Nominative from the main inflection in (42b), hence accounting for the long distance agreement between the main verb and the embedded object.

The above account of raising/ECM appears to have a natural extension to the phenomenon of pseudo-passives, illustrated in (43).

(43)   *This matter was never talked [about t]*

Supposing that the infinitival inflection *to* is related to the preposition *to*, we can take inactive *to* to reflect a more general property of English verbs consisting of the ability to render complement prepositions 'Case inactive', and hence make their domains Case transparent. On this view, structures like (43) will then satisfy Case-uniformity in English, though they will be correctly blocked by Case minimality in languages that do not confer such 'override' ability to their verbs.

In sum, I have argued that small clause complements of active verbs have Accusative subjects — another major case of GR-*in*consistency, simply because they assign subject θ-role but not Case, which must then be provided by the main verb. I have taken the fact that ECM and raising infinitivals behave like small clauses to result from a Case-inactive inflection, selected by the main verb. This enables a matrix Case assigner to connect with the subject position under Case minimality, and, when the complement is unaccusative, with the object position as well. Infinitivals with PRO, on the other hand, have the same Case properties as tensed clauses, the empty category 'PRO' being due to the fact that the inflection is defective (not for Case, but) for agreement, forcing it to function as an independent θ-role bearer, as tensed inflection does in null subject languages.

6. From EPP to BG

6.1 *Greed versus Case Uniqueness*

The above discussion has been concerned with two phenomena. One can be referred to as Case mobility, the fact that the same Case, e.g. Nominative or Absolutive, can show up on different GRs. The other is the mobility of arguments, the fact that arguments bearing a specific θ-role can show up with different GRs. Both the present approach and the one of MPLT share the goal of reducing the two phenomena to one. MPLT pursues that goal by taking argument mobility — A-movement, to be more basic, and Case mobility to follow from it. In that system, arguments move to specific Case assigning positions — the Spec of some AgrX, to get Case, and when they show up with a Case that is not the canonical one, it is because they have moved or will move (at LF) to a different-than-usual SpecAgrX. In contrast, the present proposal takes Case mobility to be the more basic phenomenon, by postulating that a Case is allowed to connect with as many GRs as necessary to link up with a θ-role, constrained only by Case minimality, and that movement is then free within single-Case domains. As we see below, the two approaches differ in their ability to account for BG. I first consider the present approach, and then turn to MPLT.

As I have argued, with verbs that do not assign subject θ-role, the EPP gives rise to a non-thematic subject position, which needs to be occupied, two options then being available: movement, or insertion of an expletive.[6] Whichever option is chosen, there will be a violation of Case-uniqueness unless one Case is suppressed, since the EPP has given rise to one more GR than there are θ-roles, and -through GR-consistency- to one more Case. N-A languages then choose to suppress the direct object Case, whence BG (1), while Ergative languages suppress the subject Case, whence the corresponding generalization in (16) above. There is still an important residue, however, concerning the specific Case that is suppressed, to which I return in 6.2 below. For the N-A languages, the question is why only the *direct* object Case can be suppressed, rather than just any object Case. The latter choice would make any object eligible for movement, or association with an expletive, contrary to fact. There is also a similar question for Ergative languages.

Considering the MPLT theory, several difficulties stand in the way of an account of BG. One is the principle of 'Greed'; another is the object movement to SpecAgrO; and a third is the analysis of expletive constructions. Beginning with the first, the principle of 'Greed' states that movement is only to get Case. But we saw in 1 above that 'move to get Case' and BG are statements of each other. If Greed is true, then movement to subject entails among other things lack of object Case. Since movement to subject also entails lack of subject θ-role, Greed is virtually a statement of BG, hence just the problem.[7] Nonetheless, an effect similar to BG is in fact derived in MPLT, as in the following passage.

(44) "Suppose that the VP contains only one NP. Then one of the two Agr elements will be 'active' (the other being inert or perhaps missing). Which one? Two options are possible: AgrS or AgrO. If the choice is AgrS, then the single NP will have the properties of the subject of a transitive clause; if the choice is AgrO, it will have the properties of the object of a transitive clause (Nominative-Accusative, and Ergative-Absolutive languages, respectively)" [MPLT: 9].

This passage states that there cannot be more Cases (Agr projections) than there are argument NPs. In addition, the MPLT theory is also committed to the existence of at least as many Cases as argument NPs. This then gives a form of Case-uniqueness: just as many Cases as arguments. Then just as Case-uniqueness yields BG in the present account, so (44) gives a form of BG, including the fact that in unaccusative structures, which have a single argument, there is no Accusative. But note that (44) is 'far sighted', rather than 'greedy', in that it defines what properties the system of AgrS must have to accommodate arguments that are elsewhere in the structure. Hence, while the facts stated by Greed (if movement, no independent Case) may be true, like BG, the notion that the system obeys a principle of 'Greed' is illusory, like the notion that there is a principle called BG. Note now that while (44) gives a form of Case-uniqueness, the form actually needed is more general. The reason is that indirect objects must be prevented from moving to subject, as in *(to) John$_i$ seemed t$_i$ that ..., and one would presume this is for the same reasons that moved direct objects cannot show up in the Accusative: *Her$_i$ was fired t$_i$. Having rejected Greed, one then needs a more general notion of Case-uniqueness barring two cases on the same A-chain, rather than (44). In this sense, (44) will become superfluous. Still, the system that (44) refers to would express correctly the distinction between the (structural) Case of direct objects, that can be suppressed, from the (inherent) one of indirect objects, that cannot. Since it seems to have no other use, it reduces to a statement of that difference, which for the present system is the question to be addressed in 6.2.

The second difficulty for MPLT arises in connection with the AgrO of (44) in ways already noted. Consider in particular that, contrary to what (44) would suggest, Nominative Case (AgrS) is neither sufficient nor necessary for Accusative Case (AgrO), as shown in (45).

(45) a. (Accusative without Nominative)
          I expected [her to hire me]
      b. (Nominative without Accusative)
          Questo$_i$ è successo t$_i$ *me/a me
          this   is happened   me/to me
          'This has happened to me'

In (45a) it is not obvious what would license the complement AgrO under (44) given the lack of an AgrS. In (45b), which repeats (19) above, on the other hand, there is no reason why the second object could not receive Accusative given that the first uses up the Nominative. The contrasts in (46) make the same point in English.

(46) a. *John talked* | **himself** *silly*
                         | **the audience** *to sleep*
      b. *The ice melted (*__the name__) off the mailbox*
          (not: 'by melting, the ice caused the name to vanish from the mailbox')
      c. *John froze (***himself**) to death*

These cases instantiate the 'resultative' construction, studied in connection with unaccusativity by Levin and Rappaport (1995). As they argue, in (46a) the NP in boldface seems to be assigned Case by the verb despite the fact that the verb is not subcategorized for it. While that kind of NP is obligatory in the resultative construction of (46a), it is in fact impossible in (46b, c) on the unaccusative reading of either verb. The grammatical variants of (46b, c) follow from the fact that the trace is serving the same function as the NP in (46a). But then the ungrammatical variants are a BG effect just like the one in (45b) that does not follow from the system in (44): there is a second object, the first being the trace, and it fails to receive Accusative despite the presence of a Nominative and the absence of any other Accusative. Similarly, allowing subjects to go to Spec AgrO in Ergative languages will fail to draw the distinction of (15b) above between subjects which are underlying objects and those which are not. The movement to SpecAgrO is problematic not only empirically, because it creates too many movement options, but as already noted also conceptually. The reason is that if the *factual* rather than theory internal cases of movement, that is those where there is an observable change in GR, are ultimately due to the EPP rather than the need for Case, then there is no conceptual reason for extending movement to objects, since we know there is no EPP for objects: in e.g., *John ate (an apple)* suppression of the object θ-role eliminates the GR altogether.

The third difficulty for MPLT concerns expletive constructions. Once BG is correctly derived for movement constructions, from the EPP and Case-uniqueness as argued, the question is how to ensure that it continues to obtain in expletive constructions (which provide the more direct evidence for it, incidentally). Both proposals require that subject Case associate with an argument, which in these constructions will be an object. However, they analyze the association differently. The present one postulates that the subject Case reaches the argument, while MPLT postulates that the argument moves at LF to reach the Case. The two proposals are obviously similar, roughly just mirror images of one another. To the extent that they are distinguishable, however, evidence disfavors the LF movement analysis. Known LF properties are not consistent with the postulated preverbal position of the argument. As noted, negation has scope over the quantifier in *There weren't many people*, and other relevant tests yield the same results.[8]

In sum, on the proposed approach based on the interaction of two general constraints: Case-uniqueness and GR-consistency, both BG and the corresponding generalization for Ergative languages are correctly derived. In contrast, there are several difficulties for the MPLT account. While those difficulties are partially independent, they all seem related to the traditional but misleading assumption that movement is to get Case. The principle of Greed is essentially a statement of that assumption; the hypothesis that there is an AgrO is the generalization of that assumption from certain subjects to objects; and the LF movement in expletive constructions also results from a generalization of movement to all instances of 'structural' Case.

6.2 *'Structural' versus 'Inherent' Case*

We now turn to the residual question of the discrimination between direct and indirect objects expressed by BG, namely the fact that only Accusative is suppressed. To come to grips with that fact, we need to consider what notion 'GR-consistency' is. For a Case C_i assigned to a GR_x to be 'consistent', there must be some other sentence in which C_i occurs in GR_x. Hence, GR-consistency is 'global', resting on a comparison among sentences. We can put it slightly differently by thinking of a sentence in which C_i occurs in GR_x as generating a bidirectional entailment $C_i \Leftrightarrow GR_x$ — a violable constraint that becomes part of the grammar. Other sentences will then be bound by that constraint, resulting in a consistent pattern. The question will be what happens when inconsistency is compelled, resulting in more than one (internally consistent) pattern. Which pattern will any individual sentence be attracted to? We would expect it to be most strongly attracted to the strongest pattern, the ones that corresponds to the largest number of generated entailments. However, we would also expect it to be attracted to other patterns, in ways proportional to their strength. Now consider what happens when Nominative direct objects are created under compulsion from Case-uniformity. Because the number of structures with Nominative direct objects can be significant, there will be a configuration of the overall system in which a large number of entailments 'Nom $\Rightarrow$ direct object' would exist. In the present formalism, this would be a constraint of a certain rank, expressing a type of GR-sub-consistency present alongside of the (higher-ranked) primary consistency 'Nom $\Rightarrow$ subject'. Such sub-consistency of 'Nom $\Rightarrow$ direct object' could be a sufficiently strong attractor to force an individual sentence to adopt it when violation of the primary pattern is compelled. The overall system would thus be stable in this configuration. Now let us apply this reasoning to indirect objects. Hypothetically, there will then be a class of cases like *He_{NOM} *was talked* t_{NOM} (Meaning 'He was talked to'), generating entailments 'Nom $\Rightarrow$ indirect object'. The number of such entailments will be smaller, however, hence translating into a lower-ranked constraint, or weaker attractor. The reason is that, across a typical lexicon, the number of indirect objects is generally much smaller than the number of direct ones, as many of the verbs that take indirect objects also take direct ones (some being unaccusative). Conceivably, then, the system would not be stable in this type of configuration, calculation of individual sentences not actually supporting the sub-consistency pattern, which would thus be eliminated. To carry out the relevant optimization, illustrated in (47) below, we need to assume that constraint violations are cumulative, as if constraints had numerical weights, as in Burzio (1994:237 ff.) rather than being 'strictly' ranked, as in Prince and Smolensky (1993). This is already implicit in the above idea that larger numbers of identical entailments translate into higher-ranked constraints. However, rather than by numerical weights, the cumulative effect can be expressed as well by taking appropriate conjunctions of constraints to yield constraints of higher rank, as in Smolensky (1997). Thus consider (47).

(47)

was told John	I. UNI C-θ	II. NOM ⇒ SUBJ	III. IO-FAITH	IV. NOM ⇒ DIR-O	V. NOM ⇒ INDIR-O
a. John$_{\text{NOM}}$ was told t_{ACC}	*				
b. ☞ John$_{\text{NOM}}$ was told t_{NOM}		*			*
c. ——			*		

was talked John	I. UNI C-θ	II. NOM ⇒ SUBJ	III. IO-FAITH	IV. NOM ⇒ DIR-O	V. NOM ⇒ INDIR-O
a′. John$_{\text{NOM}}$ was talked t_{DAT}	*				
b′. John$_{\text{NOM}}$ was talked t_{NOM}		*		*	
c′. ☞ ——			*		

Constraints (II, IV, V) read, respectively: 'If a GR has Nominative Case, then it must be a subject/direct object/indirect object'. Both tableaux are based on the hypothesis that both direct and indirect objects could be non-canonically Nominative. In each tableau, then, the first candidate violates Case-uniqueness (I) by associating two Cases with a single θ-role. The second violates (II) by placing a Nominative on a non-subject, and the third violates Input-Output faithfulness, in some fashion. For present purposes we may assume that it consists of a null string, but we could assume instead that it is an active form, perhaps with an arbitrary subject, like *They told John/They talked to John* (semantically close to the passive input). In the second tableau, candidate (c′) wins, but that cannot just be because constraint (II) dominates (III), since then candidate (c) in the first tableau should also win. Rather, on the present proposal, it is only the conjunction of constraints (III) and (IV) that dominates (II), while the corresponding conjunction of (III) and (V) is dominated by it, as stated in (48).

(48) (IO-FAITH & NOM ⇒ DIR-O) >> NOM ⇒ SUBJ >> (IO-FAITH & NOM ⇒ INDIR-O)

Again, the proposal here is that Nominative direct objects represent a sufficiently strong subcanonical pattern to successfully compete with the canonical one of Nominative subjects under certain conditions, while the numerically weaker indirect objects fail to do so.[9] Hence, while we are not in a position to actually predict that indirect objects will fail to accept Nominative, or — for that matter-that direct objects will accept it, we can — on the relevant assumptions — predict a discriminatory effect in the right direction.[10]

Similar reasoning can be applied to account for the fact that, in Ergative languages, only direct objects move, thus yielding Absolutive subjects, while other objects, which would presumably yield subjects with other Cases, let us say 'Oblique' do not. The account in (47) carries over, once the constraints that refer to Nominative Case are replaced with the ones in (49) that refer to Subject.

(49) a. Subject ⇒ Ergative   >>
     b. Subject ⇒ Absolutive >>
     c. Subject ⇒ Oblique

We take the canonical pattern (49a) to be successfully subverted by the one in (b) because -again- it is numerically substantial, unlike the one in (c). Effectiveness of the pattern in (b) to compete with the one in (a) is independently shown by the fact that in some Ergative languages it in fact prevails, thus attracting the class of unergative verbs to it, which could have followed the one in (a) instead, as was noted in (15) above. The variation between (49a) and (b) with unergative verbs would follow if the class of unaccusatives, that gives rise to (49b), and the class of transitives, that yields (a), were of comparable size.

The above considerations may perhaps also shed light on the fact that ECM, with both small clauses and infinitives, is limited to Accusative Case, excluding, for instance *I persuaded Bill of [John to see me] (versus ... of it). If ECM is percolation of the Case that would go to the whole clause down to its subject, then the asymmetry could follow from the fact that, just as with NPs, clauses are more common as direct than as indirect objects, yielding this stronger pattern of non-canonical Case.[11]

If correct, the above discussion enables us to derive the distinction between structural and inherent Case formerly taken as a primitive. Just as we have taken Case to be GR-consistent but violably, so we can take it to be θ-consistent violably, thus adding (50c) to (50b, c) (=9a, b).

(50) a. *Case uniqueness of θ-role* (UNI C-θ):
        There is exactly one Case for every θ-role and exactly one θ-role for each Case.
     b. *GR consistency of Case* (CONS GR-C):
        There is one specific Case for each specific GR and vice-versa.
     c. *θ-consistency of Case* (CONS θ-C):
        There is one specific Case for each specific GR and vice-versa.

The Cases that have been referred to as 'inherent', e.g. Dative, associated with Goals, are the ones for which no violation of (50c) is ever compelled. In contrast, the 'structural' Cases are those that witness such violations. For the violation illustrated in (51) the ultimate instigator is the EPP, with Case-uniqueness (50a) and GR-consistency (50b) as co-conspirators.

(51)   **Structural Case #1**: Nominative Patients

froze ⟨pat⟩	EPP	UNI C-θ	CONS GR-C$_{SUBJ}$	CONS C-θ
a. froze ⟨pat⟩$_{ACC}$	*			
b. [$_{No\ Case}$] froze ⟨pat⟩$_{ACC}$			*	
c. [$_{NOM}$] froze ⟨pat⟩$_{ACC}$		*		
d. [$_{ACC}$] froze ⟨pat⟩$_{ACC}$			*	
e. ☞ [$_{NOM}$] froze ⟨pat⟩$_{NOM}$				*

In (51), candidate (a) violates the EPP for lacking a subject GR. Candidates (b) and (d) violate GR-consistency of subjects, for having a subject which is not Nominative. That is remedied in both (c) and (e), but the former fatally violates Case-uniqueness. Structure (e) can then surface with the Nominative patient either moved to subject: *The river froze*, or in place, as in Italian *È gelato il fiume* 'Froze the river'.

The second type of violation of (50c), illustrated in (52), is due to the inability of small clauses and certain infinitives to assign Case to their subjects.

(52)   **Structural Case #2**: Accusative Agents

I expect [⟨Ag⟩ to win]	UNI C-θ	CONS GR-C$_{SUBJ}$	CONS C-θ
a. I expect [⟨Ag⟩$_{No\ Case}$ to win]	*	*	
b. ☞ I expect [⟨Ag⟩$_{ACC}$ to win]		*	*

In (52) Caselessness as in (a) is not an option given high-ranking Case-uniqueness. Violation of both GR-consistency for subjects and θ-consistency are thus compelled. Note that (50) above obscures what is in fact a perfect parallelism between GR-consistency and θ-consistency. In (50), Case-uniqueness (a) is in a sense just a more permissive version of θ-consistency (c). Together, those two constraints and their ranking indicate that it is best for a specific Case to associate with a specific θ-role and vice versa, but that -that failing- it is better for a Case to associate with *some* θ-role and vice-versa, rather than failing to associate. Now GR-consistency (50b) seems to lack this second provision. In fact, however, earlier discussion has provided it. We have seen (discussion of (47)) that when a canonical pattern is violated (e.g. Nom. ⇒ subjects) this only happens if a subcanonical pattern (Nom. ⇒ direct objects) can be established, and then only if that pattern is strong enough (*Nom. ⇒ indirect objects). Assuming a 'Case-uniqueness of GR' (associate Case one-to-one with any GR and vice-versa) parallel to 'Case-uniqueness of θ-role' (50a) would in fact just derive our Case-uniformity (23). That is, if there is a general imperative for GRs not to remain Caseless, then a trace will be subject to it. The identity in Case between the trace and its antecedent will come from Case-uniqueness as before, yielding Case-uniformity.

Hence it appears as if the central organizing principle is one of invariance, operating on the three-way association of Cases, GRs and θ-roles. When variation obtains, it is compelled by higher-ranking principles. These are not unlikely to be themselves just other forms of invariance. So, as already suggested, the EPP can be taken to be the invariant presence of the subject GR, presumably made possible by the fact that one major response that it triggers: raising of the object, is viable, while a corresponding response to an invariant presence of an object GR: lowering of the subject, would not be. I must leave a formal pursuit of these remarks to further work, however.

In sum, I have proposed that the fact that BG targets only direct objects reduces to GR-consistency in the sense that Nominative direct objects are the most productive category of non-canonical objects, just as Absolutive subjects are the most productive category of non-canonical (= Ergative) subjects in Ergative languages, thus yielding a substantial pattern of sub-consistency in both cases. Defaulting on an alternative, subcanonical, type of Case rather than failing to associate with Case is thus a property by which GRs parallel θ-roles, which we assumed need to maintain *some* association: Case-uniqueness (50a). The discussion has then defined the domain over which Cases can re-associate with either GRs or θ-roles, and has therefore derived the distinction between the descriptive categories of 'structural' and 'inherent' Case.

7. Quirky Subjects and BG

7.1 Case Superimposition

A descriptive characterization of the phenomenon of 'Quirky' subjects in Icelandic illustrated in (53) may consist of supposing that the effects of Nominative Case on the subject position are suspended.[12]

(53) a. *Bjögunarsveitin   biargaði strákunum*
　　　　the rescue-squad-NOM rescued the boys-DAT
　　a'. *Strákunum   var   bjargað*
　　　　the boys-DAT was-3SG rescued
　　　　'The boys were rescued'
　　b. *Strákana   vantaði   í skólann*
　　　　the boys-ACC lacked-3SG in school
　　　　'The boys were missing in school'
　　c. *Strákunum   leiddist   í skólann*
　　　　the boys-DAT bored-3SG in school
　　　　'The boys got bored in school'

Apparently, movement of an object to satisfy the EPP is free to occur in the absence of the normal competition between subject and object Case, so that object Case seems to simply show up unchanged. From the present perspective, this will be a GR-consistency effect on the moved object, which still bears its initial GR via the trace. Indeed, there is good reason to believe that those in (53), and all QSs of Icelandic, are moved objects, as also argued by Sigurðsson (1989). There is no reason to suppose instead that object Case can be assigned to the subject position directly via some 'lexical' mechanism as is sometimes proposed.[13] Thus we can take the verbs of (53b, c) to be unaccusative (in the sense of not assigning subject θ-role), with a 'theme' and an 'experiencer' object, respectively.

The lack of competition between subject and object Case will lead to the expectation that BG should be violated in Icelandic, indeed as in (54).

(54) a. *Ég fyllti bátinn*
　　　　I filled the boat-ACC
　　b. *Bátinn   fyllti*
　　　　the boat-ABS filled

Icelandic does not always behave this way, however. In other cases, it exhibits the same behavior as English and other languages, as shown in (55).

(55) a. *Ég sýndi henni bílana*
I showed her-DAT the cars-ACC
a′. *Bílarnir voru sýndir henni*
the cars-NOM were shown her-DAT
b. *Verkamennirnir breikkuðu veginn*
the workers-NOM widened the road-ACC
b′. *Vegurinn breikkaði*
the road-NOM widened

What this means is that the property of suspending the effects of subject Case (whatever that is) that results in (53) and (54) is only an option in Icelandic, evidently not taken in (55). Our task is therefore to determine what may control the choice of options, but first of course to determine what the 'suspension' consists of.

On the latter issue, there will only be two logical possibilities for characterizing the apparent suppression of subject Case: (i) Nominative is simply not assigned, or (ii) it is assigned covertly. There are at least three reasons to believe that the second hypothesis is correct and that GR-consistency for subjects is satisfied, with Nominative going to the 'quirky' subject, despite the presence of object Case. One reason is theory internal, based on our earlier discussion. If the normal subject Case were suppressed, we would expect some alternative pattern of consistency of subject Case to emerge, as in Ergative languages, were it is only the Absolutive objects that can move to subject. This is not true in Icelandic, as the above examples, as well as others below show: Accusatives, Datives, Genitives, can all move to subject. A second reason is provided by structures like (56) ((21a) above).

(56) *Henni voru sýndir bílarnir*
her-DAT were shown the cars-NOM

As Sigurðsson (1991, fn.10) notes, in such structures "for most speakers, Nominative objects cannot be in first and second person at all". Hence QSs appear to have an effect in constraining agreement possibilities. If they were not connected with inflection, there would be no reason for this, since it is not a general property of Nominative objects that they cannot be in the first or second person, as shown by simple Italian examples like (43b) above or (57).

(57) *Saremo invitati anche noi*
will be-1PL invited also we
'We will also be invited'

Rather, as argued in Burzio (1991, 1992), such limitations to third person are a characteristic of agreement relations that implicate featureless elements, here -I will argue- the QS. One element that gives rise to this same syndrome is Romance reflexive/impersonal *si/se*, illustrated in (58).

(58) a. *Si inviteranno   anche loro*
         si will invite-3PL also   they
         'They will also be invited'
     b. **Si inviteremo   anche noi*
         si will invite-1PL also   we

As I note in that work, the ungrammaticality of (58b) follows from supposing that in such constructions the inflection is connected both to the Nominative object and to the impersonal subject *si*, in contrast to the single connection of (57) (whose subject is just an empty category). The inflection in (58) will then have to agree with both *si* and the object, in effect forcing the latter two to agree with each other. This requirement will then directly reduce the contrast in (58) to that of (59), in which *si*, the same featureless element, is functionally a reflexive.

(59) a. *Loro si   inviteranno*
         they self will invite-3PL
         'They will invite themselves'
     b. **Noi si   inviteremo*
         we self will invite-1PL
         (cf. Noi ci inviteremo)
         we us will invite-1PL
         'We will invite ourselves'

The contrast in (59), indicative of a rather general cross-linguistic pattern, follows in turn from taking third person to be closer than first and second to the 'no-person' of *si*, so that (59a) will satisfy an appropriate notion of approximated agreement, while (59b) will not. This account then carries over to (58) assuming the doubly connected inflection, and in turn to Icelandic (56), on the hypothesis that inflection indeed connects with the QS, though evidently not with the features of the inner NP. Rather, it must connect only with an outer shell as diagrammed in (60), so that the two Cases, Nominative and object-Case are in fact superimposed.

(60)   Case superimposition in Icelandic Quirky subjects:

[[NP] Object-Case]_Nom

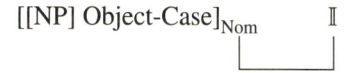

Plausibly, then, the outer shell will have no person/number features, just like a PP or a clause, but will nonetheless register its presence with the inflection, yielding the noted agreement restriction. In (60), Nominative is thus present on the subject GR, satisfying GR-consistency for subjects.[14]

A third important piece of evidence that QSs are indeed connected with the inflection is that they show up as PRO in infinitives, as in (61).

(61) a. *Hana vantaði vinnu*
her-ACC lacked job
'She lacked a job'
a'. *Hún vonast til [að PRO vanta ekki vinnu]*
she hopes to PRO lack not job
b. *Honum var bjargað*
him-DAT was rescued
'He was rescued'
b'. *Hann vonast til [að PRO verða bjargað]*
he hopes to PRO be rescued

If the correct characterization of PRO is that of an empty category connected with inflection as argued above, then, when QSs occur as PRO, they must obviously be so connected.

In contrast to the infinitivals in (61), complements of ECM verbs exhibit overt QSs, as in (62).

(62) a. *Ég tel [henni hafa verið skilað peningunum]*
I believe her-DAT to have been returned the money
b. *Ég tel [henni hafa verið bjargað]*
I believe her-DAT to have been rescued
c. *Ég tel [honum hafa verið sýndir bílarnir]*
I believe him-DAT to have been shown the cars-NOM

Here I will take the infinitival inflection in (62) to still connect with the subject as in (60). However, on the above proposed analysis of ECM complements, such inflection will be 'inactive' and hence not assign Nominative. Instead, it will allow the Accusative from the main verb to reach the subject, superimposing onto the object Case in lieu of the Nominative of (60).

In sum, then, there are three pieces of evidence that endorse the 'superimposition' hypothesis in (60): (i) There are no 'subconsistency' effects on the object Case that can appear in subject position as there are in Ergative languages; (ii) the QS has an effect on verb-agreement; (iii) The QS can be PRO. Hence, it appears that when confronted with the predicament that forces other languages to make tough choices, Icelandic succeeds in having it both ways, satisfying GR-consistency for both subjects and objects, which maintain their Case under movement. To exclude this situation in other languages and also -as we see below- to appropriately limit it in Icelandic, we must assume that it involves violation of some constraint, let us suppose the one in (63).

(63)   No C-Super: Avoid Case superimposition

The so far observed language typology would then follow from the ranking possibilities in (64).

(64)   a.   Nominative-Accusative languages except Icelandic:
              No C-Super, Cons GR-C$_{SUBJ}$ >> Cons GR-C$_{OBJ}$
         b.   Icelandic:
              Cons GR-C$_{SUBJ}$ >> Cons GR-C$_{OBJ}$ >> No C-Super
         c.   Ergative languages:
              No C-Super, Cons GR-C$_{OBJ}$ >> Cons GR-C$_{SUBJ}$

Note, however, that the nature of No C-Super (63) is unclear. It seems that, if the present general approach is correct, it should reduce to some form of 'consistency'. Consider that, while QS sentences are GR-consistent with other sentences by satisfying their entailments, like Nom ⇔ subject, Dat ⇔ indir. obj., etc., the opposite may not be true. So QS sentences should correspondingly generate entailments that a subject must be simultaneously both Nominative and Dative/Accusative/etc. These will then not be satisfied by non-QS sentences, resulting in inconsistency. Whether this is the case will depend on whether notions like subject or object refer only to the outer shell of structures like (60), or whether they refer to the inner NP as well. Also, QS sentences may violate Case-uniqueness for associating two cases with a single θ-role, though that is also unclear.[15] I am not in position to pursue these possibilities at the moment, and will thus make the simplifying assumption that there exists a specific constraint like No C-Super (63). I will also assume for concreteness that the Nominative Case is not associated with the θ-role of a QS, because only connected with the outer shell as the agreement facts suggest, so that there will be no violation of Case-uniqueness in that sense. If so, however, there must be a violation of Case-uniqueness for the failure of Nominative to associate with *any* θ-role in some cases. But that is the same violation that is incurred by impersonal passives, like *It was danced*, which Icelandic in fact permits. Case-uniqueness in this sense must therefore be independently low-ranked in Icelandic.

Before turning to the distribution of the QS option, we must consider the status of QSs for Case-uniformity (23) above. Since promotion of objects to QSs meets the usual locality canons, it must satisfy Case-uniformity if that is indeed the ultimate source of locality. This conclusion can be maintained by means of the rather simple assumption that Case-superimposition as in (60) is not limited to pre-verbal position, but obtains post-verbally just as well. Movement will then be able to both leave a Nominative trace and result in a Nominative subject, hence satisfying Case-uniformity. At the same time, the object, which is contained within the subject, will maintain its relation with the verb, via the subject's trace.

7.2 GR consistency Relativized

Considering now the variable applicability of the QS option in Icelandic, we may deal with it by assuming that No C-Super (63) is not quite strictly ranked as in (64b), but rather that its rank relative to GR-consistency for objects is indeterminate. This will account for the variation in (65), in the way shown by (66).

(65)   a.   *Vegurinn   breikkaði*
               the road-NOM widened
       b.   *Bátinn   fyllti*
               the boat-ACC filled

(66)

	widened road	Cons GR-C$_{SUBJ}$	No C-Super	Cons GR-C$_{OBJ}$
a.	road$_{ACC}$ widened t	*		
b. (☞)	[road$_{ACC}$]$_{NOM}$ widened t		*	
c. ☞	road$_{NOM}$ widened t_{NOM}			*

In (66), candidate (a) violates GR-consistency for the subject by not associating the Nominative with the subject GR. Candidate (b) satisfies GR-consistency for both subject and object by realizing both Cases, but incurs a violation of No C-Super. Candidate (c) avoids that violation by suppressing the object Case, thus violating GR-consistency for objects. Assuming the rightmost two constraints in (66) are unranked relative to one-another will make (b, c) co-optimal, indeed as (65) suggests, although the choice is set for individual verbs. If this variation were idiosyncratic, we would fix the choice for individual verbs by specifying the direct object Case in the input for the verb. Then, if Input-Output faithfulness for Case is bottom-ranked in the grammar, it will never have any effect except when the rest of the grammar is indeterminate, as in this case. Although there is likely to be some idiosyncrasy, we will see shortly that the variation in (65) is substantially predictable, however, requiring multiple rankings, rather than the indeterminacy of (66).

A ranking indeterminacy does seem to exist, however, between Case-superimposition (63) and another constraint, which I state as in (67).

(67) SUBJ θ-MAX: The subject position must host the most prominent θ-role in the sentence.

We can take (67) to be responsible for the fact that the subject takes the most prominent θ-role in general, for instance in transitive structures.[16] However, in the languages of (64a, c), in which NO C-SUPER is high-ranked, (67) will never have any effect on movement possibilities. In N-A languages, only the argument whose Case is suppressed per BG (namely the would-be Accusative) will be able to move. Similarly, in Ergative languages, only the argument whose Case is appropriate for the subject GR, the Absolutive, will be able to move. But in Icelandic (67) appears to rear its head in (68), analyzed in (69).[17]

(68) a. *Henni voru sýndir bílarnir*
her-DAT were shown the cars-NOM
b. *Bílarnir$_i$ voru sýndir t$_i$ henni*
the cars-NOM were shown her-DAT

(69)

were shown cars her$_{DAT}$	SUBJ θ-MAX	NO C-SUPER	CONS GR-C$_{OBJ}$
a. ☞ her$_{DAT}$ were shown cars$_{NOM}$		*	
b. ☞ cars$_{NOM}$ were shown t$_{NOM}$ her$_{DAT}$	*		

In (69), candidate (a) satisfies SUBJ θ-MAX (67), but violates NO C-SUPER, while candidate (b) does just the opposite. If we take those two constraints to be unranked, then the free variation will be correctly expected. Note that in (69) CONS GR-C$_{OBJ}$, satisfied by both candidates, refers to the Dative object. There is a question, however, concerning the direct object. Unlike in candidate (b), in (a) the Nominative object does not save a violation of NO C-SUPER. There would therefore seem to be no reason why that object should not be Accusative, consistently with that of the active sentence in (70).

(70)   *Ég sýndi   henni   bílana*
       I showed her-DAT the cars-ACC

I return to this question shortly. Note in the meantime that the failed alternations in (71) are indeed as predicted by SUBJ θ-MAX (67), as shown in (72).

(71)   a.   *Henni   var skilað   peningunum*
            her-DAT was returned the money-DAT
       a'. **Peningunum   var skilað   henni*
            the money-DAT was returned her-DAT
       b.   *Henni   var óskað þess*
            her-DAT was asked this-GEN
       b'. **Þess   var óskað henni*
            this-GEN was asked her-DAT

(72)

was asked this$_{GEN}$ her$_{DAT}$	SUBJ θ-MAX	NO C-SUPER	CONS GR-C$_{OBJ}$
a. ☞ her$_{DAT}$ was asked this$_{GEN}$		*	
b. this$_{GEN}$ was asked her$_{DAT}$	*	*	

In (72), both candidates violate NO C-SUPER, hence (b) loses for also violating SUBJ θ-MAX, the Genitive object being thematically less prominent than the Dative experiencer.

Returning now to the problem of the Nominative object in (68a), its solution is related to the partial predictability of the variation in (65) above. Zaenen and Maling (1990) make the important observation that the unaccusatives that preserve the object Case of the corresponding transitive, yielding a QS as in (65b), are those which are morphologically non-distinct from the corresponding transitive, while the ones that suppress that Case, yielding Nominative subjects instead as in (65a), are the ones that bear certain morphological distinctions, having for instance somewhat different inflectional paradigms than the corresponding transitive. What this means from the present point of view is that GR-consistency of Case is relativized to the independent degree of similarity among verbs (there are similar effects in morpho-phonology, studied in Burzio 1999; Steriade 1998). Even internally to a single GR, GR-consistency is thus to be viewed as expanding into a family of constraints of different rank — for our purposes, the two in (73), ranked in that order.

(73)   a.   CONS GR-C, RELATIVE: Cases must be GR consistent among verbs that share morphological properties.

b. CONS GR-C, GENERAL: Cases must be GR consistent among all verbs.

Supposing that the NO C-SUPER constraint of (63) is in fact ranked intermediately between (73a) and (73b), rather than unranked as in (66), will now account for Zaenen and Maling's observation. Where applicable, (73a) will prevail, imposing QSs as in (65b). Elsewhere, NO C-SUPER will prevail, imposing loss of object Case as in (65a) or in English.

Turning now to passives, as Zaenen and Maling also note, these are regular in always losing the Accusative of the transitive, as in (68) versus (70) above. This follows as well from the proposed ranking. Since passives have distinct morphology, they will never invoke (73a) relative to their active counterparts, being therefore free to switch Case. But what about structures like (68a), where the switch from Accusative to Nominative seems nonetheless unmotivated? Consider here that, if -QSs aside- passives systematically have a Nominative direct object (sometimes a trace, as required by Case-uniformity), then that will be the canonical direct object Case for this morphological class. Thus, while the higher-ranked GR-consistency (73a) will not apply across transitive-passive pairs, it will apply within the class of passives given their shared morphology. This will then result in the Nominative object of QS sentences like (68a) simply by consistency with other passives.

Summing up, Icelandic QSs must be analyzed as involving Case superimposition, since they are detectably connected with the Nominative-assigning inflection (or other equivalent assigner) while at the same time they bear the Case of the object GR they are connected with. The ability to move Case-marked arguments to subject dispenses with the need to suppress object Case, thus voiding BG. However, alongside of the QS behavior, Icelandic also exhibits the standard behavior described by BG. The alternation between the two behaviors is largely predictable by taking GR-consistency of Case to be sensitive to independent dimensions of similarity among verbs. Unaccusative verbs which are more highly similar to their transitive counterparts are more strongly compelled to assign the same Case to their objects, resulting in QSs. Unaccusatives which are more distantly related to the respective transitives, are freer to switch their object Case, thus avoiding the markedness of QSs. This confirms that the distribution of Case is controlled by a general principle of 'consistency' or invariance. It also shows that the distribution of QSs is not controlled by some rigid 'parameter', but rather by violable constraints, cross-linguistic variation thus following from ranking options. At the same time, the phenomenon of QSs in Icelandic shows unmistakably that movement is not to satisfy any Case requirements, since QSs have two Cases — one more than would be optimal. Rather, movement must come from the need to fill the subject position, and -as Icelandic shows further- the need for thematically prominent subjects.

8. Conclusion

In this article, I have argued that in order to achieve a principled account of BG, one needs to abandon the once popular assumption that A-movement is to get Case. Instead, one must find the motivation for A-movement in the EPP and the presence of a vacant subject position with its unassociated Case. Movement to fill that position will connect two GRs and potentially their respective Cases, in violation of the principle of Case-uniqueness of θ-role ('Visibility'). As a result, either one of the two cases will need to be suppressed, yielding BG for N-A languages, and the generalization of Marantz (1991, this volume) for the Ergative languages.

This pattern of Case reassociation carries over to expletive constructions because it is in fact not contingent on movement, but is rather due to principles internal to Case theory: Case-uniqueness and minimality. These apply equally to both movement and expletive constructions, thus yielding parallel reflexes.

One major class of cases in which the alignment between Cases and GRs breaks down, due to the EPP, thus receives a principled account. Another such class, the 'Exceptional Case Marking' of subjects of small clauses and of some infinitives, was also argued to follow from principle, given the lack of a clause-internal Case assigner. As a result, Cases can be taken to be fundamentally GR-consistent, all exceptions being accounted for. Once misalignments between Cases and both surface and underlying GRs are thus accounted for, the difference between 'structural' and inherent' Case, drawn precisely on whether or not such misalignments exist, is accounted for as well.

We have then seen in connection with Icelandic that there exists one marked mechanism — Case superimposition, that gets around Case conflicts, resulting in both Quirky subjects and suspension of BG.

The present approach based on GR-consistency of Case contrasts with others, especially the one of MPLT, in which the association between (structural) Cases and arguments is more indirect, and essentially the by-product of a complex syntactic derivation. I have argued that the MPLT extension of the traditional movement analysis of subjects of passives and unaccusatives to all subjects and all direct objects is unmotivated. If movement is caused by the presence of a GR with no θ-role, then there is no reason for it in other than the traditional cases. This conceptual argument has an empirical counterpart in the fact that the movement account of structural Case overshoots the target, allowing more freedom in the association of Cases with GRs than is actually needed.

The above discussion has revealed a complex pattern of constraint interaction by ranking, demonstrating the viability of an Optimality-theoretic approach to problems of syntax (cf. also Barbosa et al. 1998; Grimshaw 1997; Legendre et al. 1995; Legendre et al. to appear). In addition, it has introduced several constraints like the EPP, GR-consistency for subjects/objects and its relativized versions, and Case-uniqueness, which seem to strike a common theme of consistency or invariance, suggesting that maximal invariance of patterns is a central principle of language.

Acknowledgments

I wish to express my deep gratitude to Eric Reuland, Ad Neeleman, and Fred Weerman for organizing the 1994 workshop, and to Eric for steering the discussion in particularly productive and insightful ways. I am also eternally grateful to the colleague or colleagues, yet unknown, though Pesetsky, Marantz and Kayne are prime suspects, who chose to refer to an idea that was around MIT when I was as 'Burzio's Generalization'. Citation of my name in that simple connection has never failed to impress a dean or a promotion committee at any of the right moments.

While it may be late to find a collective ancestry for the generalization itself, it is not late to find a collective solution for it, and this volume should accomplish just that. This paper represents my own attempt, but is one that bears similarity to several of the other contributions as the reader will become aware, and was genuinely influenced by other discussions in ways which transcend specific agreements or disagreements. Whether or not I am fully responsible for the discovery of Burzio's generalization, I am for any error in deriving it that may be contained in this article. I did, however, give it my best try. The present article is closely related to a 1994 manuscript of mine titled 'Case-uniformity'.

Warmest thanks to two anonymous reviewers for very helpful comments.

Notes

1. I find various attempts to maintain that unergatives are covertly transitive perhaps relevant to some abstract semantic characterization, but rather unconvincing as a solution of the noted problem for MPLT. As Laka (1993, fn.4) points out, while many verbs which are intransitive in English are transitive in Basque, and hence predictably have Ergative subjects, those which are intransitive and not unaccusative even in Basque, still take Ergative subjects, showing that this kind of solution has no independent support.

2. I abstract away here from occasional lack of parallelism, e.g. *It seems that you are here*, versus **That you are here seems*. There is no prediction here that expletive and movement structures should be equivalent in all respects, since they have different LFs.

3. Although the issue is somewhat complex, a plausible account seems to me to run along the

ANATOMY OF A GENERALIZATION 237

following lines. Post-verbal Nominatives are marked. They are thus possible only under compulsion from the appropriate semantic constraints that demand that new information be given post-verbally. However, the latter would in fact plausibly require a VP-final position, rather than just a post-verbal one. Cases like (33b) would then be excluded because they have a Nominative which is neither pre-verbal, which would avoid the markedness, nor VP-final. In contrast, in the unaccusative structure (33c), the Nominative would be VP-final, assuming that the PP *on the screen* is in fact an adjunct. In turn this would follow from the hypothesis of Freeze (1992), Moro (1997) that *there* is a locative pronominal raised to subject, thus viewing *there* constructions as a subspecies of the Quirky-subject sentences of Icelandic. Taking the notion VP-final to be phonologically defined, the trace of *there* in (33c) would not interfere with VP-finality. This would leave the question of why the PP *out of order* in (33b) cannot likewise be an adjunct related to raised *there*, but that fact would presumably reduce to the fact that the latter PP cannot itself raise, as in (ia), unlike the PP of (33c) that can, as in (ib).

(i)   a.   *[Out of order] appeared some data
      b.   [On the screen] appeared some data

4. Note as well that, unlike *there*, *it* is not restricted to positions that have no θ-role, as shown by (i).

   (i)   It struck me [that ...]

I take the verb in (i) to be transitive, with a sentential subject and a direct object. The sentential subject is 'extraposed'. It then receives Nominative postverbally just as in (31).

5. PRO is either coreferential ('controlled') or arbitrary, just like certain other anaphors, e.g. Romance *si/se*, various possessives like Italian *proprio*, Russian *svoj*, etc., all of which are uninflected like PRO in the sense that they exhibit no overt agreement with their antecedents, unlike pronouns.

6. In null subject languages, the subject can be merely 'interpreted' as an expletive, requiring no insertion.

7. Note that, instead of deriving BG from the EPP as in the present proposal, it would not seem possible to simply accept BG and derive the EPP from it. The reason is Icelandic, where BG does not hold as we see in the next section, but the EPP still does.

8. What would make the movement approach tenable given the scope fact noted as well as the implausibility of the adjunction structure would be to suppose that what moves is not the NP, but rather some Case absorbing/checking feature of the NP, leaving the lexical material in place, as in fact in Chomsky (1995: Chapter 4), unpublished at the time of my original writing. In that version, the MPLT approach becomes indistinguishable in the relevant respects from the present one, since postulating a Case-absorbing feature going up the tree and postulating a Case-giving feature going down are clearly equivalent hypotheses. Note that if what moves is a Case-absorbing feature, then it would make sense to take minimality of movement (shortest move) to be relativized to Case assigners, and that would just be my Case minimality (25) above. The text argument against AgrO still stands, however.

9. One outcome not considered in the tableau is the 'impersonal passive' *It was talked to John.* This type of outcome is grammatical in various languages, and would follow from ranking I-O faithfulness above Case-uniqueness, hence compelling a Nominative with no θ-role.

10. Note that, if it is true that direct objects are more numerous than indirect ones, then a system with Nominative direct objects will ultimately yield a larger number of violations of 'Nom⇒ Subject' than an alternative system with Nominative indirect objects. This must be irrelevant for the text discussion to go through. What makes it irrelevant is that sentences are evaluated individually as in (47). There is thus no evaluation of competing configurations of the system

as a whole. A configuration is only stable or unstable depending on what evaluation of individual sentences yields.
11. ECM constructions like (i) (=37a) may seem problematic for the earlier point.
    (i)   John believed [her$_{ACC}$ to have disappeared t_{ACC}]
    In (i), the trace is taken to have non-canonical Accusative despite the fact that it represents a relatively small class — the intersection of the ECM class and the unaccusative class. To avoid this pitfall, the text must be slightly reinterpreted. As was already noted, what is relevant is not the type of Case, but the type of Case assigning relation. Thus the constraints that refer to Nominative Case in (47) must actually be taken instead to refer to a link with inflection. Then, the object trace in (i) has a non-canonical link with the inflection *to*, which is thus no different from that of any other unaccusative. Then, the fact that *to* is here not a Case assigner is independent, and will result in an extension of the Accusative assigned by the main verb automatically.
12. The Icelandic examples cited are from Andrews (1990a, b), Sigurðsson (1989, 1991), Van Valin (1991), Zaenen and Maling (1990), Zaenen et al. (1990).
13. A straightforward argument for this position, sometimes overlooked in the literature, is that all ditransitive verbs have Nominative (rather than Quirky) subjects (see Yip et al., Table 3). If QSs are always underlying objects as claimed in the text, this generalization simply follows from the independent fact that verbs have at most two objects. If QSs are not always underlying objects, there is no account.
14. For a rather different solution to the person restriction, see Taraldsen (1995).
15. Case-uniqueness is violated in this way by the Romance impersonal *si* construction of (58) above, where the *si* has a θ-role, so that Nominative is connected with two θ-roles. I attribute this violation to the relatively 'weak' referential content of *si*, plausibly resulting in a weaker θ-role.
16. This constraint must be subordinated to the one that demands that 'new information' be given post-verbally suggested in 4.1 above.
17. For related discussion, though from a rather different perspective, see van Valin (1991).

References

Andrews, A. 1990a. "The VP-complement analysis in Modern Icelandic". In J. Maling. and A. Zaenen (eds), 165–185.
Andrews, A. 1990b. "Case structures and control in Modern Icelandic". In J. Maling and A. Zaenen (eds), 187–234.
Aoun, J. 1979. "On government, case-marking and clitic placement". Ms., MIT.
Barbosa, P., Fox, D., Hagstrom, P., McGinnis, M. and Pesetsky, D. 1998. *Is the Best Good Enough? Optimality and competition in syntax*. Cambridge, MA: MIT Press.
Bobaljik, J., and Jonas, D. 1993. "Specs for subjects: The role of TP in Icelandic". In *MIT Working Papers in Linguistics 18: Papers on Case and Agreement I*, Bobaljik, J. and C. Phillips (eds).
Burzio, L. 1986. *Italian Syntax: A Government-Binding Approach*. Reidel.
Burzio, L. 1991. "The morphological basis of anaphora". *Journal of Linguistics* 27: 81–105.

Burzio, L. 1992. "On the morphology of reflexives and impersonals". In *Theoretical Analyses in Romance Linguistics LSRL XIX,* Lauefer, C. and Morgan, T. (eds). Amsterdam: John Benjamins.

Burzio, L. 1994. *Principles of English Stress.* Cambridge: CUP.

Burzio, L. 1996. "Surface constraints versus underlying representation". In *Current Trends in Phonology: Models and methods,* J. Durand and B. Laks (eds), 123–141. European Studies Research Institute, University of Salford Publications.

Burzio, L. 1998. "Multiple correspondence". *Lingua 103:* 79–109.

Burzio, L. 1999. "Surface-to-Surface Morphology: when your Representations turn into Constraints". Ms., Johns Hopkins University (ROA-341-0999).

Burzio, L. To appear. "Cycles, non-derived-environment blocking, and correspondence". In *Optimality Theory: Syntax, phonology, and acquisition,* J. Dekkers, F. van der Leeuw, and J. van de Weijer, (eds). Oxford: OUP.

Chomsky, N. 1981. *Lectures on Government and Binding.* Dordrecht: Foris.

Chomsky, N. 1986. *Knowledge of Language: Its nature, origin and use.* New York: Praeger.

Chomsky, N. 1993. "A minimalist program for linguistic theory". In *The View from Building 20: Essays in honor of Sylvain Bromberger,* K. Hale, and S. J. Keyser, (eds), 1–52. Cambridge, MA: MIT Press.

Chomsky, N. 1995. *The Minimalist Program.* Cambridge, MA: MIT Press.

Freeze, R. 1992. "Existential and other locatives". *Language* 68(3): 553–595.

Grimshaw, J. 1997. "Projection, heads and optimality". *Linguistic Inquiry* 28(3): 373–422.

Laka, I. 1993. "Unergatives that assign ergative, unaccusatives that assign accusative". In *MIT Working Papers in Linguistics 18: Papers on Case and Agreement I,* Bobaljik, J. and Phillips C. (eds).

Legendre, G., Raymond, W. and Smolensky, P. 1993. "Analytic typology of case marking and grammatical voice based on hierarchies of universal constraints". Proceedings of the 19th Annual Meeting of the Berkeley Linguistics Society, 464–478.

Legendre, G., Wilson, C., Smolensky, P., Homer, K. and Raymond, W. 1995. "Optimality and *Wh*-extraction". In *Papers in Optimality Theory.*[University of Massachusetts Occasional Papers 18], J. Beckman, D. Walsh, L. and S. Urbanczyk (eds), 607–636. University of Massachusetts, Amherst: GLSA.

Legendre, G., Vikner, S. and Grimshaw, J. To appear. *Optimality-Theoretic Syntax.* Cambridge, MA: MIT Press.

Levin, B. and Rappaport Hovav, M. 1995. *Unaccusativity: At the syntax-lexical semantics interface* [Linguistic Inquiry Monograph 26]. Cambridge, MA: MIT Press.

Maling, J. and Zaenen, A. 1990. *Modern Icelandic Syntax* [Syntax and Semantics 24]. San Diego: Academic Press.

Marantz, A. 1991. "Case and licensing". In *Proceedings of the Eigth Eastern States Conference on Linguistics,* G. Westphal, B. Ao, and H.-R. Chae (eds). Department of Linguistics, Ohio State University. [reprinted in this volume]

Moro, A. 1997. *The Raising of Predicates: Predicative noun phrases and the theory of clause structure.* Cambridge: CUP.

Prince, A. and Smolensky, P. 1993. *Optimality Theory: Constraint interaction in generative grammar*. Ms., Rutgers University, and University of Colorado.
Rizzi, L. 1990. *Relativized Minimality*. Cambridge, MA: MIT Press.
Sigurðsson, H. A. 1989. Verbal Syntax and Case in Icelandic. PhD Dissertation, Lund University.
Sigurðsson, H. A. 1991. "Icelandic case-marked PRO and the licensing of lexical arguments". *Natural Language and Linguistic Theory* 9:2.
Steriade, D. 1998. "Lexical conservatism in French adjectival liaison". Ms., UCLA.
Taraldsen, T. 1995. "On agreement and nominative objects in Icelandic". In *Studies in Comparative Germanic Syntax*, H. Haider, S. Olsen, and S. Vikner (eds), 307–327. Dordrecht: Kluwer Academic Publishers.
Van Valin, R. D. Jr. 1991. "Another look at Icelandic case marking and grammatical relations". *Natural Language and Linguistic Theory* 9(1): 145–194.
Watanabe, A. 1993. AGR-Based Case Theory and Its Interaction with the A-bar System. PhD Dissertation, MIT.
Yip, M., Maling, J. and Jackendoff, R. 1987. "Case in tiers". *Language:* 63(2): 217–250.
Zaenen, A., Maling, J. and Thráinsson, H. 1990. "Case and grammatical function: The Icelandic passive". In J. Maling, and A. Zaenen (eds), 95–136.
Zaenen, A. and Maling, J. 1990. "Unaccusative, passive, and quirky case". In J. Maling and A. Zaenen (eds), 137–152.

Name Index

A

Abney, S. 69
Abraham, W. 8, 131, 137, 142, 143, 153, 155, 156, 162, 167, 170, 172, 178, 179, 182, 188 (n.7), 188 (n.10)
Ackema, P. 136
Andersen, T. 110, 186
Anderson, J. M. 133, 134.
Anderson, S. 185, 187 (n.5)
Andrews, A. 238 (n.12)
Aoun, J. 201
Aronson, H. I. 11

B

Baker, M. 62, 95, 99 (n.18), 99 (n.21), 117, 120, 141
Barbosa, P. 236
Belletti, A. 9, 35, 36, 126 (n.11), 185, 189 (n.18)
Benvéniste, E. 64, 157
Besten, H. den 167, 189 (n.18)
Bhatia, T. 83, 98 (n.3)
Bittner, M. 47, 48, 50, 51, 106, 108, 110, 112, 126 (n.3), 126 (n.4), 126 (n.7), 151
Bobaljik, J. 2, 48, 54 (n.12), 106, 110, 112, 125, 126 (n.2), 212
Bok-Bennema, R. 76 (n.1), 91, 99 (n.15), 99 (n.21)
Borer, H. 124
Branigan, P. 99 (n.16)
Bresnan, J. 16, 98 (n.1), 99 (n.16)

Burzio, L. 1, 5, 8, 9, 11, 38, 44, 52 (n.1), 104, 114, 131, 132, 134, 135, 136, 139, 140, 141, 142, 143, 144, 146, 147, 148, 159, 166, 167, 168, 169, 174, 175, 177, 178, 180, 185, 186, 188 (n.6), 189 (n.18), 201
Butt, M. 148, 152, 212, 214, 221, 228, 233

C

Catford, J. C. 168
Chomsky, N. 1, 11, 33, 40, 48, 58, 62, 64, 72, 73, 90, 94, 99 (n.11), 104, 105, 108, 109, 112, 118, 121, 125, 126 (n.8), 144, 145, 175, 178, 195, 197, 199, 201, 214, 237 (n.8)
Comrie, B. 131, 132, 157, 187 (n.5)

D

Dahl, Ö. 188 (n.8)
Davison, A. 98 (n.2)
DeLancey, S. 150
Dikken, M. den 106
Dixon, R. M. W. 110, 122, 123, 126 (n.7), 127 (n.12), 131, 132, 134, 135, 147, 149, 157, 159, 165, 173, 178, 182, 184, 187 (n.2), 187 (n.5)
Doane, A. N. 171, 172
Dryer, M. 143, 147, 148

E

Egede, P. 187 (n. 3)
Enç, M. 155, 162
Ezeizabarrena, M. J. 127 (n. 13)

F

Farrell, P. 148, 150, 153, 154, 155, 156
Freeze, R. 237 (n. 3)
Fukui, N. 112

G

Gawronska, B. 168
Geenhoven, V. van 161, 187 (n. 3)
Grewendorf, G. 167, 185
Grimshaw, J. 76, 236
Groos, A. 76 (n. 1), 99 (n. 21)
Guéron, J. 62, 76 (n. 5), 151, 158, 159, 161, 162, 183
Gurtu, M. 82, 98 (n. 4)

H

Haider, H. 6, 7, 31, 33, 36, 53 (n. 9), 76 (n. 4), 90, 93, 95, 137, 168
Hale, K. 47, 48, 50, 51, 57, 70, 71, 72, 73, 106, 108, 110, 112, 117, 123, 125 (n. 1), 126 (n. 4), 126 (n. 7), 151, 175, 178
Halle, M. 19, 24
Halliday, M. A. K. 133, 134, 185
Harris, A. 11, 29 (n. 1), 48
Haspelmath, M. 181, 182
Hedlund, C. 45
Heim, I. 155, 183, 187 (n. 3)
Hestvik, A. 82
Higginbotham, J. 69
Hoekstra, T. 6, 7, 8, 58, 61, 62, 63, 64, 76 (n. 5), 90, 93, 94, 95, 97, 99 (n. 19), 142, 151, 159, 188 (n. 13)
Holisky, D. 124
Holloway King, T. 106, 110, 124, 152
Hoop, H. de 4, 127 (n. 11)

Hopper, P. 187 (n. 5), 188 (n. 15)
Hornstein, N. 183
Hout, A. van 124

J

Jaeggli, O. 22
Jayaseelan, K. A. 98 (n. 6)
Jelinek, E. 48, 123
Johns, A. 60, 91, 99 (n. 15)
Johnson, K. 95, 126 (n. 3), 141
Jonas, D. 212

K

Kachru, B. 83, 98 (n. 3)
Kachru, Y. 83, 98 (n. 3)
Kalmár, I. 187 (n. 3)
Kayne, R 62, 64, 67, 73, 74, 94, 112, 157, 159, 160, 175
Keenan, E. 45, 98 (n. 3), 110, 126 (n. 6)
Keyser, S. J. 57, 70, 71, 72, 73, 117, 123, 125 (n. 1), 131, 135, 136, 175, 178
Khalayli, S. 76 (n. 9)
Kitagawa, Y. 112
Klimov, G. A. 157
Koopman, H. 69, 99 (n. 11), 112
Kotin, M. 180
Kubo, M. 15, 16, 98 (n. 1)

L

Laka, I. 2, 7, 8, 99 (n. 11), 103, 106, 108, 123, 125, 149, 236 (n. 1)
Lamontagne, G. 106
Larsen, T. 49, 50
Larson, R. 117
Lasnik, H. 33
Legendre, G. 203, 236
Levin, B. 110, 119, 125 (n. 1), 198, 219

M

Mahajan, A. K. 74, 75, 84, 90, 93, 94, 98 (n. 2), 98 (n. 4), 99 (n. 9),

99 (n. 18), 99 (n. 19), 110, 123, 131, 134, 135, 148, 149, 150, 154, 155, 156, 157, 158, 159, 160, 162, 163, 164, 165, 169, 173, 179, 180, 188 (n. 6)
Maling, J. 18, 53 (n. 11), 233, 234, 238 (n. 12)
Marantz, A. 2, 5, 7, 13, 21, 31, 91, 97, 98 (n. 1), 99 (n. 12), 106, 108, 119, 122, 150, 151, 188 (n. 6), 189 (n. 18), 196, 199, 203, 204, 234
Menuzzi, S. 74
Milner, G. B. 167
Mohanan, T. 82, 83, 98 (n. 2)
Moro, A. 237 (n. 3)
Moshi, L. 16, 98 (n. 1)
Mulder, R. 58, 64

N
Norman, W. 49, 50

O
Ortiz de Urbina, J. 110, 120

P
Pandharipande, R. 98 (n. 2), 150
Partee, B. 183, 189 (n. 22)
Perlmutter, D. 104, 114, 131, 132, 134, 135, 136, 143, 146, 147, 159, 174, 175, 177, 180, 184, 186, 189 (n. 18)
Pesetsky, D. 67, 185, 189 (n. 18)
Phillips, C. 123
Picallo, C. 75
Plank, F. 143
Pollock, J.-Y. 3, 4
Postal, P. M. 69
Prince, A. 197, 221
Pullum, G. 134, 187 (n. 2)

R
Rappaport Hovav, M. 125 (n. 1), 198, 219
Reuland, E. J. 189 (n. 20), 189 (n. 22)
Rindler-Schjerve, R. 137, 169
Rizzi, L. 35, 36, 207
Roberts, I. 95, 141
Roeper, T. 131, 135, 136
Rooryck, J. 151, 159, 188 (n. 13)
Rumsey, R. 153

S
Safir, K. 22
Saksena, A. 98 (n. 2)
Schoorlemmer, M. 136
Schumacher, T. 171
Seefranz-Montag, A. 144, 177, 178
Seler, E. 60
Shibatani, . 187 (n. 5)
Sridar, S. N. 98 (n. 1)
Srivastav-Dayal, V. 98 (n. 4)
Sievers, E. 171
Sigurðsson, H. 18, 21, 207, 238 (n. 12)
Silverstein, M. 153
Smolensky, P. 197, 221
Speas, P. 112
Sportiche, D. 99 (n. 11), 112, 189 (n. 17)
Srivastav, V. 84
Steriade, D. 233
Stowell, T. 70, 112

T
Taraldsen, T. 238 (n. 14)
Tatian 171
Tenny, C. 124
Thieroff, . 188 (n. 8)
Thompson, S. 187 (n. 5), 188 (n. 15)
Thráinsson, H. 18

Timberlake, A. 45
Trask, R. 50, 132, 157, 161, 163, 166, 167, 168, 188 (n. 12)
Travis, L. 106, 124

V
Vanden Wyngaerd, G. 176, 179
Van Valin, R. D. jr 238 (n. 12), 238 (n. 17)
Verkuyl, H. J. 124

W
Weerman, F. 2
Williams, E. 36, 76 (n. 7), 112
Woodbury, A. C. 110, 126 (n. 6)
Wunderlich, D. 51

Y
Yadroff, M. 124
Yip, M. 26, 199

Z
Zaenen, A. 18, 53 (n. 11), 233, 234, 238 (n. 12)
Zwarts, J. 69

Subject Index

A
Abstract verb 70
Accomplishment 59, 169
A-chain (*see* chains)
Achievement 169
A-conditions 184
Active passive construction 80, 81, 83, 85, 87, 89, 91, 92, 95
Activity 59
Adjacency 112
Adjectival participle 170
Adjectival predicate 206
Adjunct 83, 88, 96
Adjunction 176, 211
Adjunct predicate 61
Adverbial accusative 181
Adverbial clauses 83
Adverbial 168
Agent 71, 73, 83, 132, 137, 138, 153, 155, 178, 179
Agentivity 141
Agr 22, 26, 27, 28, 42, 46, 196, 217
AgrO 48, 58, 59, 60, 62, 105, 106, 200, 219, 220
AgrS 48, 50, 58, 60, 62, 105, 106, 218, 219
Agreement 5, 11, 14, 22, 27, 33, 42, 45, 50, 75, 89, 106, 113, 140, 207
Aktionsart 59, 124, 143, 146, 148, 172
Anaphoric time relation 183
Antekerrepenhe 51
Anti-ergative 41

Anti-passive 58, 59, 120, 121, 122, 125
Antisubject 82
Aorist 12, 13, 14, 124
A-position 92, 96
Argument, external 8, 36, 48, 57, 63, 66, 67, 71, 72, 74, 75, 80, 85, 105, 109, 120, 144, 177, 178
Argument, internal 7, 57, 119, 120, 121, 146, 147, 174, 179
Argument position 11
Argument structure 37, 38, 48, 57, 68, 71, 72, 73, 118
Aspect 75, 106, 107, 109, 111, 115, 118, 123, 124, 125, 142, 143, 146, 159, 166
A-structure (*see* argumentstructure)
Auxiliary 69, 74, 81, 89, 90, 93, 94, 95, 135, 137, 138, 139, 140, 142, 151, 153

B
Balochi 135, 148, 153, 154, 155, 156, 173
Southern/Eastern Balochi (*see* Balochi)
Western Balochi (*see* Balochi)
Bare plurals 139
Basque 13, 25, 106, 108, 110, 118, 119, 123, 149, 157, 165
BE 61, 63, 95, 138, 157, 158, 166
Big Syntax 70, 71, 72
Binding 36, 184
Binding (anaphor) 81

SUBJECT INDEX

Binding (theory) 183
Boundedness 137
by phrase (see also demotion) 65, 96, 120

C
Case 195
  Case, absolutive 5, 43, 50, 51, 58, 59, 107, 110, 120, 121, 122, 124, 150, 154, 185, 199, 204, 208, 227
  Case absorption 97, 141
  Case, abstract 11, 14, 16, 17, 18
  Case, accusative 1, 3, 5, 7, 9, 11, 12, 15, 17, 23, 24, 28, 31, 35, 39, 40, 41, 43, 57, 59, 60, 65, 74, 79, 90, 95 105, 109, 112, 116, 120, 124, 152, 167, 177, 182, 196, 199, 200, 202, 204, 205, 209, 213, 214, 216, 218, 219, 223
  Case alternation 120, 121
  Case assignment 2, 3, 17, 31, 89, 90, 92, 93, 94, 207, 211
  Case as a functional category 112
  Case checking 3, 65
  Case, dative 12, 17, 18, 23, 31, 142, 163, 205, 224, 232
  Case, default 20, 51, 145
  Case dependency 32, 33, 35, 36
  Case, dependent 7, 24, 91, 92, 93, 97
  Case, ergative 5, 7, 11, 12, 13, 14, 24, 25, 26, 28, 41, 51, 58, 59, 60, 74, 80, 93, 105, 110, 111, 113, 115, 116, 121, 122, 123, 124, 132, 137, 147, 150, 151, 203
  Case feature 23, 24, 26, 50, 113, 124
  Case, genitive 18, 39, 91, 157, 202
  Case hierarchy 26

'Case in Tiers' (CT) 199, 200, 204, 205
Case, inherent 9, 199, 224, 225
Case, instrumental 93, 95
Case, lexical 31, 199
Case licensing 31, 33, 34, 42, 58, 60, 63, 113
Case marking 12, 74, 75
Case, morphological 3, 5, 7, 11, 12, 15, 16, 17, 18, 22, 86, 93, 97
Case, nominative 5, 12, 23, 28, 35, 50, 58, 63, 65, 74, 90, 95, 105, 106, 112, 113, 114, 123, 145, 150, 199, 206, 208, 216, 218, 222, 226, 227
Case, oblique 59, 63, 74, 153, 163
Case, quirky 18, 23, 25, 91
Case realization 24
Case, structural 1, 4, 5, 6, 7, 9, 16, 33, 34, 35, 39, 40, 47, 90, 150, 196, 220, 225
Case superimposition 228, 229, 230, 235
Case, theta blind 117–122, 125
Case theory 2, 7, 17, 19, 22, 28, 103, 105, 106, 111, 113, 117, 119, 123, 125, 185, 235,
Case (T-related) 6, 58
Case uniformity 205–212, 216, 225, 231
Case-uniqueness(see visibility hypothesis)
Case (V-related) 6, 33, 58
Case, zero 33
Catalan 75
Cataphoric time relation 183
Causative 71
Causative alternation 105
Cause 72, 73
C-command 174, 200, 207
Chains 25, 121, 202, 203, 205, 206, 218

SUBJECT INDEX

Checking 32, 43, 47, 50
Checking, functional 6
Checking, lexical 6
Chinese 43
Clitic 2, 158, 160, 165, 184
Compositionality 37, 113
Conative 59
Consistency (general principle of) 234
Control (*see* also object control) 83
Coreference 82, 86, 184

D

Danish 46
Dative 157
Definiteness 155, 184
Delimiting 182
Demotion (of arguments) 81, 88, 92, 95, 96, 103, 120, 146
Dethematization 2, 92, 94, 96, 97
Detransitivization 49, 63
Deverbal noun 39
Direct object 41, 143, 166, 177, 180, 198, 225
Discourse themata 184, 185, 186
Discourse-functional relations 186
Distributional properties 138, 141, 148, 149, 174, 177
DO (*see* direct object)
Double object construction 16, 35, 36, 38
DP features 47
DS 16, 19, 96, 205
D-structure (*see* DS)
Durativity 167, 179
Dutch 3, 38, 62, 132, 138, 139, 140, 142, 143, 148, 158,166, 167, 176, 180
Dyirbal 110, 122, 133

E

ECM (exceptional case marking) 20, 26, 177, 196, 214, 215, 216, 223, 229, 235

Economy 2, 6, 17, 32, 39, 42, 43, 44, 47, 51, 65
ECP 70, 84
Ellipsis 180, 182
Empty category 214
English 3, 20, 33, 38, 46, 50, 62, 69, 75, 79, 80, 92, 93, 94, 95, 96, 112, 123, 136, 139, 162, 182, 196, 219, 226
EPP 2, 3, 5, 11, 17, 18, 19, 20, 21, 28, 40, 42, 43, 72, 145, 172, 177, 182, 197, 200, 201, 202, 209, 210, 212, 217, 220, 224, 225, 226, 235, 236
Erg-Abs languages 58, 59, 60, 107, 133, 153
Ergative construction 50, 51, 57, 81, 83, 85, 87, 88, 89, 91, 92, 93, 95
Ergative grammar 120, 122
Ergative languages 2, 6, 9, 25, 32, 50, 149, 151, 155, 162, 199, 201, 202, 203, 218, 219, 223, 230, 232
Ergative marker 93
Ergative verb 38, 63, 136, 167, 169
Ergative system 107, 109, 110, 118, 119, 121, 125, 146
Ergativity 8, 15, 106, 133, 134, 137, 138, 140, 141, 148, 154, 156, 161, 162, 165, 166, 174
Ergativity (diagnostics for) 133, 134, 137, 138
Ergativity, lexical 74, 133, 143, 168
Ergativity, phrasal 143
Ergativity, split- 14, 26, 27, 28, 131, 132, 153, 156, 159, 167, 208
Ergativity, syntactic 131, 135, 136, 147, 148, 159, 180
Ergativity, typological 131, 133, 147, 149, 159, 178, 180
Eskimo 60, 75, 133
Event 145, 167, 175, 184

Experiencer 178, 226, 233
Expletive 38, 43, 44, 46, 47, 84, 139, 209, 210, 211, 212
Extended projection 22, 76
Extended projection principle (*see* EPP)
Extraction (*see* also *wh*-extraction) 83, 84, 85, 88
Extraposition 83, 84, 88

F

F-category (*see* functional category)
Feature
   Feature, active 107, 108–113, 114, 115, 118, 123, 124, 125, 216
   Feature, functional 42
   Feature, phi 32, 42
   Feature, strong 108, 109, 124
   Feature, weak 108, 110, 124
Focus 37, 175
French 38, 44, 62, 75, 165, 166
Frisian 143, 158, 166, 167, 176
Functional category 68, 69, 70, 73, 146
Functional domain 75
Functional element 74, 75, 108, 109, 111
Functional head 34, 68, 70, 74, 113
Functional morphology 43
Functional projection 92, 112, 124

G

Georgian 11, 12, 13, 14, 15, 25, 27, 28, 48, 106, 110, 124, 150
German 3, 6, 31, 34, 37, 38, 40, 41, 62, 69, 132, 135, 136, 137, 138, 139, 140, 142, 145, 147, 155, 158, 166, 167, 168, 176, 177, 181, 186
Germanic languages 79, 158
Global 220
Gothic 131
Government 112, 149

Government and binding (lectures on) see LGB
Government and binding (theory of) see also LGB 104, 105
GR (grammatical relations) 196, 197, 200, 207, 213, 217, 220, 229, 232
GR-consistency 202, 203, 204, 205, 210, 214, 220, 221, 223, 224, 225, 229, 230, 233
Greed 206, 209, 218
Greek (ancient) 168
Greenlandic Eskimo 119

H

HAVE 63, 64, 74, 156, 157, 158, 161, 162
Have vs be 151, 173
Head parameter 106
Hearer/speaker properties 147
Hindi 7, 13, 14, 25, 79, 80, 82, 86, 89, 90, 91, 92, 93, 94, 95, 96, 97, 106, 110, 123, 124, 135, 148, 149, 150, 151, 155, 157, 158, 159, 164, 165, 169, 170, 173, 202, 204
Hurrian 133

I

Icelandic 18, 19, 23, 206, 209, 226, 227, 228, 234, 235
Imperfective 59, 123, 180
Impersonal 119, 120, 144, 228
Impersonal construction 47
Impersonal passive 138, 230
Incorporation 46, 65, 66, 67, 68, 70, 73, 74, 75, 76, 93, 95, 96, 97, 117, 120, 121, 123, 139, 140, 152, 159, 160, 162, 163, 164, 165, 175, 176, 178
Indefinite 141, 152, 167
Indefinite object deletion 121, 122
Indic Indo-European Languages 79

Indo-European languages 153, 186
Indirect object 220, 221
Indo-Aryan languages 131, 135
INFL 15
Inflection 45, 50, 60, 150, 196, 208, 214, 215, 234
Ingression 67, 70, 73
Ingressive aspect 73
Input-output faithfulness 222, 232
Instrumental marker 80, 91
Interminative 172
Intransitive 12, 26, 40, 47, 57, 104, 143, 147, 148, 149, 167, 172, 177
Inuit 50, 110, 116, 161
Inuktitut 26, 49, 50, 161, 162
Italian 44, 136, 138, 139, 140, 143, 148, 167, 168, 196, 227

J
Japanese 15, 16

K
Kichaga 16
Kuikuró 110

L
Late Latin 171
Latin 116, 157, 158, 160, 168, 177
L-category (*see* lexical category)
Lexical category 68, 69, 70
Lexical conceptual structure 37
Lexical decomposition 158
Lexical syntax 70
Lexicon 108
Lezgian 133, 181, 182
LF 33, 82, 109, 211
LFG 17
LGB 97, 195
Licensing 9, 11, 17, 20, 38, 39, 40, 48, 57
  Licensing (Categorial vs functional) 35, 40, 41, 43, 46, 47, 49, 50, 51

Licensing, free 41
Licensing, functional 33
Licensing system (Positional vs non-positional) 42
Linear adjacency (see also linear order) 94, 97
Linear order 200
Linearity 139, 162, 166, 173, 179
Linking 1
Locality conditions 211
Locative 64, 157
L-related 146

M
Macushi 110
Maya 49, 60
Middle construction 35, 38, 39, 105
Middle Dutch 3
Minimal chain link condition (*see also* chains) 62, 64
Minimalism 65, 73, 108
Minimalist Program for Linguistic Theory (*see also* minimalism) 33, 195, 196, 197, 199, 200, 204, 206, 209, 211, 217, 218, 220, 235
Minimality 211, 214, 216, 217
Monadic predicate 109, 114, 125
Mood 146
Morpho-phonology 24, 233
Movement 121, 196, 205, 218, 220, 223, 231, 235
  A-movement 195, 196, 206, 209
  Head-movement 64, 66, 73
  Head-movement constraint 70
  LF movement 82, 211, 217, 220
  NP-movement 2, 3, 23, 35, 45, 90, 95, 109, 208
  Object movement 90
  X^0 movement 117
MS (morphological structure) 20, 22, 50

N

New information vs old information 209
Nez Perce 51
Nom-Acc languages 3, 6, 48, 58, 59, 60, 61, 133, 151, 153, 203, 208, 209, 217, 232
Nom-Acc systems 48, 49, 50, 51, 75, 106, 107, 111, 201
Nom-Erg systems 32, 43, 48, 51, 75, 106
Nominalization 65, 66
Nominal participle 75
Nominative first 3, 4, 6, 9, 58
Nominative grammar 119, 120, 121
Nominative objects 18, 228
Nominative system 108, 118, 122, 125
Non-perfective 147, 150, 180
Non-specificity 141
North Caucasian 168
Norwegian 46, 47
Nuclear scope 179, 184
Nuclear stress 37
Null-subject 44, 109

O

Object 31, 104, 115, 116, 123, 167
Object agreement 16, 49, 88, 89, 90, 91, 165
Object, structural 81
Object control 87, 159
Old High German 171
Old Saxon 171
One-place predicates 149, 169, 178, 185
Ontological class 69
Optimality 156
Optimality Theory 8, 236
Optimization 221
OV languages 74, 75, 110

P

Päri 110

Participial agreement 62
Partitive nominal 141
Passive 1, 2, 3, 4, 12, 16, 35, 40, 45, 47, 48, 59, 61, 75, 79, 105, 119, 120, 180, 234
Passive auxiliary 91
Passive morphology 2, 234
Passive, participial 61
Passivization 59
Past participle 92, 93, 95
Patient 132, 146, 224
Perfect participle 93, 176
Percolation 213
Perfect participle construction 90, 95, 141, 167
Perfective 124, 132, 146, 147, 148, 154, 159, 168, 169, 172, 173, 178, 180, 182, 184, 185
Periphrastic perfect 151, 166
PF 5, 20, 21, 109
Pivot 174, 182
Polish 6, 45
Polynesian languages 167
Possessive 64, 160, 161
Possessive pronoun 82
Postposition 93, 94, 163
PP 212, 229
Pragmatics 147
Prefix 137, 139, 147, 176, 180
Prepositional 93, 183
Principle A (*see* also binding) 183, 184
Principle B (*see* also binding) 82, 183
Principles and Parameters Theory 11, 33
PRO 20, 21, 22, 33, 214, 215, 217, 229
Pro 22, 214
Processual passive 148
Pro-clitic 163, 170
Promotion (of arguments) 81, 88, 231
P-stranding 47
Psych verb 12, 35, 36, 37

SUBJECT INDEX

Psych verb, causative 67
Psych verb, transitive 35, 36, 38

Q
QS (*see* subject, quirky)
Quasi passive 132
Quiche 49, 50
Quirky subjects (*see* subject, quirky)

R
Raising 94, 105, 182, 214, 216
Ranking of constraints (*see* also Optimality Theory) 201, 202, 221, 232, 233, 234
Reference time 183
Reflexive 2, 38, 39, 154, 184, 228
Relational Grammar 12, 17, 58, 104, 143
Relativized minimality 207
Resultative 180, 183
Resultative construction 175, 219
Rhematic (*see* also thema/rhema) 142, 186
Romance languages 38, 44, 62, 69, 75, 79, 158
Russian 3, 6, 20, 45, 133, 168, 180, 181, 182

S
Samoan 167
Scandinavian languages 44, 45, 46, 47, 82
Scope 212
Scrambling 37, 155
Semantic transitivity 64
Shortest move 209
Simple past 12
Slavic languages 44, 45, 148, 168
Small clause 147, 166, 169, 170, 172, 173, 174, 175, 177, 180, 182, 184, 185, 212, 213
SOV language 50, 145, 149, 150, 152, 153, 154, 155, 163, 165, 184

Speakers time 183
SpecAgrO 197, 200, 218, 220
SpecAgrS 200
Spec-Head relations 33, 34, 197, 207, 217
Spell Out 108, 109, 110
Split S-system 123
SS 19, 21, 22, 33, 108, 110
S-structure (*see* SS)
Statal 179
Statal passive 146, 148
Stata144, 145, 168
Stress 175
Subject 1, 26, 31, 33, 39, 70, 94, 95, 104, 115, 122, 139, 159, 166, 170, 196, 203, 210
Subject, absolutive 223, 225
Subject, accusative (*see* also ECM) 197, 203
Subject argument 36, 136
Subject, derived 26, 182
Subject, ergative 81
Subject, expletive 44, 45
Subject, instrumental 79, 81, 96
Subject, nominative 14, 81, 205, 222
Subject, non-nominative 79, 197
Subject, non thematic 14, 15, 16, 17, 26, 217
Subject, oblique 49, 79, 157, 223
Subject position 2
Subject post verbal 44
Subject (PP subject) 96, 97, 159
Subject, quirky 209, 226–235
Subject, structural thematic 2, 7, 79
Subject, transitive 58, 166
Subject, VP-external 96, 139
Subject, VP-internal 136, 139, 141, 144
Super raising 208, 209
Suppression of theta role 220
SVO language 43, 50, 165, 180, 184
Swedish 45, 46

SUBJECT INDEX

T
T (*see* tense)
Telicity 59, 142, 144, 148, 166, 182
Tense 34, 62, 68, 74, 75, 106, 107, 109, 111, 113, 123, 124, 125, 146, 159
Terminative 185
Thema/rhema 155, 179
Thematic role (*see* theta role)
Theme 71, 146, 179, 226
Theta assingment 3, 31, 33
Theta consistency 224
Theta free 35, 39
Theta marking 144, 177
Theta position 36
Theta role (*see* also agent, cause, experiencer, patient, theme,) 1, 9, 105, 112, 116, 124, 146, 174, 179, 197, 210, 217, 225
  Theta role, external 1, 2, 3, 79, 105, 116, 185
  Theta role, internal 155
  Theta role, subject 209
  Theta theory 2
Tibeto-Burman languages 150
Time-modification ("in/for an hour") 59
Tolai 110
Topicalization 34, 40
Trace 206, 211
Transitive verb 7, 13, 67, 74, 115, 120
Transitivity 63, 71, 75, 122, 123
Trigger 1, 2, 28, 33
Two-place predicates 149, 150, 169, 185
Typology 109, 133, 146, 149, 155, 157, 182, 230

U
UG 43, 44, 52, 79, 105
Ukrainian 3, 6

Unaccusative 1, 3, 12, 13, 36, 40, 48, 116, 122, 133, 146, 149, 180, 185, 203, 207, 212, 221,
Unaccusative alternation 119
Unaccusative predicates 104, 105, 114, 118, 123,
Unaccusativity 103, 131, 132, 136, 147, 174, 185
Unergative 12, 13, 57, 104, 149, 175, 176
Unergative predicates 106, 109, 113, 122, 123
Universal grammar (*see* UG)
Urdu 135, 148, 151, 152, 155, 173

V
V2 (verb second) 34
Vacuous branching 144, 145
Valency 148
Verb, dyadic 51
Verb, monadic 51
V-features 47
Visibility (hypothesis) 197, 200, 202, 203, 204, 205, 206, 207, 209, 210, 212, 213, 214, 220, 221, 224, 225, 236
V-marginal language (*see* also SOV, VOS, and VSO) 155, 157, 163, 173, 179, 180
V-medial language (*see* also SVO) 110, 155, 157, 158
VO languages 74, 110
VOS languages 163
VP external/ outside VP 50, 139, 146, 150, 155, 162, 167, 179, 180, 186, 204
VP internal/ inside VP 38, 50, 93, 141, 142, 146, 151, 153, 155, 167, 180, 184, 186, 196, 207
VP internal subject hypothesis 96, 109
VSO language 50, 149, 154, 155, 163

W
Warlpiri 48
Waurá 110
West Germanic (*see* also Germanic languages, English, Dutch, Frisian, German, Yiddish) 132, 135, 147, 177
West-Greenlandic Eskimo 136, 139, 140, 141–142, 161, 166, 186
wh-extraction 49, 85

Y
Yiddish 166

Z
Zero-verb 74

In the series LINGUISTIK AKTUELL/LINGUISTICS TODAY (LA) the following titles have been published thus far, or are scheduled for publication:

1. KLAPPENBACH, Ruth (1911-1977): *Studien zur Modernen Deutschen Lexikographie. Auswahl aus den Lexikographischen Arbeiten von Ruth Klappenbach, erweitert um drei Beiträge von Helene Malige-Klappenbach.* 1980.
2. EHLICH, Konrad & Jochen REHBEIN: *Augenkommunikation. Methodenreflexion und Beispielanalyse.* 1982.
3. ABRAHAM, Werner (ed.): *On the Formal Syntax of the Westgermania. Papers from the 3rd Groningen Grammar Talks (3e Groninger Grammatikgespräche), Groningen, January 1981.* 1983.
4. ABRAHAM, Werner & Sjaak De MEIJ (eds): *Topic, Focus and Configurationality. Papers from the 6th Groningen Grammar Talks, Groningen, 1984.* 1986.
5. GREWENDORF, Günther and Wolfgang STERNEFELD (eds): *Scrambling and Barriers.* 1990.
6. BHATT, Christa, Elisabeth LÖBEL and Claudia SCHMIDT (eds): *Syntactic Phrase Structure Phenomena in Noun Phrases and Sentences.* 1989.
7. ÅFARLI, Tor A.: *The Syntax of Norwegian Passive Constructions.* 1992.
8. FANSELOW, Gisbert (ed.): *The Parametrization of Universal Grammar.* 1993.
9. GELDEREN, Elly van: *The Rise of Functional Categories.* 1993.
10. CINQUE, Guglielmo and Guiliana GIUSTI (eds): *Advances in Roumanian Linguistics.* 1995.
11. LUTZ, Uli and Jürgen PAFEL (eds): *On Extraction and Extraposition in German.* 1995.
12. ABRAHAM, W., S. EPSTEIN, H. THRÁINSSON and C.J.W. ZWART (eds): *Minimal Ideas. Linguistic studies in the minimalist framework.* 1996.
13. ALEXIADOU Artemis and T. Alan HALL (eds): *Studies on Universal Grammar and Typological Variation.* 1997.
14. ANAGNOSTOPOULOU, Elena, Henk VAN RIEMSDIJK and Frans ZWARTS (eds): *Materials on Left Dislocation.* 1997.
15. ROHRBACHER, Bernhard Wolfgang: *Morphology-Driven Syntax. A theory of V to I raising and pro-drop.* 1999.
16. LIU, FENG-HSI: *Scope and Specificity.* 1997.
17. BEERMAN, Dorothee, David LEBLANC and Henk van RIEMSDIJK (eds): *Rightward Movement.* 1997.
18. ALEXIADOU, Artemis: *Adverb Placement. A case study in antisymmetric syntax.* 1997.
19. JOSEFSSON, Gunlög: *Minimal Words in a Minimal Syntax. Word formation in Swedish.* 1998.
20. LAENZLINGER, Christopher: *Comparative Studies in Word Order Variation. Adverbs, pronouns, and clause structure in Romance and Germanic.* 1998.
21. KLEIN, Henny: *Adverbs of Degree in Dutch and Related Languages.* 1998.
22. ALEXIADOU, Artemis and Chris WILDER (eds): *Possessors, Predicates and Movement in the Determiner Phrase.* 1998.
23. GIANNAKIDOU, Anastasia: *Polarity Sensitivity as (Non)Veridical Dependency.* 1998.
24. REBUSCHI, Georges and Laurice TULLER (eds): *The Grammar of Focus.* 1999.
25. FELSER, Claudia: *Verbal Complement Clauses. A minimalist study of direct perception constructions.* 1999.
26. ACKEMA, Peter: *Issues in Morphosyntax.* 1999.

27. RŮŽIČKA, Rudolf: *Control in Grammar and Pragmatics. A cross-linguistic study.* 1999.
28. HERMANS, Ben and Marc van OOSTENDORP (eds.): *The Derivational Residue in Phonological Optimality Theory.* 1999.
29. MIYAMOTO, Tadao: *The Light Verb Construction in Japanese. The role of the verbal noun.* 1999.
30. BEUKEMA, Frits and Marcel den DIKKEN (eds.): *Clitic Phenomena in European Languages.* 2000.
31. SVENONIUS, Peter (ed.): *The Derivation of VO and OV.* n.y.p.
32. ALEXIADOU, Artemis, Paul LAW, André MEINUNGER and Chris WILDER (eds.): *The Syntax of Relative Clauses.* 2000.
33. PUSKÁS, Genoveva: *Word Order in Hungarian. The syntax of $\bar{A}$-positions.* 2000.
34. REULAND, Eric (ed.): *Arguments and Case. Explaining Burzio's Generalization.* 2000.
35. HRÓARSDÓTTIR, Thorbjörg. *Word Order Change in Icelandic. From OV to VO.* n.y.p.
36. GERLACH, Birgit and Janet GRIJZENHOUT (eds.): *Clitics in Phonology, Morphology and Syntax.* n.y.p.
37. LUTZ, Uli, Gereon MÜLLER and Arnim von STECHOW (eds.): *Wh-Scope Marking.* n.y.p.
38. MEINUNGER, André: *Syntactic Aspects of Topic and Comment.* n.y.p.
39. GELDEREN, Elly van: *A History of English Reflexive Pronouns. Person, "Self", and Interpretability.* n.y.p.
40. HOEKSEMA, Jack, Hotze RULLMANN, Victor SANCHEZ-VALENCIA and Ton van der WOUDEN (eds.): *Perspectives on Negation and Polarity Items.* n.y.p.